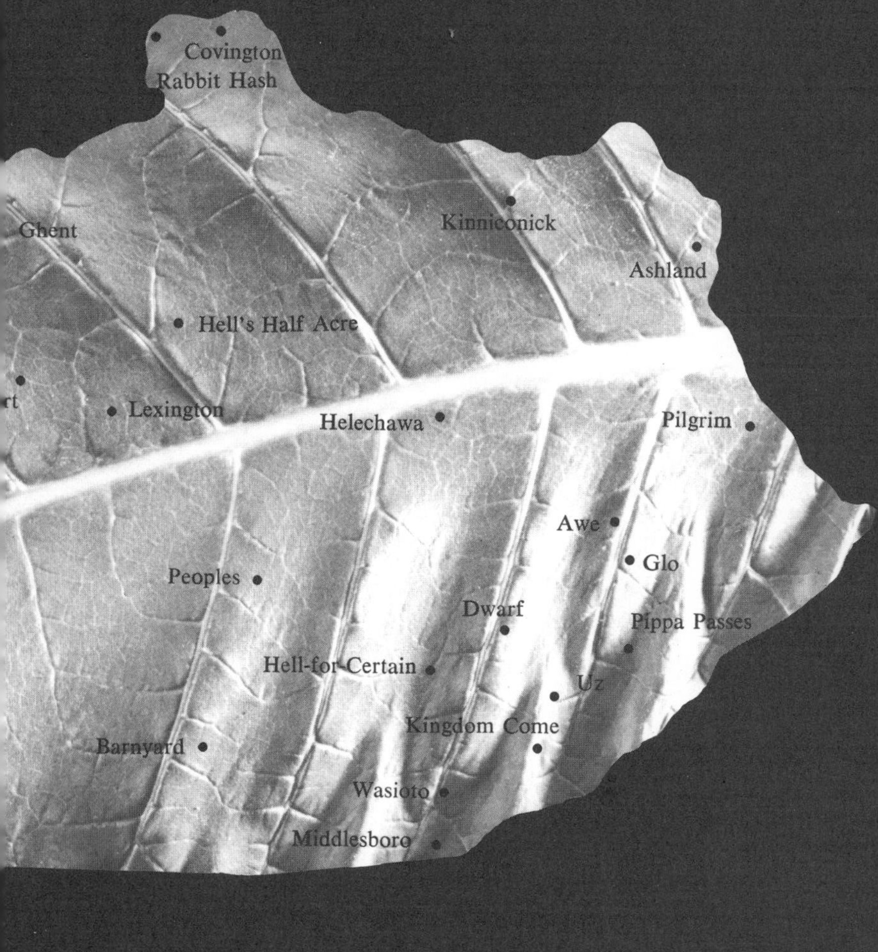
Covington
Rabbit Hash
Ghent
Kinniconick
Ashland
Hell's Half Acre
Lexington
Helechawa
Pilgrim
Awe
Glo
Peoples
Dwarf
Pippa Passes
Hell-for-Certain
Uz
Kingdom Come
Barnyard
Wasioto
Middlesboro

Joe Creason's
Kentucky

Joe Creason's Kentucky

By Joe Creason

Foreword by Jesse Stuart

Published by

The Courier-Journal
The Louisville Times

This book is dedicated with humble and grateful appreciation to those readers who have responded to my column over the years with more than 35,000 letters and especially to the dear lady who noted: "I never miss your column because each one is better than the next."

Joe Creason dedicated the first edition of his book with his usual unashamed humility. This second printing is dedicated to the memory of the Commonwealth's best known goodwill ambassador, who died most unexpectedly on August 14, 1974. His columns are missed by his readers; he is missed by his friends and colleagues.

𝕿𝖍𝖊 𝕮𝖔𝖚𝖗𝖎𝖊𝖗-𝕵𝖔𝖚𝖗𝖓𝖆𝖑
THE LOUISVILLE TIMES
525 West Broadway, Louisville, Kentucky 40202

Library of Congress Catalog Number: 72-88786
Design and Illustration: Joseph V. Rigsby
Printing: Pinaire Lithographing Corporation, Louisville, Kentucky
First Printing: October, 1972
Second Printing: March, 1975
Third Printing: February, 1976

Contents

FOREWORD   7

PREFACE   9

ACKNOWLEDGMENTS   11

1. PEOPLE ARE THE FUNNIEST CRITTERS   13
   The Humor of Folks Caught in the Act of Being Themselves.

2. AND POLITICS THE DAMNDEST IN KENTUCKY   45
   With an Election Every Year, What Else Could You Expect?

3. 100 PROOF — AND HOME MADE   65
   Moonshine Doesn't Always Mean by the Light of the Silvery.

4. SCHOOL DAZE   79
   Children Tell It Like It Is.

5. THE WAY WE TALK   103
   *If Shakespeare Was Still Alive, He'd Feel
   Right at Home Here.*

6. THE SPORTING SET   121
   *Racing, Football, Basketball, Crap Shooting —
   Name Your Sport, Sport.*

7. FROM PARADISE TO HELL-FOR-CERTAIN   145
   You Just Won't Believe Some of These Place Names.

8. WHAT'S A COMMONWEALTH, DADDY?   157
   *Features about an Incredible State, Including Why It
   Is a Commonwealth.*

9. MOVE OVER BURLINGTON LIAR'S CLUB   179
   Stories in which the First Teller Doesn't Stand a Chance.

10. WHAT BUGS ME . . .   193
    If I Couldn't Get Some Things Off My Chest I'd Bust.

11. THE WAYS OF FOLKWAYS   213
    *Legends, Myths, Fairy Tales, and Superstitions Passed Down
    through Seven Generations.*

12. WIT, WISDOM AND OTHERWISE   233
    *Crossroads Philosophy, Ironics, and a Catchall of
    This and That.*

INDEX   254

Foreword

Joe Cross Creason has been a reporter, feature writer, and what-have-you for *The Courier-Journal*. I can't imagine anything he couldn't do for that Louisville paper or any other big newspaper in the United States — for he's a natural born writer who has his eyes and ears ever alerted, and even a nose for news. *The Courier-Journal* never sent a better goodwill ambassador into the field. He'd get a story, I believe, where no other man could find one. Even if the story were on the critical side, the person or persons it was about would still like the man who wrote it. And it was not an unusual thing in earlier years, when he was making lengthy field trips on feature story assignments, for a newspaper man to be roughed up, black-jacked, shot at or even shot in my part of this Commonwealth where they didn't trust writers and were suspicious of strangers. But Joe, with his smiles, his friendly words — at least sixty per minute — became one of their beloved writers. Thousands know him personally; hundreds of thousands know him through his writing.

There is an old saying: Let a man be born into a minority group and let him choose a good wife and he will be a success in any vocation. To be born a Republican as Joe was in Benton, in western Kentucky's Marshall County — where in some precincts there once weren't enough Republicans for election officials — well, he's really in a minority.

Joe Creason has been and is a happily married man because he chose Shella, a beautiful woman, with as strong and positive character as any woman of Naomi's or my acquaintance. Shella has been and is always by Joe's side. And we should know this for Joe and Shella have visited us and we have visited them many times during the 26 or more years we have known each other.

I first met Joe Creason in 1946, when he came to our home, W-Hollow, to do a story for *The Courier-Journal Magazine*. Besides establishing a friendship that has lasted over the years, I recall the visit well because he had the first seat belts I ever had seen in a car.

The next time Joe Creason came was to do a feature about the real-life characters in my book *The Thread That Runs So True*. We spent two or three days together on that one, and I had a close-up look at his technique in interviewing people, his ease in talking with them, his

7

ability to get facts. He has returned to W-Hollow many times since then.

Was there ever a person with whom Joe Creason couldn't level? If he'd not been born to write, he'd have been great in the political field. But so many in politics are too soon forgotten. He won't be. Joe Creason is now public domain. Everybody owns and loves the man.

Before he stopped his *Magazine* writing, I know that he covered each of Kentucky's 120 counties many times. I doubt any man has ever been in more places in Kentucky.

Since he was called in off the road to do a daily column, people all over this Commonwealth have missed tall, affable Joe Creason. But they have never forgotten him, and they certainly still read him.

And now Joe will have a book published of his selected writing. He's done so much quality writing the selecting will be hard to do.

When I think of my friend Joe Creason — a writer with natural talents if one was ever born, a man who reaches the people through the printed page, a goodwill ambassador with a sense of humor who brings sunshine when the day is cloudy — I really can't say enough for this Kentuckian who is a legend in his day and time.

Jesse Stuart
W-Hollow, Kentucky

8

Preface

This collection of real-life vignettes of Kentucky humor, politics, sports, history, folklore, tall tales, and a few other categories was excerpted from a daily column that made its debut in *The Courier-Journal* on October 1, 1963. The column first was called "JOE CREASON'S KENTUCKY." That later was simplified to "joe creason," and I'm still trying to decide if someone was telling me something with that lower case spelling.

Anyway, with the news dominated then as now by Vietnam, inflation, riots, and assorted other crises, there was need for at least one spot in the paper to focus daily on humorous, ironic, and off-beat incidents that otherwise might never get into print but which are important since they show Kentuckians as they really are.

So, I was summoned from the lush pastures of newspaper feature writing, where I had grazed placidly for 15 years, and given the opportunity, as a fellow columnist once phrased it, "to dig a grave daily."

Perhaps on that first day I should have prepared a mimeographed reply suitable for instant mailing, setting down what I hoped the column might accomplish, because several times each year I receive letters almost identical to this one from 1968:

"Every day you pass on your quota of humorous little stories and trivia about Kentucky. But do you really believe such escapism is proper in a time of crisis? Using humor or telling us the philosophy of the courthouse whittlers and spitters in an effort to take our minds off the grave realities of the moment will not make them any less grave."

I agree that my repeating a funny story involving someone from Harlan or Louisville or Turkey Neck Bend, passing on a fact of history, providing a sample of folklore, or undertaking a ridiculous lost cause won't make the troubles that beset us disappear. But, since there's something therapeutic in laughter, these stories might cause our grave realities to seem less mountainous. I doubt a chuckle will do much to bring peace or cool to a long hot summer, but it might not do any harm, either.

Aside from hoping to provide a forum for items that couldn't compete for space with hard news developments, there was one other reason why I was pleased at the chance to have a go at column writing. I hoped that by calling attention to the genuine differences that exist in Kentucky as compared even to surrounding states — differences in attitudes, customs, traditions, the way humor creeps into every facet of life — I might kindle the pride of Kentuckians in the rich heritage of our Commonwealth.

My own feeling is that in an age of conformity, such as the period in which we now are living, when everyone is expected to act, think, and react alike, there's a glory in being different if those differences are natural and genuine.

Still, not all Kentuckians feel that way. Some seem to regard our being different as evidence that this is a backward, hayseed state; the fact we aren't a carbon-copy of the Californian or the New Yorker is, to them, something to be ashamed of, a hair shirt we must wear. With their perspective thus blurred, they look around and on every hand encounter examples of Kentucky's folk culture — speech, patterns, stories — and apologize, never realizing these characteristics mirror the pure Anglo-Saxon beginning of this state.

While I realized Kentucky had appalling shortcomings that couldn't be laughed away or glossed over with a veneer of Old-Worldism, by referring to the uniquenesses of the state, I hoped to counter in a small way the negativism some Kentuckians felt. High sounding motives, I realize, but it costs no more to dream first class.

From the outset it was my intention to use the scatter-shot approach to column writing; that is, to publish five or six relatively short stories daily on the theory that any reader might find at least one of interest to him.

Gathering material to slake the voracious appetite of such a column has been a many-splendored thing. My years of feature writing, during which time I have traveled some 500,000 miles in Kentucky, left me with a backlog of facts and contacts. I have spent an average of two days per week away from the office, scrounging for material. Moreover, I have received an average of 350 letters a month from readers, offering tips, leads, stories, and suggestions.

Has the column come within a long-distance telephone call of its lofty goals? I don't know. Reading the compilation of stories which follow will put you in position to judge for yourself.

Joe Creason
Louisville, Kentucky

Acknowledgments

I am indebted to many people associated with *The Courier-Journal* for their extreme patience in seeing the column this book came from worked down into a format with which I, at least, felt comfortable. They include Barry Bingham, Sr., former editor and publisher; Barry Bingham, Jr., present editor and publisher; Norman E. Isaacs and Robert P. Clark, former and present executive editors; and George Gill, managing editor.

Others on the newspaper who also deserve my special thanks are John Herchenroeder, James N. Roberts, and Cary Robertson, who as Sunday editor assigned me to do many of the feature-type stories that appear here.

Ted Weil, a long-time friend, should be thanked for suggesting years ago that someday I should publish excerpts from my columns in book form.

The production was handled by Dr. Samuel W. Thomas, an experienced hand in such matters since it was he who put together the impressive *Views of Louisville since 1766*, another book published by *The Courier-Journal* and *The Louisville Times*, and he also is associated with the G. R. Clark Press, a Louisville group active in historical publications.

My thanks also go to Joe Rigsby, of Doe-Anderson Advertising Agency, for his design of the book and for the drawings that appear throughout it, and to Evelyn E. Gordinier for her thorough copy reading.

And I would be remiss if I did not recognize the part played by my wife, Shella, in helping me dig laboriously through miniature mountains of clippings to select the material used to illustrate the humor, the folklore, and the history of Kentucky.

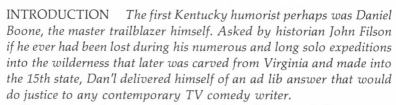

INTRODUCTION   *The first Kentucky humorist perhaps was Daniel Boone, the master trailblazer himself. Asked by historian John Filson if he ever had been lost during his numerous and long solo expeditions into the wilderness that later was carved from Virginia and made into the 15th state, Dan'l delivered himself of an ad lib answer that would do justice to any contemporary TV comedy writer.*

"I never was what you could call real lost," he mused, "but once or twice I was pretty confused for several days."

From that early day to this, a keen wit, a penchant for turning a colorful (if often uniquely worded) phrase has been the trademark of the Kentuckian. But Kentucky humor isn't the custard pie-in-the-face variety; it's more subtle, natural, unaffected, unexpected, and under-stated than that, often depending as much on things that are not said as upon things that are said.

For instance, there was the way John Campbell, an old mountain farmer, expressed his personal philosophy: "When I works, I works hard; when I sets, I sets loose; and when I think, I go to sleep."

And there was almost O. Henry-type drollery in the case of a Louis-ville woman, once a chain smoker, who had given up cigarettes after her husband, armed with the surgeon general's scare report, had con-vinced her she should quit. However, her halo rested precariously on her head, as a bit of soul-searching revealed.

"When my husband dies," she said, "I know exactly what I will do. I'll phone the funeral home, tearfully instruct them to come and get him. Then I'll ask them to stop on the way over and get me a carton of cigarettes!"

Here, then, are samples of the everyday, low-key, often offbeat humor of people caught in the act of being themselves.

12

CHAPTER 1

PEOPLE ARE THE FUNNIEST CRITTERS

Paul Barry of New Haven tells about the funeral of a
highly successful businessman who died a few years back
in nearby Bardstown. When his funeral procession left
the church for the cemetery, an armored car, which comes
from Louisville weekly to deliver currency to the town
banks, was caught in the middle of the motorcade.

As the procession passed down the street, a local
character, who had treated himself to one too many at
the tavern, spotted the line of vehicles.

"Get a load of that," he lisped, pointing to the armored
car, "who says you can't take it with you!"

As you perhaps know, flat land is an extremely scarce
commodity in the mountainous eastern quarter of
Kentucky and the towns are strung out, often two streets
wide and miles long, parallel to the highways. Consequently, a multitide of signs — No Littering, School
Crossing, Speed Zone, Railroad Crossing and others —
adorn the roads' rights of way.

When he taught at Loyall in Harlan County, William
McKay asked a student where he lived.

"Oh," the boy answered, "I live down the road a way
in Congested Area."

An out-of-state relative who is an amateur artist visited
Mrs. H. B. Broida in Louisville and, to expose her to some
of the flavor of Kentucky, they made a tour of back roads

13

where they came upon one of the 16 covered bridges that remain in the state.

The visitor was enthralled and they got out for a closer look at the wooden bridge. An old man who lived nearby came over to see what was up.

"I certainly would like to paint this bridge," the artist enthused as she viewed the picturesque old span from all angles.

"You do," the native replied, "and it's sure gonna take a lot of paint!"

The late Johnson Musselman was a Louisville magician of some considerable note who had one trick in his collection he never used.

It seems that at a convention of magicians, Musselman saw a new wrinkle of the old sword box illusion — the one where murderous-looking swords are thrust into a cabinet holding the magician's assistant. He bought the trick for a goodly price, but never put it into his act.

"I'll tell you," he explained in nonmagical candor, "I just don't see how it can work!"

All of us share a positive passion for rationalizing, attempting to apply logic to everything we do. As in the case of a group of salesmen who were sitting in the lobby of the Grand Hotel in Hazard some 15 years ago.

In those days, dozens of salesmen who visited various coal company commissaries stayed at the hotel and their after-dinner conversations were better — and often just as disconnected — as a segment of "Laugh-In."

"Man alive," one salesman this particular night enthused, "this sure was a great day for me. I made an awful lot of new friends."

"Yeah, I know," another rationalized, "I didn't sell anything, either."

How happy must a person be to be happy? Must he be just barely happy, fairly happy, or very happy?

That perplexing point arose in western Kentucky after a notorious local scoundrel had seen the light, repented of past misdeeds, and was ready to join the congregation of a rural church at a creekside baptismal service. The preacher marched the reformed rascal into the stream and plunged him under the water.

"Now tell us, brother," the preacher said when he'd come up. "How happy are you right now?"

"Preacher," the man gasped, "I'm happy all right, but I ain't what you'd call damn happy!"

If, as they say, true beauty is in the eye of the beholder, then it should stand to reason that the true meaning of words is in the ear of the listener. That is to say, a conversation of even the simplest words can be misunderstood totally when those involved aren't on the same wave length. A situation told by Dr. Ralph Congleton of Lexington is an example.

A few years back, his story goes, a lady from out of the state was visiting in Lexington. Since she'd heard so much about Kentucky, she was interested in learning more about the state, its history, culture, etc. So she went to the Lexington Public Library for assistance.

"This is my first time in Kentucky," she said, "and I wonder if you might suggest to me a good book on the state."

"I would recommend," the librarian told her, thinking of James Lane Allen's classic story, "that you check out 'A Kentucky Cardinal.'"

"Oh," ohed the visitor, a good Catholic, "I don't want a book on church history."

"You misunderstand," smiled the librarian, "this cardinal was a bird.

"Well," retorted the visitor, somewhat indignantly, "I most certainly don't want a book on church scandal!"

While visiting a friend in the hospital, George Trotter of
Lebanon saw a car roar up to the emergency entrance
and come to a tire-screeching halt. An excited young man
leaped out, raced up the steps three at a time, and spun
through the revolving door.

"What's the trouble?" an anxious nurse asked.

"My wife's going to have a baby!" he panted.

"Well, bring her on in," the nurse told him.

"Oh," the guy replied, "the baby isn't due for a month
— I'm just timing myself to see how long it will take
to get her here!"

The writing of a check is truly a ho-hum, everyday
occurrence and yet we all react differently to this act when
a sizeable sum of money is involved. Which explains the
puzzling reaction of a Louisvillian when it came time
for him to sign a check for a considerable sum of money
some time back.

This fellow was ready for the final signing of the papers
involved in the buying of a new house. A light drizzle
was falling the morning he and his wife met downtown
with a battery of bankers and lawyers to wind up the deal.

After all the legal matters had been explained and the
papers signed, the time came for the buyer to produce the
down payment. This he did with a flourish by whipping
out his checkbook and, with a nonchalance that suggested
he dealt in such sums several times a day, made out a
check for $5,000. Then, stifling a bored yawn, he flipped
the check on to the banker's desk.

That done, he arose, shook hands with all present and
started out the door, trying all the while to pull on his
wife's powder-blue raincoat!

Jack Dougherty, a Louisvillian whose secret ambition,
since he's in the business, is to blacktop the world, tells a
story which he vows is gospel true. And even if it really

didn't happen, it should have.

Anyway, two men who live across the street from each other in Louisville backed out of their facing driveways at the same time and came banging together in the middle of the street. They climbed out of their cars, surveyed the dented fenders and broken glass and decided they'd better call in the police to make a report of the accident.

The cops were called, and while they were waiting one of the men opened the glove compartment of his car, pulled out a bottle of good Bourbon and suggested that they have a belt to fortify themselves against the cold until the law arrived.

Being conscious of good health practices, the other man was agreeable and took a long swig before handing back the bottle. The first fellow tightened the cap, returned the bottle to the compartment and locked it.

"Aren't you going to have a drink?" asked the puzzled man who had indulged.

"Not right now," came the smirking answer. "I think I'll just wait until after the police have been here!"

It sounds for all the world like a trade joke, but a middle-aged man, dressed in work clothes, came into the lingerie department of a Louisville shopping center store and announced he wanted to buy a corset for his wife.

"What bust?" the clerk asked him.

"The zipper," he replied, "is what bust!"

All who aren't overly nimble even when wide awake know how painfully slow of wit they are for the first minute or so after being roused from a sound sleep. For that reason, most of us have boundless admiration for those parties who can cast off the drug-like effect of sleep quickly and come up bright-eyed and bushy-tailed as soon as their eyes are open. As in the case of a fellow

Larry Stone of Central City tells about.

When TVA was building the world's largest steam electric power plant on the Green River near Central City, the work force included one goldbricker who was notorious for his ability to find a quiet place to take a nap every afternoon. One day the foreman found him seated in a remote spot, his head bowed over almost touching his chest, sound asleep.

Not wanting to risk creating an incident with the union, the foreman tip-toed away and returned with a steward to bear witness to the work violation as he fired the man.

Just as the foreman was about to rouse him and lower the boom, the goldbricker awoke on his own and, while his head was still bowed, saw two feet standing in front of him.

But he didn't panic. Instead he said "Amen" in a firm voice, arose and walked piously back to work.

Those who have been in that part of Kentucky know that Ghent, Warsaw, Sparta, Florence, and other towns with exotic foreign names are located only a few miles apart in the Carroll-Gallatin-Boone County area in the northern part of the state.

The story is told that early in World War II, after Hitler had invaded Poland, a man came running into the hardware store operated by the late G. G. Woods in Carrollton and ordered all the shotgun shells he had on hand. He was asked why all the ammunition.

"I just heard on the radio," he said breathlessly, "that the Germans are in Warsaw, but they'll get a helluva fight from me if they try to take Carrollton!"

Being the type myself who invariably seems to think of penetrating remarks well after it's too late to make them, I've always admired agile-minded individuals who have a spontaneous remark on the tip of their tongue to fit any situation. This talent isn't restricted to any particular group, and may be found in what at first might appear to be the least likely setting.

For instance, there was Sister Bona Vita Murphy, a little Irish-born Catholic nun who taught at Nazareth College near Bardstown from 1890 to her death in 1928. The more I've heard of her, the more I realize she was forever delivering the kind of suitable, off-the-cuff remarks I wish I might have said.

Nazareth is located in the distillery area of Nelson County. In fact, the college property adjoins a distillery on the back side. Sometime in the early 1920's Cardinal Glennon of St. Louis was visiting the college and, after a tour of the campus, was talking to teachers, including Sister Bona Vita.

"I am well pleased with Nazareth," the cardinal said, then added in a joking voice, "but I noticed there is a well-beaten path from here to the distillery."

"Faith," cut in Sister Bona Vita, a twinkle in her eyes, "and it didn't take Your Grace long to find the path, now did it?"

One characteristic inborn in most Kentuckians is a streak of honesty that at times can be as blunt as a sledge-hammer blow. As in a story Charles E. Whittle, Sr., a Brownsville lawyer, tells on himself.

It was in the 1920's and Whittle had just opened his law office. A short time later, he says, one of the first clients he had represented came into his office for a full explanation of why the bill he had received had come to a certain figure.

"Well," Whittle started, "I have a family to support. The overhead here in this office is heavy. Paper is expensive and there's lights and heat and this typewriter here cost $100. My furniture came high, too.

"And there are these law books," he continued, waving his hand at the rows of publications covering one wall, "they're awfully expensive. Why, the law books in just this one room cost thousands of dollars."

The client sat silent for several seconds after that oration.

"Them law books," he finally said in a solemn voice. "You ain't never read most of 'em, have you?"

Down in the hills of Jackson County they tell about a boy who was called for induction into the army. At the induction station, a sergeant was asking the usual questions. "What were you in civilian life?" he inquired.

"I," came the short but sweet answer, "was happy!"

All of us tend to get uptight with worry when faced with changes or new situations. Take the story Mrs. Kate Purvis, Central City, tells.

When her father, J. W. Bastin, married in 1886, he was very young and understandably nervous about the matter.

"I hate to marry and leave home," he confessed to his father.

"But I married and left home when I was about your age," he was told.

"That was different," the apprehensive groom-to-be rebutted. "You married Maw — you didn't marry a total stranger!"

Early in the year customers who came into a Louisville bank that operates a Christmas Club were asked if they'd like to participate in the savings plan.

"Wouldn't you like to join our Christmas Club?" a teller at one of the bank's suburban branches asked an old gentleman.

"No, ma'am," he replied simply. "I doubt I'd get to come to many of the meetings."

20

Fred Burkhard, who edits a weekly newspaper at Liberty, tells a story which illustrates how there's more humor in real life than in the contrived, hoked-up situations on which TV comdey shows thrive.

Back around the turn of the century, Burkhard says, matches weren't as refined as today and sometimes entire boxes wouldn't strike. Merchants were constantly badgered with complaints from customers.

Such was the situation when a woman returned a box of faulty matches to Henry Harmon, who ran a store at Dunnville. Taking a match from the box, Harmon swiped it across the seat of his pants and it burst into flame. He tried a second match and it, too, struck.

"These matches seem to be striking all right to me," he said to the disgruntled customer.

"For you, maybe," the woman admitted grudgingly, "but you're crazy if you think I've got time to come down here and rub a match across the seat of your pants every time I want a light!"

Ed Hasenour, Louisville restaurant operator, was taking applications for jobs at his place. Each applicant was told to fill out a form which asked for information regarding where the prospect had worked previously, for how long, etc.

One applicant was almost painfully honest when he came to the question: "Why did you leave previous job?"

He wrote: "Too hard."

Arthur Chandler of Frankfort passes on a story involving a notorious old reprobate — gambler, whisky drinker, cusser, brawler — who was about to pass on to his reward, if any. The preacher was called in and asked if he would like "to renounce the devil."

"Guess not," he replied feebly. "In the condition I'm in, and according to the way I've lived, I ain't in no position to create hard feelings from nobody!"

One of nature's true noblemen is Ray Wimberg, Louisville's most ardent civic booster. Hardly an event is held in the city — sports, theater, music, lectures, political rallies (either party) — but that he's on hand to meet and greet people and make them feel welcome.

Being in the restaurant supply business, Wimberg also keeps his ear close to the ground as far as his line of work is concerned. He and Mrs. Wimberg were having dinner downtown in a restaurant when a waiter dropped a tray loaded with dishes.

"Listen, Mama," he said to his wife over the sound of the breaking china, "they're playing our song!"

Since my waistline is beginning to look more like a wasteline, it's clearly obvious that I have a hearty appetite. One of the few times I've really lost my relish for food occurred some years back when I was at the Kentucky Maximum Security Prison at Eddyville — on assignment, let me add — and the late Wilton W. Thomas, the warden, asked me to have dinner with him.

The meal was delicious and Thomas told me one of the prison trustees was his cook.

"What's he in for?" I asked.

"Oh, he tried to kill his wife and mother-in-law," Thomas replied casually. "He poisoned their food!"

Dr. Troy Eslinger, a former Lexington Presbyterian minister who now is president of Lees Junior College at Jackson, is a man with a deep sense of humor and a stock of stories to prove it.

One of his stories concerns a time he was dickering with a Lexington automobile dealer for a new car. They had gotten fairly close together on the deal, but still were several dollars apart.

"Come on now, surely you can do better than that,"

Eslinger said he coaxed the dealer. "After all, I'm just a poor Presbyterian preacher."

"I know," he vows the dealer replied. "I've heard you preach!"

Until I came across a hotel clerk in Ashland some years ago, I'd always felt the most confident person extant surely must either be one who would work a crossword puzzle with a fountain pen or a Marine from Texas. However, this clerk topped them with room to spare.

I was trying to do some work in my room and called the desk to ask if the hotel happened to have a set of encyclopedia handy.

"No, we don't," the clerk said. "What did you want to know?"

Seems four residents of Dosker Manor, a housing project for senior citizens in Louisville, were at a particularly crucial spot in a bridge game.

When one man made an especially daring bid, his partner, who is deaf and wears a hearing aid, reached hurriedly into his pocket for a tranquilizer. It was only after he'd gulped it down that he realized what he had swallowed wasn't a nerve pill, but a bean-sized spare battery for his hearing aid!

Greensburg is probably the most art-conscious town its size in Kentucky. In 1955, the Greensburg Art Club was organized by Mrs. Russell Phillips and a sizeable colony of talented local artists has been active ever since.

A few years back a big batch of paintings by club artists were on display in town.

"Wuz these pictures took or drawed?" an old man asked.

23

Upon being assured they were "drawed," he passed the most sincere compliment at his command.

"I'll be dogged," he marveled, "they look just like they was took!"

Years ago, when some people really didn't understand banks, an old mountain man in Perry County finally was convinced he should take the money he kept buried in a coffee can in the back yard and put it on deposit in a Hazard bank. The very next morning, however, he appeared at the bank to withdraw his treasure.

When the money was handed to him, he stood at the cashier's window and slowly counted it twice.

"Isn't it all there?" the cashier asked.

"Yep," came the grudging reply, "but just barely!"

Mankind has been nibbling at forbidden fruit since the days of Adam and Eve, as a story told by J. R. McAfee, a Kentucky Methodist minister for some 50 years prior to his retirement, proves.

When he was about 12, his story goes, a favorite pastime of the boys at the country church he attended was to gather around the stile block and watch the women and girls, burdened down as they were by hoopskirts, dismount from the horses most of them rode in those days. One Sunday a girl was sliding from her horse when one of her skirt hoops caught on the pommel of the side saddle and she hung suspended, face down, in a sea of petticoats.

The minister of the church saw what had happened and came running toward the crowd of gawking boys.

"Look the other way, boys," he warned sternly, "or you're liable to be struck blind!"

"By golly," one of the older boys giggled as he slapped a hand over the left side of his face, "I think I'll risk one eye!"

A breakdown in communications between individuals, groups and even nations is one of the problems facing the world today. That being the case, it's amazing how uncomplicated and clear many situations can seem once they have been explained in precise, easy-to-understand language. Julian Van Winkle, the former head of Stitzel-Weller Distillery in Louisville, illustrates the point with a story.

Seems that a small company was trying to start a new insurance program for employees and the plan had to have unanimous participation. However, one man was an adamant holdout. Other workers and low-tier officials tried to reason with him, but he continued to refuse.

Then one day the boss of bosses called him on the carpet and told him bluntly that he'd be fired unless he got on the band wagon. Needless to say, the man saw readily that his previous unbending posture might have been a mistake. Later fellow workers wanted to know why he'd changed his mind so quickly.

"Well," he answered reasonably, "I just never had the plan explained to me so clear before!"

Talk about embarrasing moments....

A funeral director in south central Kentucky was handling a funeral some time back and the preacher performing the service was notoriously long-winded, one given to reading from the Scriptures and then explaining the passages in infinite detail.

While the minister was reading his text, the funeral director drove out to the cemetery to check on last minute details. He returned to the church by a side door and noted the preacher had stopped talking. So he marched to the casket, motioned for the pallbearers to step forward, and the body was removed. Not until the funeral had been completed at the cemetery did he learn he'd made a slight goof.

"You remember back there at the church?" the preacher said in a deeply injured voice. "Well, I hadn't started to preach!"

The Most Reverend Thomas J. McDonough, archbishop of Louisville, is an ardent golfer. Some time back he was preparing to play with two friends when a man, obviously a non-Catholic as it turned out, arrived on the tee. Since one of the trio knew him, he was asked if he'd like to join the group.

"Archbishop," said the player who knew the late arrival, "this is Paul — —."

The foursome played the round.

"It," the man who'd joined the group said later, shaking the archbishop's hand, "was nice to have met you, Arch!"

All those who come from a small county seat town know that by long-standing tradition the first Monday of the month is County Court Day, a time when people come to town whether or not they have any court-related business and the streets usually are jammed.

W. B. Timmons, a former resident of Lebanon, the seat of Marion County, who now lives in Miami, tells about a merchant from his county who made the first of many succeeding trips to New York years ago to visit wholesale outlets to buy goods for his store. He arrived by rail late at night and couldn't tell too much about the Big City then.

But when he arose the next morning and looked out his hotel window, he saw the streets were swarming with people rushing to and fro.

"This," he mused, "must be County Court Day in New York!"

This is a noisy world in which we're surrounded by a constant clatter of sounds, some restfully soothing and some so marrow-chilling they can turn the stoutest spine to pure jelly.

According to Larry Stone, some of the loafers at one of the barber shops at Central City were discussing this and that and especially the most frightening sounds a man can hear.

"There's nothing can scare you worse than hearing a groan in the dark when you know nobody's there," one man said.

"The sudden buzz of a rattlesnake at your feet when you don't have on boots is scarier than that," another of the talkers suggested.

"I know a sound worse than all yours put together," a third man in the group spoke up. "It's a long, low whistle from a mechanic lookin' under the hood of your car!"

All who have tried to shake the cigarette habit can sympathize with Bill Lewis, Anchorage.

"I tried to give up my addiction to cigarettes by chewing mints," he moaned. "Now I'm addicted to both!"

Hardin McLane is a former high school basketball coach and in that line of work he was exposed, he no doubt thought, to every kind of unexpected experience in the book. But his basketball background was barely a warm-up for some of the oddball things that happened to him after he became city judge of Elizabethtown.

For instance, on a weekend police arrested for the 129th time the town's most consistent drunk and jail patron. On the citation the arresting officer noted that the man had been quite, but not quiet, vocal in reciting how he was "going to run for city judge and change a few things around here."

When the man was brought into court at 9 a.m. on the following Monday, McLane was ready with a psychological ploy of the type he had used in coaching.

"I want you to come over here and sit in my chair," he said to the then-sober boozer. "You said you wanted to be judge, so I'm going to let you try this case. You're going to be me, and I'm going to be you."

They exchanged places and McLane took the role of defendant.

"Your Honor," he began morosely, "I know I've been arrested 129 times for public drunkenness in the city of Elizabethtown, seven times in the last two months alone. Now you've been good to me, judge. You've given me light sentences and you've tried to straighten me out. I know I haven't been much of a citizen, but I'm sorry and I'm going to throw myself on the mercy of the court."

That said, McLane sat down in the chair that had been occupied by the defendant.

"I want you to know," the accused drunk said, taking the role of judge, "that I think all this stuff in the past about you is a mistake. I think you're a fine fellow and since the court is supposed to be compassionate, I'm letting you go. Case dismissed!"

With that he arose and walked out the door.

"Let him go," the out-psyched Judge McLane said to the officers. "He'll be back in a week and I'll be judge again then!"

Fred Burkhard tells about a boy from rural Casey County who never had been more than 15 miles from home until he visited relatives who lived in Cincinnati. Upon his return, acquaintances gathered around to hear his impression of the city.

"Well," he mused meditatively, "it's a right interesting place, but it's too far away ever to amount to anything!"

A lady walked into a fruit-vegetable market in St. Matthews.

"Do you all have any home-grown peaches?" she asked in a heavy accent that literally dripped with the aroma of magnolia blossoms.

"No, ma'am," the clerk said, "the peaches we have

were grown in Georgia."

"Well, mah goodness," the lady drawled, "that's just what ah mean!"

T. C. Dedman, who runs the Beaumont Inn at Harrodsburg, tells about a fellow he once knew who seemed destined to become an eternal college student. He liked school so much he'd already hung around for eight years, slowly sipping at the fountain of knowledge.

"What's he going to be when he graduates?" someone asked his father.

"I guess," came the sad reply, "he's gonna be an old man!"

If you've ever been mired in one of those traumatic how-do-I-get-out-of-this-one situations, then you'll appreciate the predicament in which a young Louisville mother once found herself.

It all started when, after resisting mightily, she finally was conned into becoming a Cub Scout den mother. The initial meeting of new sponsors was scheduled in a room at a suburban church where assorted community organizations assembled regularly.

She had been gone from home nearly an hour when someone from the Cub Scouts telephoned and asked her husband if she planned to attend the meeting. Later a second call was received, stating she still hadn't arrived. Her husband was beginning to worry when, more than two hours after she'd left, she finally returned home.

"You just won't believe what happened to me," she sighed, sinking into a chair. "When I got to the church, I followed a bunch of other people into a room in the basement and took a seat. I hadn't been there long before I realized I was with the wrong group, but then I didn't dare get up and leave for fear of making myself conspicuous.

"You see," she blushed, "I had gotten in on a meeting of Alcoholics Anonymous!"

Mrs. T. Jeremiah Beam of Louisville grew up in Anderson County and as a girl she remembers hearing heated arguments between Union and Confederate veterans as they rehashed Civil War battles in which they had fought. But she always felt there was more sound than fury in their recaps because of a statement made by an aged Confederate as he placed a wreath on the grave of a Union veteran who had just died.

"The enemy," the old man said, a trace of a sob in his voice, "is slowly advancing backward!"

It's strange how attitude sometimes can change certain catastrophe into joyous exuberance.

Jim Morrisey, who is involved in the weight-watching business, tells about a woman member of a class in western Kentucky who lost 71 pounds, ending a life-long weight problem. At one meeting of the class she was telling about coming home with her arms full of packages, unlocking the door and having her unmentionables fall off.

"It was," she sighed, "the happiest day of my life!"

In earlier, less sophisticated days, old-time peddlers (or hucksters) did a thriving business in some rural sections of Kentucky. These vendors would load a varied stock of staples, ranging from baking soda to bolts, aboard a truck or van and take their portable store door to door on certain days each week.

For years one certain peddler had been making the rounds in western Kentucky. Because the items he offered were of good quality, many women came to depend on him for various things, including cosmetics.

One week the regular peddler was sick and so a substitute driver was covering his route. Being new, he wasn't too familiar with the wide assortment of goods on the van.

"Do you have any pancake make-up today?" one woman asked him.

"I don't remember puttin' any of that on this morning," the novice peddler said, "but I do know I got some instant pie-filling!"

Louisville restauranteur George Imorde, Sr., recalls a philosophical conversation years ago between his father, Henry, and Young E. Allison, the famed author. The two men were riding to town together one morning when Allison broke out a pack of cigars and offered one to Imorde.

"No, thanks," he declined, "I never smoke in the early morning."

"Isn't habit a funny thing?" Allison mused. "Look at the habit you've gotten into — not smoking a cigar first thing in the morning!"

No matter how long they've been in the profession, doctors, dentists, lawyers and others, including journalists, are said to be practicing their trade. And that phrase can be confusing.

Mrs. George W. Wilson, III of Lexington is an attorney. Some time back her housekeeper answered the telephone. Although Mrs. Wilson could hear only the housekeeper's half of the conversation, the caller must have asked if Mrs. Wilson was now practicing law.

"She's not practicing," the housekeeper said, "she's lawin' for real!"

Elizabeth Spalding, Bardstown, reported that a woman customer in a department store there didn't have enough cash to cover a purchase she had made.

"Would you like to give us a check?" the obliging clerk asked.

"That would be nice," the woman replied.

"On which bank?" the clerk pressed.

"Oh, it doesn't matter," the customer replied seriously, "I don't have any money in any of them!"

The cartoon image of the Boy Scouts of America is of a bunch of kids helping a poor old lady across a street — whether she wants to go or not. But the Scouts are strong on stressing other things, including loyalty, patriotism, honesty, and ingenuity.

And when it comes to ingenuity, a Lexington Scout showed that in great abundance when he came before a board of review to test his qualifications for a merit badge in life saving. As part of the test, a hypothetical emergency was set up and he was asked how he'd react.

"This building is on fire and the blaze is spreading," the boy was told. "On the second floor there's a man with a compound fracture of the leg. He's unconscious. What would you do?"

The boy thought hard for a few seconds.

"Second floor . . . burning building . . . fractured leg," he mumbled almost under his breath as he mentally reviewed the desperate situation. "Gee, I guess the only thing to do would be to sound 'Taps'."

The 80-mile drive from Louisville to Lexington used to take the driver through Middletown, Eastwood, Simpsonville, Shelbyville, Graefenburg, Frankfort and Versailles. Today by using I-64, it's possible to by-pass that string of towns.

Which sets up a story from Lexington. A furniture dealer there was coming to Louisville to pick up a truck load of items for a wholesale firm. Because of the load size, he hired a town odd-job man to go along with him.

The helper was impressed with the new interstate, which he never had been on before, but he was somewhat discombobulated by the fact that all the old familiar landmark towns along the route were missing. As they got near to Louisville, he began to fidget and looked furtively out the window. Finally he asked the question burning in his mind.

"Jack," he blurted out, "what in hell have they done with Shelbyville!"

Wendell Butler, Kentucky Commissioner of Agriculture, tells about an old man who lived in Metcalfe County, whose eyes were failing, but whose deep sense of prideful vanity kept him from admitting it and going to a doctor for glasses.

One day he went out to the barn, saddled a mule and was about to mount and ride off when a grandson ran out of the house.

"Grandad," the boy shouted, "you got the saddle on backwards!"

"Danged little smart aleck," the old man spat, "you just couldn't wait to see which direction I was headed, could you?"

Because he is bald, the president of a bank in central Kentucky always wears a hat, even at work. He did, that is, until a chance conversation with the bank porter, a long-time employee.

"Why is it that after all these years of working here you still don't have an account with the bank?" he asked the porter one day.

"Because," the porter replied, glancing at the ever-present hat on his head, "you always look like you're about to go somewhere!"

Kentuckians are somewhat phlegmatic critters who seldom get carried away by the excitement of the moment. Either that or we have the faculty for putting first things first.

At any rate, Julian Goodman, who just happens to be president of a small eastern-based corporation by the name of the National Broadcasting Company, comes from Glasgow. A story he tells concerns his father, the late Charles A. Goodman, Sr. and the day he was named to head NBC. He called his father to tell him the good news.

"Dad," he said, "I want you to be the first to know that the directors of one of the world's largest corporations have just met and elected me president of NBC."

"That's wonderful, son," Mr. Goodman replied, "and when I have the time, I want you to tell me all about it. But I don't have the time to talk right now. This is Mule Day in town, I'm already late and there won't be another one for a month!"

Brother John Joseph, a teacher at St. Xavier High School in Louisville, tells a story about a priest who received a call to a small parish in the hills of eastern Kentucky. In order to start out impressively, he prepared an inspiring sermon for his first Sunday in the parish.

However, a heavy snow fell the night before and only one man, a farmer, made it through the drifts to church next day.

"Do you think we should go ahead with the service?" the priest asked the man.

"Well, your reverence," the parishoner replied, "I never was one to advise the clergy. All I know is farming. But I do know that if I was to go down to the field to feed the cattle and only one cow showed up, I'd feed that one cow."

34

Taking the hint, the priest laid the whole one-hour-plus service on the congregation of one. Afterwards he asked him how he liked it.

"As I said before," the farmer replied, "I never was one to advise the clergy. All I know is farming. But I do know that if I was to go down to the field to feed the cattle and only one cow showed up, I wouldn't feed her the whole darn load!"

It's amazing how sometimes certain circumstances can arise and make even a serious situation seem much less hairy than it appears at first. Louisville attorney Ed P. Jackson, Jr. passes along a story told by printing company executive W. I. Gibbs to prove the point.

Some years back on a state road in Leslie County an elderly mountain farmer in a mule-drawn wagon was involved in an accident with an auto. Claiming to have been grievously wounded, the farmer filed an action for injuries against the car driver.

"But isn't it true after the accident," the defendant's lawyer asked, "you said you never felt better in your life?"

"Well," the claimant started out evasively, "that morning I got up, hitched up my wagon, put my hound dog in the wagon and..."

"Give us a yes or no answer to my question," the lawyer interrupted.

"I'm comin' to that," the farmer snapped. "That morning I got up, hitched up my mule, put my hound dog in the back of the wagon and jest had got over the rise in the road when this big car barreled into my rear end.

"My mule was knocked to one side of the road, my hound dog to the other, and I was pinned under the seat. Directly here come a policeman, seen my mule had its leg broke, pulled out his gun and shot it dead. He went over to my dog, seen it was bad hurt, and shot it in the head.

"Then," the farmer continued, "he come over to me and asked, 'Well, how are you feelin'?' and, shore enough, I said 'I ain't never felt better in my life!'"

When he was a boy, Dr. Ben Hollis, now a Louisville physician, worked part time in a West End drug store. Early one morning the telephone rang when only he and the porter who cleaned up were there. After several rings, the porter answered.

"Do you have any trichlorophenoxyacetic acid?" the caller asked.

"Ma'am," the porter apologized as he tripped over the jaw-breaking drug, "I done told you all I know when I said hello!"

In the mid-1950's, Green County was the locale of one of the most fantastic oil strikes in the nation. High production wells were brought in at depths of 150 to 300 feet in front yards, side yards, gardens, barn lots, corn fields, and even the five-acre plot owned by a small, remote church.

The church's one-eighth share of the income from the 15 or more wells drilled on its land soon came to represent a tidy sum, and disposition of the money posed a mild crisis. A meeting of the entire congregation was called, and three resolutions were approved:

1 — Pay off all church debts immediately.

2 — Put a tidy sum in the bank, then divide the remaining money, plus future income, among the members.

3 — Take in no new members for the time being.

Years ago Thomas S. Waller and the late Jack E. Fisher occupied law offices on different floors of the Citizens Bank Building in Paducah. Both being great talkers, their greetings away from the courtroom often would be shot from the hip, so to speak.

One day when the elevator stopped at his floor to pick him up, Waller found Fisher was the only other passenger aboard.

"Hello, Tom," Fisher greeted him. "What do you know?"

"Everything, Jack," he replied modestly, "Ask me something."

"Well, sir," came the equally modest retort, "if there was anything I didn't know, I certainly would ask you."

By then the elevator had reached the lobby and the operator had been completely brainwashed. As they headed for the door, Waller heard him speaking to another operator.

"You know," he said admiringly, "there go the two smartest men in town!"

Since I'm so absentminded that when I pass a mail box I instinctively search my pockets for letters I've forgotten to post, I have great admiration for an aged mountain man I heard about who reportedly knew everything. However, he shrugged off his accomplishments.

"I just heard things here and there," he explained, "and I was too lazy to forget 'em!"

Coleman E. Smock, Simpsonville, recalls tidbits of crossroads advice he acquired years ago from characters he knew in the St. Mary section of Marion County, where he grew up. One was "Guinea" Mudd, a master horse-and-buggy chauffeur who, before autos were common, was in great demand among the salesmen who came into the area via train and then needed transportation to reach the rural stores in the county. Guinea had a way with horses, and he could use a whip with great skill. In fact, he kept the drummers amused as they drove along with his philosophical monologues and his feats with the whip.

One day he was driving a salesman for the first time. Guinea was in rare form with his whip. He leaned out of the buggy and flicked the blossom off a dandelion clean as a whistle. A horse fly lit on the horse's ear and he cut it off with nonchalant ease.

37

"Let's see you cut that down," the drummer said, pointing to a round object the size of a football hanging from a limb just up the road.

"Mister," Guinea replied, "that's a hornet nest, and they's something you always want to remember. A dandelion is a dandelion and a horse fly is a horse fly, but a hornet nest — that's an organization!"

It is a well-known fact that Kentuckians are notorious for the regard and devotion they feel for dogs. And one who felt those emotions deeper than most was John Pritchard, of Mayfield, once the loving owner of a big, rawboned hound dog named Tiger.

Now Tiger wasn't any great shakes as a hunter. In fact, the only time he ever showed even mild interest in anything was when a cat was around. Then Tiger would turn into a flop-eared counterpart of his name. He'd lay back his ears and pursue the cat to any extreme.

One day Pritchard and Tiger were walking down by the Illinois Central Railroad tracks when Tiger spotted a big yellow tomcat. Tiger lit into the cat and the two were at it hot and heavy when a freight train hove into sight. The cat saw the train in time and leaped clear. But poor Tiger was so wrapped up in his mission of extermination that he never saw what hit him.

"I hate losing Tiger, sure," the sad owner said later. "But what I hate most is that he died thinkin' that tomcat had done it to him!"

Izzy Goodman, Louisville, tells about a race horse that lost a race it was supposed to win easily.

"Why didn't you go to the front?" the trainer roared at the jockey.

"Because," the rider answered, "I wanted to stay with the horse!"

The total assets of a backroad farmer in Green County
had been reduced to an aged mule worth maybe $10. In
desperation, he decided to run a lottery on the mule and,
to his surprise, raised $300 by selling chances on the beast
for 25 cents each. A drawing was held, but when the
winner came to claim his prize, the mule was dead.

Later the farmer was asked if he hadn't gotten a lot of
lip over selling chances on a dead mule.

"Only from the feller that won," he admitted, "he raised
so much hell I finally had to give him back his quarter!"

Take it from Sam Houston Watkins, an Elizabethtown
man of many parts, it's a mighty thin line that separates
saying just barely enough from saying just barely too
much.

He learned that great truism some years back on a
vacation to Texas, the state where Sam Houston, the man
whose name he bears, is the number one hero.

Anyway, Watkins was driving near Amarillo when he
was stopped by a state policeman who thought he might
have been going a mite too fast. The trooper started
writing out a ticket and asked to see his driver's license.

"Where did you get that name?" the trooper smiled as
he prepared to tear up the ticket after he'd glanced at
the driver's license.

"I got it from my grandfather," Watkins replied, then
pressed his luck a trifle too far by adding facetiously,
"and my grandfather got it from a man who left Tennessee
for a little state out west a long time ago and never
was heard from again."

What do you think happened after that?

Garland McKinney is a Louisville resident now, but he
lived long enough along the Green River in Green County
to lay in a plentiful supply of earthy stories with a
crossroads flavor.

One story concerns his cousin named Buck, who, at an early age, developed a salty vocabulary that would have put a veteran sailor to shame.

Buck's proudest possession was a young goat to which he would hitch a small wagon and enjoy a ride occasionally. Those occasions, however, were rare since the goat was stubborn as a mule, if you'll pardon the mixing of barnyard types, and usually couldn't even be caught.

One hot summer morning, Buck decided he'd like a ride, but the goat, refusing to cooperate, was taking appropriate evasive action. Finally after chasing him all over the lot, Buck stopped running and proceeded to lecture the animal, and the surrounding world, with words that all but peeled the bark off the trees.

It happened that his grandfather was resting under a nearby tree and heard Buck's dissertation.

"If you don't stop that cussin'," the old man warned, "the devil will get you and that goat, too."

"He might get me," Buck rationalized, "but he'll play hell catchin' that #!*+* goat!"

The word "club" has such a pliable meaning that sometimes it should be used with a word of explanation. The late Otto Rothert, who for years was secretary of The Filson Club, Louisville's celebrated historical society, became aware of that the first time he returned to Notre Dame, his alma mater, for a reunion.

"I suspected," he used to say, "that when I said I worked for The Filson Club, most people thought I was a bartender at some night club."

Although I'm really not as old as some, nevertheless I can remember when you'd see as many horses as automobiles around the courthouse square in Benton, the western Kentucky town where I was born. For when I was a boy, that section of far western Kentucky was isolated and roads which only Model-T's could traverse were the rule rather than the exception. Farm trucks were downright rare and horse-drawn wagons and buggies still were widely used.

Horses could be hitched anywhere around the square in the middle of town except for one space reserved for George Homer Wyatt, the Santa-sized town marshal who rode a cast-off World War I motorcycle. The space was marked with a warning sign and George Homer guarded it zealously.

However, one day while the one-man law department was out in hot pursuit, a farmer hitched his team of horses in the forbidden space. George Homer was furious when he returned.

"Don't you know you can't hitch here?" he chewed on the man.

"And just why not?" the farmer reasoned, pointing to the words painted inside the reserved spot. "Don't that there sign say 'Fine For Hitching?'"

It is a well-known fact that people in central Kentucky dearly love to follow the horses. They also have been known, on occasion, to partake of our most renowned liquid product, and I don't mean spring water. And that, horses and Bourbon, is a lead into a story told by C. Robert Yeager, Middlesboro native, University of Kentucky graduate, and now president of a jewelry manufacturing company in Attleboro, Massachusetts.

When he was in school at UK, Yeager says, a nearby rural church hired a new preacher from out of the state. His first sermon came at the time in the spring when the race meeting was starting at Keeneland Race Track and so he delivered a ringing oration on the evils of gambling, especially betting on horses. The message went over like a lead balloon, as did his second sermon when he spoke on the evils of drinking whisky, even 7-year-old, mellowed-in-the-barrel, Kentucky Bourbon.

Sensing things weren't going too well, before his third

sermon he consulted one of the elders of the church for advice.

"The thing is," he was told, "you don't know this state. Most Kentuckians like to bet on horses and take a nip or two. What you ought to do is preach for a while on something that isn't controversial."

"Give me a subject," the new preacher pleaded.

"Well," the old man mused, after some thought, "why not preach a sermon on the Chinese. We don't have many of them around here!"

Since I'm a great hand myself at holding in reserve and not using items I'm especially proud of, I can appreciate the feeling of a woman a friend in Lexington was telling me about. The woman is a cook and one day she reported for work wearing a beautiful set of new store-bought teeth.

However, at noon the lady of the house noticed she removed the new choppers and gummed her food the same as before.

"Why don't you use your new teeth?" the cook was asked.

"Well, I paid $250 for them teeth," came the answer, "and I sure ain't gonna wear 'em out eating!"

In and around Marion County, Judge Joe C. Jarboe is noted for his dry sense of humor.

A case in point is the time he was riding on a bus between Bowling Green and Hopkinsville. The man in the seat next to him was a bragging Texan who insisted in belittling everything he saw. Kentuckians, he kept insisting, are slow, never get anything done.

"In Texas," he insisted, "we get things started and finished quick."

About then the bus passed the 351-foot-high monument that stands at the birthplace of Jefferson Davis at Fairview.

"What in the world is that?" the Texan asked.

"Beats me," Judge Jarboe replied. "I was by here yesterday and it hadn't been built then!"

Then there was the poor slob who came home from work with only half of his pay in hand. His wife began chewing him out royally.

"I spent the rest of it," he explained, "to buy something for the house."

"Why, that's wonderful," the wife bubbled, reversing her field. "What did you buy for the house?"

"I bought," he answered, ducking for cover, "another round of drinks!"

It doesn't tie in with a roundup of native Kentucky humor, but a warning I read years ago in one of the late Bennett Cerf's collections of jokes perhaps should be fitted in about here. It went:

"STOP! Don't read too many jokes at one time. They're funnier in small does."

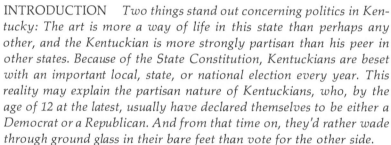

INTRODUCTION   *Two things stand out concerning politics in Kentucky: The art is more a way of life in this state than perhaps any other, and the Kentuckian is more strongly partisan than his peer in other states. Because of the State Constitution, Kentuckians are beset with an important local, state, or national election every year. This reality may explain the partisan nature of Kentuckians, who, by the age of 12 at the latest, usually have declared themselves to be either a Democrat or a Republican. And from that time on, they'd rather wade through ground glass in their bare feet than vote for the other side.*

An example of how partisan the Kentuckian can be is pointed up in a story told by Dr. Tim Lee Carter, the Republican Congressman who represents the Fifth District. Some years back Dr. Carter was called to the bedside of his area's most ardent Republican, an old man in his mid-80's who for 65 years had worked for the party. After an examination, the doctor had a serious pronouncement to make.

"You've got only a month at most to live," he said, "and I'd advise you to get your affairs in order as soon as possible, starting with the most important."

"In that case," the old man replied, "the first thing I better do is go to the courthouse and change my registration from Republican to Democrat."

The doctor was astounded, and asked for an explanation.

"Well, I look at it this way," the old man replied. "If somebody has got to go, I'd rather it was one of theirs than one of ours!"

Of such stuff is Kentucky-style politics made.

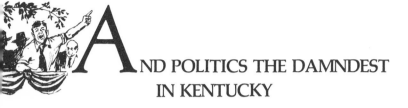

AND POLITICS THE DAMNDEST
IN KENTUCKY

Kentucky doesn't require that those running for the office of coroner be a doctor. The only requirement is that the coroner be able to recognize if a body is dead or not.

Because of this, some years back in one of the eastern Kentucky counties three former coal miners were candidates for coroner. Two of the men had been injured during World War II and they were using their war wounds in an effort to gain the sympathy of the voters. But since the third candidate had not even been in the war, he was more or less up the creek without a paddle.

At speakings held around the county, one of the war injured would call attention to his missing right arm.

"I lost my arm fightin' for my country in the big war," he would say. "I was a coal miner before, but I can't mine no coal now. I got a big family and I need your vote."

"I was a coal miner, too, before the big war," the second man would say, calling attention to the right leg he had lost, "and if you think it would be hard minin' coal with just one arm, think how it would be trying to work in a mine with just one leg. I got a big family too, and I need your vote."

The non-veteran was really faring badly in such oratorical exchanges until he hit upon his own way to gain some of the sympathy vote.

"Now I wasn't in the war," he said, "and I didn't lose no arm nor no leg. But I want you to know, I'm about the worst ruptured man in this whole county!"

The matter of political party loyalty, so pronounced among Kentuckians, was the subject of a story Charles Aaron, who distributes oil in the Lake Cumberland area when he isn't fishing or trading yarns, was telling at his place in Russell Springs.

"My grandfather was about the strongest Republican that ever lived," he figured. "A year before his death, one of his best friends decided to run for sheriff on the Democrat ticket, and he came to grandfather and asked if he could expect his support and vote.

"'Well, it's like this,' grandfather told him, 'I never voted for but one Democrat in my whole life and, by damn, that year the corn never got knee high and turned yaller as a pumpkin!'"

In the interest of providing equal time to the other side, Louisville Mayor Frank W. Burke, a former U.S. Congressman, calls attention to the old saying that holds, "to err is Republican, to forgive is Democratic."

A story told by Louisville attorney Arthur W. Grafton illustrates how a Kentuckian can rationalize his partisan instinct. There have been times, admits Grafton, a Democrat, when he was sorely tempted to vote for the other side, but each time he recalls a chilling warning once given to former Federal Judge Roy M. Shelbourne during a moment of similar soul-searching.

Judge Shelbourne was a young man then, living in Bardwell, Ballard County. One day he was discussing politics with a group of older men and he happened to say he just might vote for the Republican in an upcoming election.

"Young man, don't do that," the elder statesman of the group pleaded. "I voted for a Republican once 40 years ago and my coffee hasn't tasted the same since!"

Partisanship to the contrary, there is something different
in the way any election in Kentucky is conducted.
Because politics is such a way of life in this state, a
campaign for an office takes on an urgency that almost
defies the imagination. It is when local county offices are
up for grabs every fourth year that electioneering reaches
a fever pitch, with signs, slogans, mottoes, and sayings
adding a distinct flavor to the goings-on.

A few years back a candidate in central Kentucky had
as his campaign motto this solemn promise: "I will be
the last one to let you down." Ironically, he was an
undertaker running for coroner.

In a mountain county, a candidate for magistrate
offered this take-it-or-leave-it proposition to the electorate:
"If you elect me, I promise to stop getting drunk, picking
fights, and toting a gun."

This pledge to wage a clean fight was made by a man
offering himself for sheriff in a Purchase-area county:
"I have never campaigned on anybody else's shortcomings
and mistakes and I never will. I will win on my own."

And a county judge candidate in a Bluegrass county
passed out handbills containing only these words: "I have
made no wild promises except one — honest government."

For the most part, those who have been elected to high
office in Kentucky have been men — and some women —
who were far better than green hands at talking; they've
also been quick-witted, had a good sense of humor, and
they've been able to laugh at themselves when the time
was right.

Alben W. Barkley was one man who possessed all these
traits, and more. In public life for 50 years, he rose from
local office to be speaker of the House of Representatives,
majority leader of the Senate, and vice president of the
United States.

One story he told in which he was the butt of a joke
took place in Rockcastle County during one of his races
for the Senate. When the very Democratic Mr. Barkley
arrived at the courthouse in that strongly Republican

county to make a speech, he was elated to find all seats in the circuit courtroom taken and people were standing around the wall.

"Don't be too pleased, Alben," cautioned Circuit Judge Roscoe Tartar. "These people aren't here to hear you speak — I've subpoenaed them all as witnesses in some moonshine whisky cases I'm going to try when you're finished!"

The mere fact that people in the audience don't yawn openly or shake their watches should never lull a political candidate in Kentucky into believing he has his listeners eating out of the palm of his hand. John McKenzie Moss, who went on to become Congressman and assistant secretary of the Treasury under Coolidge, learned that when he ran for judge of the Warren-Edmonson County circuit in the early 1900's.

One night he made a speech in a one-room country school in Edmonson County. The room was packed and on the front row was a little old deaf lady who seemed to be hanging on to his every word by means of an old-fashioned brass ear trumpet. When Moss moved back and forth across the platform, she shifted the trumpet from one ear to the other so as not to miss a word.

Seeing how appreciative she was, Moss was inspired to scale new heights of oratory. As soon as he'd finished he sought out the lady.

"I saw how closely you followed what I had to say," he said in a loud voice, speaking into the ear trumpet. "What did you think of my speech?"

"Well," she replied in a toneless, high-pitched voice, "I've hearn better!"

Nor is it ever safe for persons holding even the highest offices in Kentucky to assume that their names are exactly household words.

During World War II, Louisville stores were so low on clerks that many would hire just about anyone who could fill out an order slip. One day Mrs. Keen Johnson, whose husband then was governor, came into a store and bought several items which she asked to have charged to their account.

"What is your name?" the clerk asked, laboriously filling out the charge slip.

"Mrs. Keen Johnson."

"And your address."

"Governor's Mansion, Frankfort, Kentucky," Mrs. Johnson replied.

"Governor's Mansion," the clerk mused. "Is that an apartment building?"

John Sherman Cooper, who retired after long service in the U.S. Senate, is a man with a deep and abiding sense of humor and a wealth of stories from back home in Pulaski County. These he relishes telling.

A favorite concerns his return to Somerset from Harvard Law School in the 1920's. He'd hung out his shingle, but clients hadn't exactly beaten a path to his door; in fact, he still was waiting for his first client when a long-time friend burst into the office.

"Johnny," he said excitedly, "a woman just ran smack into my car. It was her fault and she admits it!"

The more he described the mishap, the more apparent it was that this indeed was an open and shut case. Cooper admits his mouth watered in anticipation of the nice fee he'd certainly get for handling the matter in court.

"Now, Johnny, we've been friends for years," the aggrieved concluded. "Tell me straight: where can I find myself a good lawyer?"

A couple of farmers, dressed in faded overalls, were among those listening to a long, dull speech being delivered by a candidate down in Henderson. After nearly an hour, he finally finished.

"What was that speech all about?" one man asked
the other.

"I don't know," his friend replied. "He didn't say!"

The pressure of local politics is shown in an incident
involving the judge in a northern Kentucky county who
imposed a stiff fine against two teen-age boys for drag
racing. The only trouble was that the boys belonged to a
couple of fathers who pretty well controlled politics in the
county and both objected to the fine and demanded that
the judge reconsider his action or suffer the consequences
at the next election.

"Well," the judge reasoned as he rescinded his decision,
"I guess if I can fine 'em, I can unfine 'em!"

Perhaps no political hopeful ever came across a rebuff
with a note of finality in it equal to the one an old man in
Marshall County hung on a candidate who was running
for local office. The old man never had liked the candidate
and he was waiting for him when he came to campaign
at his home.

"I hope," the candidate said in leaving, "you won't
forget to vote for me."

"I won't forget you," the old gent spat. "I done done it!"

Speaking of Marshall County, during the early innings of
the Franklin D. Roosevelt administration, one of the
leading farmers in the county also was the most vocal
Republican. The policy of paying farmers not to raise
certain crops in an effort to keep produce prices up had
just been introduced and this created an interesting inner
conflict between political conviction and financial reality.

50

One day this man walked into a store in Benton, waving a check he'd just received for not raising any corn that year.

"That's the Democrats for you," he ranted, "paying a man not to do something."

"Well, what are you going to do with the check?" he was asked.

"Oh, I'll keep the check," he fumed, "but damn the idea!"

Two of the most colorful men ever to run against each other in Kentucky were Edwin P. Morrow, a Republican, and A. O. Stanley, a Democrat, who faced each other in several elections, including the race for governor in 1915. In that election, they went around the Commonwealth debating the issues from the same platform and from their hectic battling, countless stories developed.

Now while the two were warm friends away from politics, and even traveled together from one debate site to another during that campaign, on the platform they verbally ripped each other to shreds.

It was the habit of Stanley to fortify himself with a good belt of Bourbon before taking the platform, a ritual he performed before an outdoor debate they staged one hot August afternoon in Pulaski County. While Morrow was making his opening remarks, the hot sun beaming down on his head made the Bourbon inside Stanley act up and suddenly he became sick in full view of the audience.

But he never lost his composure. When he was feeling better, he stepped to the front of the platform and held up his hands.

"Ladies and gentlemen," he said solemnly, "this just proves what I have been saying all over Kentucky — Ed Morrow plain makes me sick to my stomach!"

The matter of his drinking habits was underscored in a remark made by Mr. Stanley in one of his last public

51

appearances years after his memorable race against Morrow.

"Water is good to take a bath in," he allowed, "but there is a much more tasty Kentucky beverage for drinking."

Although he wasn't one of the great humorists to occupy the office, former Governor Louie B. Nunn, nevertheless, was no raw rookie at using his own brand of sometimes barbed humor to spice talks and flay his political opposition. On top of that, he didn't mind telling stories in which he was the butt of a mild joke.

It is Nunn's contention that many people have no idea that being governor is a rigorous, 24-hour-a-day job and not just an endless round of kissing beauty contest winners and awarding trophies to Derby winners. To prove the point, he tells about an aged client he had in Glasgow, where he practiced law before being elected governor.

Some weeks after his inauguration, Nunn says, the old gent walked into the law office he had shared with his partner, Joe Travis.

"The judge in?" the man asked.

"No, sir," Travis replied. "He's governor now and is in Frankfort."

The man left, but the next week he was back in the office to ask the same question and get the same answer. The following week he appeared for the third time.

"My goodness," he exclaimed after Travis had patiently told him once again that the judge was governor and in Frankfort, "is that a full-time job the boy has got up there?"

A politician always needs to have his first-string brain on him, says Clay Wade Bailey, the dean of Kentucky political newspaper reporters. One who did, he claims, was Tom Mobley, once a power in Elliott County political circles.

During one campaign in which he was running for office, Mobley was verbally set upon by an opponent at a big "speaking."

"They's a lot of better men than you, Tom Mobley!" the man shouted.

"That's right," replied Mobley, keeping his cool, "but they're not running!"

Two men running for the state legislature in eastern Kentucky several years ago agreed to meet in an open debate to give their views on the various issues. The Democrat was first to speak and he launched into a lengthy, detailed and ambiguous oration on state finances.

"My Democrat opponent has undertook to talk finances," the Republican said when his turn came. "Now he ought not to of did that 'cause they ain't no way in this world he can understand it. The Lord's truth is, folks, it's about all I can do to understand that myself!"

Another successful politician who was willing to be the fall guy in stories he told was former governor and Federal Judge Bert Combs. Like in the speech he made after completing his term in Frankfort in which he said the best thing about not being governor is that folks no longer expected him to say something brilliant every time he opened his mouth.

Along the same line, there's an incident Combs recalls that took place after his term as governor when he taught a class in political strategy at Amherst College for one semester. In the main, he drew upon his own experiences for material.

At first, he says, his lectures were based on happenings in which he was the hero. Since most of the students were New Englanders and not familiar with Kentucky politics, they provided a perfect audience for that sort of discussion, always laughing at the right time.

However, he was forced to revise his format after a month or two when he kept noticing one boy who sat on the front row wasn't doing much smiling and laughing along with the other students. Finally, Combs asked him pointedly why he wasn't even grinning at his best stories.

"Because I'm from Louisville," he said, "and I'm saving my big laughs for when you tell how you ran for governor in 1955 and Happy Chandler beat the hell out of you!"

Kentucky's most knowledgeable political reporter undoubtedly was Allan M. Trout, who, until his retirement, was head of *The Courier-Journal's* Frankfort bureau. Not only was he a skilled reporter, Trout also was an endless source for stories about political figures he had known or heard about during his distinguished career.

Shortly before the turn of the century, one of his stories goes, members of the legislature were guests at a sumptuous banquet in Frankfort. Present was a senator from an eastern Kentucky county who never had been out of the hills until coming to the Bluegrass for the session.

The first course was consommé, which the senator drank, though somewhat reluctantly. Then someone passed a tray of hearts of celery, which he took and, following the lead of others seated nearby, ate. Finally the main course was brought on and the waiter placed a large broiled lobster in front of him. The senator took one look at the lobster and rose to make an announcement.

"Gentlemen," he said seriously, "I've drank the dishwater and I've et the bouquet, but I'll be durned if I'll eat this here bug. Take 'er away!"

In addition to being one of the youngest (37) and later one of the oldest (73) to be elected governor, James B. McCreary no doubt was also one of the most cautious men ever to hold the office. It was said that he seldom committed himself positively in any matter. Late in his second term as governor, he was riding a train through central Kentucky and one member of his party bet another $5 that he could cause the governor to utter some kind of positive statement before the day was over. Minutes later the train rolled past a field full of jet-black sheep.

"Governor," the bettor said to him, seizing on the opportunity to put him in a corner, "aren't those the blackest sheep you ever saw?"

"Well," hedged McCreary, "they do appear to be black on this side."

Although politics in Kentucky today still is unique compared to most other states, according to those who should know, it's different now than in earlier, less sophisticated days. That's perhaps truest in county-level politics. Before radio and TV was anything but a gleam in the eye of some mad scientist, all candidates for office used to travel over the county and debate each other from the same platform. Such eyeball to eyeball confrontations led to some highly original verbal exchanges.

Like the time in 1927 Daniel Boone Smith, the long-time commonwealth's attorney in Harlan County, ran for the state legislature in Knox County and was elected. His opponent in the Republican primary was a Holiness preacher.

"Before I'm through with him," the preacher boasted at one of the speakings, "Boone Smith's knees will knock like old Nebuchadnezzar's when he read the handwriting on the wall."

"My opponent claims to be a minister of the gospel," Smith chided when his turn came to talk, "yet he doesn't know that the handwriting on the wall was in the unknown tongue and Nebuchadnezzar had a prophet read it for him.

"Now," Smith continued, warming up, "that prophet was named Daniel. My name is Daniel, and I suspect that if you send my opponent to Frankfort, he'd have to call for me to do the reading for him!"

It probably is true that even hell hath no fury like that of a political partisan who suddenly has gone sour and turned against a former ally. When that happens, the result is pure venom, with no rumor being too wild to be circulated and nothing too bad to be said.

Charles E. Whittle, Edmonson County Attorney, learned that while he still was a political novice.

When he first went into politics, Whittle says, one man in the county was his strongest supporter. There literally was nothing he wouldn't do for him. "Charley Whittle," he'd say to anyone who would listen, "is the smartest man, the best speaker, and the most capable lawyer ever to come down the road."

Then, as fate would have it, the man got into trouble and, as county attorney, it was Whittle's duty to prosecute him. Which he did. Vigorously. The result was an about-face of classic proportions. Overnight the man began traveling about the county mean-mouthing Whittle.

"I guess," he said at every crossroads in the area, "I've heard that Charley Whittle speak a hundred times, and he ain't never told me nothin' I didn't already know!"

William C. Campbell of Russellville has been an observer of the political scene in various parts of Kentucky for a lot of years, and he can spin stories faster than a horse can trot.

A favorite Campbell political story concerns the way a local political boss controlled elections in his part of Boyd County years ago. Every time a new man moved into his territory, he'd send a notorious bully out to give him a sound thrashing as a foretaste of what to expect thereafter if he didn't vote right in elections.

Well, a newcomer moved in and the tough rode his horse out to call. Seeing the stranger seated on the porch, he hitched his horse on the other side of a low picket fence that enclosed the front yard.

"I've come to whup you," he announced matter of factly.

"That sounds like a fair proposition," the newcomer

said. "Come in and let's eat supper first and then we'll feel more up to it."

With that he arose from his chair, and he turned out to be about 6′7″ and bounded on all sides by nothing but muscle. He strolled casually over to the fence, picked up the horse and set it on the other side. Then he opened the gate for the bully, who had watched it all in stunned silence.

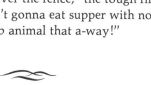

"Put that horse back over the fence," the tough finally managed to croak. "I ain't gonna eat supper with no man who'd treat a poor, dumb animal that a-way!"

Almost as important as campaign cards and handshakes to a Kentucky politician is a goodly supply of stories that point up his humble beginning, his humility, industriousness, and assorted other all-American virtues to impress the voters. Another of the hundreds of political stories from the middle Green River country told by Charles Whittle, of Brownsville, concerns the way the late Senator M. M. Logan could tell tales that would produce a laugh, bring a tear to the eye, or cause his audiences to ponder the nation's future, as the occasion dictated.

He was, the senator used to say, born far off the main road in Edmonson County and he was 13 or 14 years old before he ever saw a railroad train since the nearest rail line barely touched the southern tip of the county some 15 miles away.

One day he and a friend named Cal Johnson hiked to Rocky Hill, which was on the railroad, just to see one of the steam-spouting marvels they'd heard so much about, the senator would relate. They got down on their hands and knees to examine the rails and the spikes. As they sat on the rails, resting before their long walk back home, a train rounded a bend and bore straight down upon them. Logan said he leaped off, but Cal started running down the track in front of the oncoming train.

"Get off, Cal, get off!" Logan said he shouted to his friend.

"I ain't gonna do it," he vowed Cal yelled back as he started running in high gear. "If I get over there in the plowed ground, that thing will catch me sure!"

For some reason or other, the office of county jailer always has appealed to Kentuckians. Most often when local elections are held, more hopefuls will enter for jailer than any other office.

The field seldom gets more crowded, however, than was the case in Monroe County some years back when 28 men ran for jailer. With so many out scrounging for votes, anytime a crowd of more than 50 people would gather anywhere in the county most of the would-be jailers would be there to shake hands and pass out cards.

All 28 were in the crowd one Sunday when a rural church scheduled a creekside baptizing and some 500 witnesses were expected. After the preliminaries, the minister stepped to the edge of the creek.

"Will the candidates please follow me," he said as he moved into the water, his back to the spectators.

A few feet from the bank he looked back and saw what appeared to be a veritable host of people at his heels.

"Are all of you candidates for baptism?" he asked in a puzzled voice.

"Not all of us," replied one man as he turned and trudged back to the bank, "28 of us is candidates for jailer!"

Since they both are articulate, skilled campaigners, the stories flew thick and fast when the old pros, John Sherman Cooper and John Young Brown, Sr., ran against each other for the U.S. Senate in 1948.

In pointing out how certain things, like voting for him, just made good sense, Brown told about two maiden sisters who were inmates at Eastern State Mental Hospital in Lexington. One sunny day they were seated on the front lawn knitting in silence.

"You know what," one sister said, breaking the silence, "I wish some tall, big-fisted, 200-pound man would come along here, grab me up and hug me till it hurts."

"You keep talking like that," the other sister replied, "and you'll be out of this place in another month."

Cooper, in turn, used a story about Brother John, an old Baptist preacher he had known in Pulaski County to illustrate how, while he didn't like to boast, he certainly wasn't one to underestimate himself.

Seems a group of the brethren were attending a conference and one night they were speculating on the greatest preacher each of them had ever heard. All had spoken except Brother John. Then he was called upon for his nomination for greatest preacher.

"Well," he said after due consideration, "to tell you the truth, brothers when I'm feelin' right, I do believe I'd as soon listen to myself as anybody ever I heard preach!"

While Kentuckians take politics at all levels seriously, there is perhaps more genuine interest in the races every four years for local offices — sheriff, county judge, jailer, clerk, magistrate, etc. When such offices are up for grabs, no hand in the county will remain unshaken nor any baby unkissed as the candidates woo the voters before the final showdown.

John Sherman Cooper tells a story which illustrates how, under such circumstances, even the dispensing of justice can be clouded by how a man votes.

In 1933, when he was a candidate for re-election as judge of Pulaski County, a massive rally was held in Somerset for him on election eve. During the course of the rally, a fight broke out among his supporters and those backing his opponent. As a result, a number of men were thrown into jail.

Early the next morning several of Cooper's boosters called on him and suggested that some of the brawlers be released in time to vote.

"Actually," Cooper told them, "I plan to let them all go."

"No, don't do that," his supporters urged in unison, "just let our friends out!"

Former Governor Louie Nunn is one politician who usually weighs his words carefully. But under the pressure of the moment, any man's tongue is apt to get wrapped around his eyeteeth until he can't see what he's saying, Nunn says.

Like the flustered fellow he once knew who was trying to express his deep feelings after having been given an award of some kind.

"I don't appreciate it," he floundered, "but I do deserve it from the bottom of my heart!"

In earlier years, the Fourth of July used to be the big day in Kentucky for flag waving and long-winded oratory about patriotism and loyalty and the national heritage. As we've grown more sophisticated, we seem to have put these simple things behind us. Sometimes we even appear to think that feeling a tingle of pride when "The Star Spangled Banner" is played or saying something good about America is a sign of immaturity.

And speaking of old-time Fourth of July oratory, Mack Sisk, the Dawson Springs-Frankfort product, tells about the spellbinder who was invited to make a nonpolitical address at a convention at Kentucky Dam Village state park on that great day a number of years ago.

Being an orator of the old school, the speaker did not come with notes; instead, it was his plan to speak from the heart as the spirit moved him. In keeping with the day, he titled his talk "Our Flag and What Its Colors Symbolize."

He was introduced and embarked upon his speech.

"Ladies and gentlemen," he began, the words rippling melodiously off his marinated tonsils, "keep your eyes on

Old Glory flying here beside the platform while I direct
your thoughts to the virtues its colors symbolize.

"First, there's the red stripe, symbolic of the blood
spilled on far-flung battlefields to keep this nation free.

"Second, there's the white stripe which represents the
purity of this nation in foreign relations.

"And third, there's the blue field which stands for . . ."

Suddenly his voice trailed off as he could think of
nothing the blue represented.

"And then, there's the blue field which stands for . . ."
Again he drew a blank.

A cold sweat broke out on his forehead, and he cleared
his throat before making another run at it.

"And then there's the blue field," he blurted finally,
"and that's what makes it the red, the white and the blue!"

When the first 90 miles of the splendid 127-mile-long
Western Kentucky Parkway was officially opened in
1963, Governor Bert Combs, Lieutenant Governor
Wilson Wyatt, Highway Commissioner Henry Ward, and
various other political dignitaries were on hand for the
ribbon-cutting.

Shortly before the ceremony started, Combs vows, he
overheard two old men talking.

"Sure are a lot of big wheels here today," one of the
men said.

"Yeah," replied the other, "but I figure a little rain
would do us a lot more good!"

During World War II Kentucky had a rigid law, aimed at
conserving gasoline and rubber for strategic war use,
which required that trucks of a certain size be equipped
with governors to regulate their speeds at no more than
55 miles an hour.

One day, the story goes, a State Highway Patrol
trooper spotted a truck blazing along U.S. 60 between

Versailles and Lexington going 70 miles an hour or faster. The officer finally was able to get the truck pulled off the highway. Then he walked over to the driver, ready to give him a stern lecture and a ticket.

"Do you have any idea how fast you were going?" he asked the driver.

"Naw," answered the driver, "my speedometer don't work."

"You mean to tell me," the officer said, somewhat aghast, "you don't have a governor on this truck?"

"Nope," the driver replied innocently. "The governor's in Frankfort; that's fertilizer you smell!"

During the 1963 campaign when he was defeated for governor by Edward Breathitt, Louie Nunn (he was elected four years later) was the guest at a big buffet dinner and rally in Morehead. Since each of the women present had brought her favorite dish for the table, Nunn felt constrained to take something from every bowl.

As he walked to his seat, his plate filled to overflowing, he heard two old women whispering to each other.

"That's Judge Nunn, the candidate," one said.

"My, my," the other marveled, glancing at his plate, "he's a hungry devil, ain't he?"

George Silliman, county attorney of Boyle County, isn't exactly a midget; in fact, he's downright robust. Some years back while campaigning for the office, he met a young boy in a grocery store and was reminded forcefully how big he actually is.

"Son," Silliman said to the boy, who was with his mother, "how would you like some ice cream?"

"I'd like some best in the world," the frank little shaver answered, "but maybe I'd better take the money — I don't want to get fat like you!"

The phone in my office rang not too long back and the caller was a man who was registering a complaint about a humorous item I'd used in my column the day before on the art of political campaigning.

"I like funny stories but not when they involve politicians," he said seriously. "The trouble with political jokes is that too many of them get elected."

That statement set me to thinking — no simple task, to be sure — about how politics and those who practice the profession in Kentucky or any state have been maligned over the years. For some reason, the average American seems to have a log-size chip on his shoulder in regards to politicians and many of us go out of our way to say bad things about them.

In fact, it often seems to me that those who make up class jokes and snappy putdowns must labor overtime in producing material for the let's-all-kick-a-politician trade. A few tired, old samples of such material include these:

A politician is a guy who works his gums before election and gums up the works after election . . . When we look at the candidates running for office, we can be thankful that only one can get elected . . . Politics is the most promising of all careers — nothing but promises, promises, promises . . . The time when many a politician stumps his state is after it has elected him.

And on and on.

All of which is pure irony, of course, since in this country we're great on talk but not too much on action. We complain about politics and politicians, but then don't have enough interest to bother voting. When less than 60 per cent of those eligible bestir themselves to vote in an election for president of the United States, we can't disassociate ourselves from whatever may happen and try to play Pontius Pilate and wash our hands of the entire matter.

Which points up an observation Will Rogers or some such shrewd mind once made: "Bad politicians are made by all the good people who don't vote."

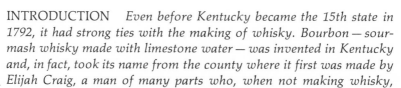

INTRODUCTION   *Even before Kentucky became the 15th state in 1792, it had strong ties with the making of whisky. Bourbon — sour-mash whisky made with limestone water — was invented in Kentucky and, in fact, took its name from the county where it first was made by Elijah Craig, a man of many parts who, when not making whisky, was a Baptist preacher of considerable renown.*

Many of the pioneers who came to Kentucky in the days prior to statehood were fleeing from the so-called "Whisky Rebellion" in the East, the uprising that followed the first imposition of a government tax on distilled spirits. Here they continued doing what they did best — making whisky. Some set up small distilleries to meet the increasing demand for sour-mash whisky in the ready markets of New Orleans; others merely put together small stills behind the barn to meet their own family needs for medicinal and drinking whisky.

Thus the state traditionally has been associated with whisky making, legal or otherwise.

Today Kentucky's 56 active distilleries produce 80 per cent of all Bourbon. On the other hand, numberless moonshiners, their crude but effective stills hidden in remote hollows, produce white lightning which, while illegal, still finds a market, especially among those who developed a taste for this kind of liquor during the arid days of Prohibition.

The fact is, some Kentuckians regard whisky making as something akin to an inalienable right and they continue to make it, legal or not.

Vigorous law enforcement has cut deeply into the ranks of the moonshiners. But stories of their deeds in other days add a distinctive flavor — and a 100 proof wallop, one might add — to the rich regional history of Kentucky.

CHAPTER 3

1 00 PROOF — AND HOME MADE

Charles M. Summers, now a Campbellsville attorney but for years a moonshine whisky still-busting "revenuer" for the Treasury Department, calls attention to a badly deteriorated farm situation that no doubt has escaped the eagle-eye of Congress.

He points out that some industrious farmers who used to run off an occasional batch of moonshine — and who, consequently, he came to know professionally — have stopped making the stuff. And their farm income has suffered drastically as a result. So, he wonders, if some farmers are paid not to raise various crops by taking their land out of production and putting it in the soil bank, why not a similar payment for farmer-moonshiners who take their stills out of production?

It was a conversation in the privacy of his law office that made him aware of the seriousness of this situation. Each year Summers prepares income-tax returns for a number of farm people who once did a bit of moonshining on the side and who were the targets of some of the investigations he used to conduct, usually with his long-time partner Quinn Pearl. This particular day a farmer who had been nailed once years back by Pearl on a raid he missed came into Summers office to have his tax computed.

"Did you make a lot of money farming last year?" Summers asked.

"Naw," the client replied. "I ain't made no money on that farm since Quinn Pearl chopped up my last still!"

Just what kind of elixir is this moonshine, this white lightning that's been made for so long and remains so illegal?

For those who never sampled it, perhaps a description by Irvin S. Cobb, the Kentucky humorist, will suffice.

"It smells," he once wrote, "like gangrene starting in a mildewed silo; it tastes like the wrath to come; and when you absorb a deep swig of it you have all the sensations of having swallowed a lighted kerosene lamp. A sudden jolt of it has been known to stop a victim's watch, snap both of his suspenders, and crack his glass eye right across—all in the same motion."

Putting aside the matter of what moonshine itself is like, what manner of men — or women, as the case may be — are moonshiners?

Actually, the moonshiner is about the last surviving undaunted soul in today's complex, rule-fettered society. Although his action strictly is illegal, he is — except when doing time in some federal pokey after having been caught — the blithe spirit of this day. He is an independent person who continues to concoct his tonic in spite of the ever-present threat of the law, which by now has cut deeply into his number in Kentucky.

From having been on countless raids with such legendary moonshine chasers as W. B. "Big Six" Henderson, Quinn Pearl, Charley Summers, Mark Holmes, Elmer Davis, and other federal agents, and having seen them arrest second, third, and even seventh-time offenders, I would label the moonshiner as one lawbreaker who doesn't discourage easily.

An example is the Nelson County man who was hailed before a federal judge for making non-taxpaid whisky.

"What kind of record do you have?" the judge asked him.

"My record is puffect, Judge," he replied. "I've been in court five times and I've been sent to the pen five times!"

So many offenders play repeat performances that they and the revenue agents, the feds, get to know each other on a first-name basis.

Henderson tells about raiding a still and recognizing a young man who escaped up the hill.

"Stop, John!" he yelled. "I know it's you!"

John kept running, but next day he appeared at the local sheriff's office.

"Why did you run?" Henderson asked. "You knew I recognized you."

"That's what my head knew, Mr. Big Six," the boy replied, "but my feets just won't stand still when I see the law!"

There was a time when it was a dead-serious game the moonshiners played with the revenuers. Shootings in the old days were common. Now gunplay is infrequent. The agents treat the moonshiner with firm respect and he repays in kind.

As you might suspect, the typical moonshiner isn't much on books and such. A story is told about an old gent named Joshua who was brought before Federal Judge H. Church Ford, a great Bible student.

"So your name is Joshua," Judge Ford mused. "Are you the Joshua who made the sun stand still?"

"No, sir, Judge," came the answer. "I'm the Joshua who made the moonshine still!"

But despite his shortcomings in formal education, the moonshiner usually has the native intelligence and cunning of a fox. This he shows in the cat and mouse game he plays with the revenuers.

Some moonshiners are craftsmen of a sort who take a left-handed kind of pride in their produce. Like the man who was seized at a Monroe County still. While they were wrecking his still, the agents filled a jar with whisky, explaining it would be sent to a lab for analysis.

"Fellers," said the moonshiner seriously, "have that man at the laboratory test it keerful and if he finds anything wrong to let me know 'cause I've always made the best 'shine in this country and I don't want to lose my reputation!"

Big Six Henderson, who participated in the seizure of more than 5,000 stills in the 28 years he was a federal agent (he now is U.S. Marshal for the Western District of Kentucky), was typical of the breed of lawmen who worked as enforcers of the ban on non-taxpaid whisky.

Working hours, terrain, and weather meant nothing to these agents. They were ready to go day or night, any time a tip was received about a still, and once on the trail they were relentless. Many would lie in the woods in summer heat or winter cold for 24 hours at a time, observing a still and figuring just the right time to swoop down on it.

"I really came to respect the moonshiners I chased," Henderson says. "When I broke in, William H. Kinnaird, then in charge of the Louisville office, gave me some advice I never forgot. 'You're going to be arresting people who often can't read or write,' he said. 'But if you give them credit for having at least 10 per cent more brains than you do, you'll get along.'"

"In almost every raid," Henderson points out, "there was at least one foot race. Track coaches talk about the 4-minute mile as something new, but I knew a dozen moonshiners in the old days who could do it."

On one raid, Henderson covered himself with leaves and lay not more than 10 feet from the still pot all night. At daybreak, three men appeared and began to work.

"Man alive," one of the men joked as the first bit of white lightning came out of the still, "wouldn't old 'Six-Gun' Henderson like to see me now!"

The man almost collapsed when, with the words barely out of his mouth, Henderson grabbed him by the ankles!

As proof (100 proof, of course) of how foxy a moonshiner or a bootlegger can be, there's the story of the out-of-town prohibition agent who was imported into a Western Kentucky town to lay a trap for a man suspected of being a peddler.

Shortly after arriving, the agent spotted the suspect standing on a street corner. Apparently he'd been shopping since he was carrying a shoe box under his arm.

"Could you tell me where a man could buy a pint of whisky in this town?" the undercoverman whispered, sidling up to him.

"Gimme two dollars and hold these shoes for me," the suspected bootlegger said, handing him the box, "and I'll see what I can do for you."

The agent did as instructed. The suspect disappeared. An hour passed and the agent stood, patiently holding the box, waiting for the man to return. After two hours he began to smell a king-sized mouse and he opened the box.

Sure enough, there was his pint of whisky!

Some of the favorite tales told by Clay Wade Bailey, the Frankfort newsman, concern moonshine trials heard in the federal court presided over by the late A. M. J. Cochran.

During Prohibition, he recalls, several men were tried at one time in a case; all were found guilty and the judge doled out rather stiff sentences for all hands.

"You know," Bailey heard a relative of one of the moonshiners say as he left the courtroom, "that judge shore is generous with other people's time, ain't he?"

Although moonshine was relatively common in all parts of Kentucky in earlier years, during the arid years of Prohibition the narrow strip in far western Kentucky bounded by the Cumberland River on the east, the Tennessee River on the west, the Ohio on the north and the Tennessee line to the south was known all over the country. For that was the Golden Pond region, the so-called Land Between the Rivers which became famed for its moonshine whisky making.

From 1920, when the country went dry, until 1933, when repeal came, Between the Rivers moonshine brought top prices in such dry cities as Chicago, Detroit, Cleveland, and Gary.

Tucked tightly between unbridged rivers, the sparsely populated strip was tailor-made for the home industry that sprang up there. Three ferries were the only means of crossing the Cumberland and Tennessee in those days, and sentries on horseback were posted at the landings to spread the alarm when strangers who might be agents appeared.

If anyone faintly resembling an agent was spotted, the sentries would ride to the nearest farmhouse and start ringing the dinner bell. The alarm would be picked up and passed along by others until the entire area echoed to the slow, metallic clang of dinner bells.

Almost as if by magic, still fires would be extinguished, barrels of mash would be hidden and bottled stock concealed. Once the danger was past, the all-clear would be sounded by firing three blasts from a shotgun.

The home distillers became so open that one operator even printed his own label: "Genuine Golden Pond Kentucky Whisky." A huge sign bearing the words: "Whisky Ridge Distilling Co. — No Trespassing" stood along one trail east of Golden Pond.

It was rumored that the Al Capone mob relied so heavily on Golden Pond whisky that a landing field was set up east of the Cumberland River and planes from Chicago used to make regular pickup stops.

Even after repeal, the area for years remained a moonshiner's paradise. It took establishment of the Land Between the Lakes National Recreation Area to finally end the practice.

They tell the story about a time not too many years ago when a politician running for statewide office was talking to voters at Golden Pond.

"I'll tell you," one man said, more or less giving away his profession, "I'm for you 110 proof, and that's as high as I can make it!"

Agent Tom Quinn was with Big-Six Henderson on one big raid when a man was caught red-handed at the still.

After Quinn had made the arrest, the man called him aside.

"That mean anything to you?" he whispered knowingly, pointing to a ring he wore that bore a Masonic emblem.

"No, and it'll mean even less to the agent over there in charge of this raid," Quinn said, motioning to Henderson. "He's a Catholic!"

Years ago a bunch of the boys in the Short Creek section of Grayson County set out to drink all the moonshine around. When one of the men passed out cold, the other revelers deposited him among the tombstones in Shain Cemetery and went on with their carousing.

They returned to him early the next morning just as he was prying open his bloodshot eyes and viewing his surroundings.

"I'll be damned," they heard him mutter in a semi-stupor, "resurrection mornin' and I'm the first one up!"

To illustrate the ingenuity and know-how of the moon-shiner, consider an invention a couple of Laurel County teen-agers came up with in the most unlikely of locations a few years back.

You see, these boys — one 17, the other 18 — were confined in the jail at London and their feat was the fashioning of a miniature moonshine whisky still from such odds and ends as coffee cans and copper tubing from their cell commode.

The two claimed to have run off nearly a quart of whisky before the operation was disrupted by their transfer to the State Reformatory at LaGrange.

Their still was a lesson in ingenuity. The boiler was shaped from a pipe tobacco canister which also served as the mash or still barrel. The thumper, into which the alcoholic steam from the still barrel passes, was a soft-drink can, and the condenser, where the vapor is reduced to liquid normally by flowing through copper tubing, was a coffee can.

The hollow handle of a safety razor was the connecting pipe between the thumper and condenser, and the furnace was a flat tobacco can in which a circle had been cut to let the heat, made by burning scraps of paper, reach the boiler.

Mash from which the whisky was derived was made by adding water to crumbled cornbread and sugar salvaged from their meals!

Some years back, inadvertently, I started a novice on his way to a moonshining career that ended in prison almost before it had begun.

After going on a raid with federal agents, I wrote a story for *The Courier-Journal Magazine* which included a rather precise recipe for moonshine. A few weeks later a man was arrested in Shively on a moonshine charge. When he was brought to court, Federal Judge Roy M. Shelbourne asked where he'd learned to make the stuff.

"I read it in *The Courier-Journal Magazine*," the man confessed.

"Well," the judge concluded as he sentenced the man to a vacation in Atlanta, "from now on I advise you to stick to the comic pages!"

They say a hangover from over-indulging in moonshine is one of the most severe head-throbbers that can be inflicted on mortal man. Many are the remedies that have been prescribed to counter it, one of the most unusual being the antidote passed on to R. B. Campbell, a Hyden banker, by a notorious moonshine quaffer who lived on Trace Branch in Leslie County.

"The only way to keep from feelin' bad after gettin' drunk on moonshine," he reasoned, "is to get drunk again the next day!"

William Short, an aide to Lieutenant Governor Julian Carroll, comes from Casey County and, like most natives of that area, he has more stories than Boston has beans.

One yarn concerns a young farm boy who had such a drinking problem that he kept all the local moonshiners working overtime just keeping up with his consumption. Since his parents knew of his habit, he had to hide his liquor all over the place — in the straw stack, the corn crib, anywhere.

This day his father was working on the barn when in a stall he found a whisky bottle which, ironically, didn't contain booze but brake fluid the boy had drained into it. The father uncorked the bottle and took a deep swig.

"Gad," he sputtered almost gagging, "no wonder this stuff's a-killin' poor Fred!"

In western Kentucky some years back a new cafe in a dry county was raided the very first week it opened and the proprietor was charged with bootlegging whisky. The next day some of the local citizens, including one unfortunate who wasn't exactly the smartest guy around, were talking about how surprised they were by the development.

"I didn't know he was bootleggin'," remarked this poor unfortunate, "but I knowed he was servin' an awful good Coke in there!"

It was in Paducah I heard the story of a man who repeatedly was hauled into court for being drunk in public from indulging well if not wisely in moonshine. Finally, the judge got tired of seeing him so often and called him into his chambers for a stern lecture.

"Have you ever thought of giving up drinking this rot gut and trying Alcoholics Anonymous?" the judge asked.

"No, Judge," the drunk replied, "but I doubt I could afford any of them expensive brands!"

Once after having been on a raid in Cumberland County, Big Six Henderson decided, on his way back home, to stop off at a remote crossroads store where, according to reports sifting into his office, moonshine was being peddled. Since he was dressed in clothes dirty and grimy from the raid, he had to do little more to disguise himself. He thought. He rubbed some smudge on his face, poured a little of the whisky he'd seized on his shirt for aroma, and entered the store.

After passing the time of day with the keeper, he got down to business.

"I wonder where a man could get a good drink of moonshine around here," he asked in a low voice.

"My gosh, Bix Six," the store proprietor replied innocently, "if anybody knows, it ought to be you!"

It may come as a shock, but the day of that moonlight enterpriser, the barrel dogger, is about at an end, the victim of several imponderable circumstances, including the foreign-export trade.

You never heard of a barrel dogger? Or even a barrel steamer, roller, sweater, or burner, other job classifications for the same operator?

Well, a barrel dogger is a sort of second cousin by marriage to a moonshiner. He traffics — that is to say, he used to traffic — in illegal booze, but he's more a retailer than a start-to-finish producer.

Let me explain.

Although he works outside the law, ironically the barrel dogger depends on the law to keep him in business. Since until recently when new white whisky was introduced, the law required that whisky made in this country had to be stored in new charred white-oak barrels, what to do with barrels after they were used one time was a vexing problem for distilleries.

At times in earlier days, hundreds of empty barrels, each costing $25 or more, would be stacked outside distillery bottling rooms. In order to get rid of them, they would be burned or sold as rain barrels to farmers for from 10 to 25 cents each.

74

The dogger helped the distilleries solve their used-barrel headache. On the pretense of needing lots of barrels to catch rain water or put to other farm uses, he would acquire 200 or more. Then he'd line the barrels up in two rows and build a low-burning fire between the rows. He would wait three or four hours for the fire to steam out the whisky that had been absorbed in the charred interior of the barrels while they were in storage during the long whisky-aging cycle.

The final step in dogging the barrels was to remove the bung, strain the whisky that had settled inside through some kind of filter — often the felt hat the dogger was wearing — to remove foreign matter, put it in jugs or jars and sell it for $5 to $12 a gallon. Each barrel would yield from a pint to a gallon or more of real aged-in-the-wood whisky that found a ready market among those given to drinking anything they could lay their hands on except maybe water.

There was nothing illegal about buying used barrels. The crime was selling the steamed-out whisky in containers that didn't bear a federal tax stamp. The first step in controlling this came some 15 years ago when the Internal Revenue Service required distilleries to keep a record of all large sales of barrels to individuals. But it was the export trade, and then the new white whisky that can be stored in used barrels, that really did in the dogger. Today a growing market for used barrels in which to store spirits has been developed in the United Kingdom and Canada, where the new-barrel law doesn't apply.

And so another ancient Kentucky home industry has about run its course.

Robert Bolds, who now lives in Louisville, came from a section along the Ohio River in Daviess County known as Tiwoppity Bottom. The area is called that because of the "tiwoppity, tiwoppity" sound made by waves when they slap against the bottom of an old-fashioned johnboat.

Some years back, Bolds claims, the local Catholic priest met one of his parishoners, a man noted for his intemperate habits. Since the man was in his cups even then, the priest was revolted by the sight.

"Drunk again!" the priest fussed.

"Me, too Father," the drunk lisped, "me, too!"

A man was nabbed by the feds at his still in eastern Kentucky for the ninth time. When he came up for trial, he was found guilty and ordered to stand before the judge for sentencing.

"You know," the judge said, "this is getting to be something of a habit, your appearing before me like this. Before passing sentence on you, I just want you to know that you have given this court more trouble than anyone else in the whole state of Kentucky."

"Thank ye kindly, Judge," the accused replied, "And I just want you to know that I couldn't have gived you one whit of trouble more than you've gived to me!"

The saddest indictment against mountain strip, or surface, coal mining that I've heard yet was delivered by a man at Lotts Creek in Perry County. He looked around at the once heavily forested mountains which have been denuded by stripping and sadly shook his head.

"It's gettin' so," he mused, "that a man can't hardly find a safe place around here no more to make whisky."

It doesn't have to do with moonshining, but since it still has to do with whisky making, let me tell you a story I heard in Anderson County.

A short prologue is needed to set the stage.

Although the work of government gaugers and checkers at distilleries now is done with professional and impersonal efficiency, that wasn't always the case. In fact, in less strict days it wasn't uncommon for the government men to sample the end product from time to time during their work day.

Years ago, before automobiles were too common, an old gent who lived in Lawrenceburg worked as a gauger at a distillery on the Kentucky River near Tyrone, some five miles away. He drove to and from work each day in a one-horse phaeton, an open buggy-like rig with rear wheels that were perhaps twice as large as the front wheels. It was his custom to nip along as the day progressed, and sometimes he'd be feeling no pain, as the saying goes, by the time he started home.

One day his fellow workers played a joke on him. They removed the wheels of his buggy, putting the larger wheels in front and the smaller ones on the rear of the rig. All the way home that afternoon he realized something was different, but he couldn't quite pin it down. Finally, as he pulled up at his house, it came to him.

"You know," he confided to a friend, "I've been making that round trip to Tyrone for 35 years, but this is the first time I ever realized that the drive back is uphill all the way!"

Down in Owensboro they tell about a temperance lecturer who appeared there in a series of meetings in the days before Prohibition. One night the speaker had gotten especially eloquent in describing the evils of strong drink — how it destroys the stomach, disrupts the digestive process, addles the mind.

In the middle of his speech, a man on the front row pulled a bottle of moonshine from his pocket and took a deep swig in full fiew of the audience.

"Brother, why did you do that?" the lecturer asked.

"Because you've said such awful things about what liquor will do to a man," came the reply, "I needed a drink to steady my nerves!"

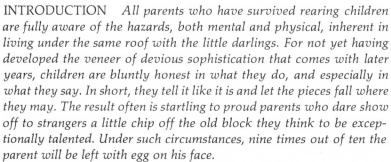

INTRODUCTION   *All parents who have survived rearing children are fully aware of the hazards, both mental and physical, inherent in living under the same roof with the little darlings. For not yet having developed the veneer of devious sophistication that comes with later years, children are bluntly honest in what they do, and especially in what they say. In short, they tell it like it is and let the pieces fall where they may. The result often is startling to proud parents who dare show off to strangers a little chip off the old block they think to be exceptionally talented. Under such circumstances, nine times out of ten the parent will be left with egg on his face.*

Consider the case of a northern Kentucky mother who was certain her 2½-year-old son was a true prodigy because of the way he could parrot nursery rhymes. A friend she hadn't seen in years stopped by the house and she called upon her child to perform for the company. The kid stood self-consciously in front of the stranger without uttering a word.

"Little Boy Blue come blow . . . ," the mother coached to get him started. When that failed, she tried again. "Little Boy Blue come blow . . ."

"Little Boy Blue come blow . . . ," the child started, then hesitated before racing on to a hasty conclusion. "Little Boy Blue come blow your nose!"

Those who have had exposure to children — parents, grandparents, neighbors, teachers, total strangers — should find recollections, fond or otherwise, of their own experiences in the following stories.

78

CHAPTER 4

SCHOOL DAZE

We live in a fast age, but it still isn't quite fast enough for 6-year-old Waynetta Cheek of Dunnville. After her second day of school, she came home crying.

"How long," she asked her mother, "does it take a little girl to graduate?"

Robert and Smith Broadbent, III of Cadiz are identical twins whose close friends have difficulty telling them apart. In fact, Sarah, the then-3 daughter of Smith, III, sometimes was confused as to who was who. However, she had one sure-fire way of distinguishing them, a secret she shared with her great-grandmother, Mrs. Sarah Holmes of Lexington.

"Daddy and Uncle Bob look alike," she said, "but Daddy spanks and Uncle Bob doesn't!"

A substitute was pinch-hitting for the regular first-grade teacher at a school in Kenton County. Having a few minutes before the lunch break, she let the children pass the time by sharing what she called happy thoughts.

"Does anyone have a happy thought they'd like to share with the rest of us?" she asked.

Up went the hand of a little girl.

"At breakfast this morning," she related in an excited voice, "my mother said 'I think I'm pregnant' and my daddy said, 'Well, that's a happy thought!'"

Any mention of the blunt honesty of Kentuckians in general wouldn't be complete without several examples to prove the same characteristic has been inherited by their children.

According to Elizabeth Spalding of Bardstown, a teacher in the Head Start program for pre-school children at nearby Bloomfield was flashing pictures of various animals on a screen and asking the kids to identify them.

The 5-year-olds recognized a giraffe, tiger, lion, elephant, etc., but no one could identify a deer when the picture was shown.

"If your father was away for several days and came home," the teacher said, trying to give them a hint, "what would your mother call him?"

"Oh," one little boy piped up, so that's what a *!#*! is!"

This Louisville family I know has two children, one a baby and the other a 3-year-old boy who is entering the question-asking stage. Every remark aimed at him draws a what, why, or how question.

It had been an especially trying day for the mother. Finally after the 3-year-old had asked "why" for the 1,000th time, she'd had it.

"If you don't stop asking questions," she moaned, "I'm going to jump in the lake!"

Which merited this reasonable response from the little boy: "What lake?"

At the risk of being branded a male chauvinist pig by those in the movement, I might venture the timid opinion that Women's Lib may have its point of diminishing returns. After all, I've never seen a gal changing a flat tire alongside the road while a man sat in the car.

For enough sometimes is enough, as Louisville fifth-grader Peggy Boeck learned at the relatively tender age of 10.

Peggy goes to Longfellow School and she eagerly
volunteered her services when the males-only requirement
was dropped and it was announced that girls could serve
as street crossing guards at her school. However,
becoming a guard required that those interested get to
school each morning at 7:30 for a training session.

After that had been going on for a week or so, Peggy
was still half asleep when her mother roused her one
morning to start to school half an hour before the others.

"Your know," she mused as she sat at the breakfast
table, staring glassy-eyed at her cereal, "sometimes I don't
think Women's Lib is such a good thing!"

Diane Clark, a Jefferson County first-grade teacher,
admits she is constantly refreshed by the honest simplicity
of 6-year-olds. And to underscore her point, she tells
about assigning her class to write an account of their
favorite TV program.

"If you need help in spelling a word," she told them,
"come quietly to my desk and I'll help you."

Immediately a little boy tip-toed to her and whispered,
"How do you spell 'Ultra Man'?" She told him and a
minute or two later he was back to ask, 'How do you
spell 'egg'?"

"Why do you need to spell egg?" she wondered.

"You know," the kid replied logically, "for
'egg-splosion'!"

After 5-year-old Margie Fields of Louisville had been
given a mild spanking by her father, she ran to her
mother, Mrs. J. T. Fields.

"Mommy," she sobbed, "we married the wrong man!"

Ed Hust, editor of *The Providence Journal-Enterprise*, tells
about a small boy who was caught red-handed in a
mischievous act by his mother.

"How do you expect to get into heaven acting that way?" she asked.

"Well," he replied, remembering a method that had worked many times before, "I'll just run in and out and keep slamming the doors 'til they say, 'For goodness sake, come in or stay out.' Then I'll go in!"

Out of the mouth of veritable babes truly do come pearls of purest wisdom. Mary Louis Read of Louisville, then 12, was invited to one of the showers given before her sister Nancy was married. The various guests were asked to write down household tips for the benefit of the bride-to-be.

The best tip of all, and no question about it, came from Mary Louis: "Get a maid."

Yes, indeed, TV certainly has jaded the entertainment appetite of children. Four-year-old Mary Ellen Hodapp was taken to Ringling Bros. and Barnum & Bailey Circus when it came to Louisville.

Right in the middle of the death-defying lion act, when it seemed the poor tamer would be devoured by the savage beasts, Mary Ellen nudged her mother, Mrs. William Hodapp.

"I've seen this movie before!" she whispered.

Parents aren't the only members of a family to have things tough, as Brent Thompson of Cadiz learned in a conversation with his son Mark, then 8.

"Is it hard being a daddy?" Mark asked.

"It's the hardest job I ever had," his father confessed.

There was a short silence before Mark added this food

for thought: "You know, Daddy, it's not easy being a little boy!"

The 7-year-old son of a Louisville friend was fascinated by that TV commercial that shows a pretty girl going around blowing kisses on the cheek of all the boys in sight in the interest of selling a brand of toothpaste that promises to "give your mouth sex appeal." After bugging his father to get him a tube of the stuff, old dad broke down.

The kid could hardly wait to try out the toothpaste, which is extra frothy and has a biting taste. He loaded down his brush and began to scrub away. A few minutes later he reported back to his father, his face covered with lather and his eyes watering.

"If this is sex appeal," he said dramatically, "I don't want any more of it!"

Dorothy Gentry of Hartford tells about a little boy she knows who was being kept by a neighbor while his mother went shopping. At lunch time he seemed to be having trouble cutting the meat on his plate, and the hostess asked if he needed any help.

"That's O.K." he replied frankly, "we have meat this tough at home sometimes!"

Always expect children to say the unexpected. Erwin McDonald, who once was on the staff of the Southern Baptist Theological Seminary in Louisville, tells about taking a vacation trip to the Grand Canyon with his family some years back when his daughter was about 4.

All the way across the country McDonald kept telling her about the Grand Canyon, how it was a wonder of the world and something she'd never forget. When they finally reached the first observation point, she was in a swivet of excitement. As soon as the car stopped, she leaped out, rushed to the hand rail, gazed down into the mile-deep gorge and then jumped back with a bewildered look.

"My goodness," she gasped, "what happened!"

Some years back the Louisville radio station WAKY (pronounced "Wacky") offered a prize to persons who answered their telephones by saying "Hello, WAKY." All over town, a phone call, especially those answered by a child, would start with the "Hello, WAKY" greeting.

"I've had to tell our children to quit answering the calls that way," said the wife of a Louisville doctor. "It's driving away my husband's patients."

You see, her husband is a psychiatrist.

I know from painful experience that children see, and remember, much more than parents think they do. That was pointed up in a classic report my youngest son, Bill, then 8, wrote many years ago for Catherine Crutcher's fourth-grade class at Chenoweth School on the subject "What I remember most about my vacation."

That summer we had taken Bill and his older brother to Chicago for a week of baseball games, the zoo, and living it up in the Big City in general. None of that, however, impressed Bill nearly as much as a slight misadventure we had on the way home when we spent a couple of hours wandering all over Indianapolis trying to find US 31, and which he described fully in his report when school started in the fall.

"We went to Chicago on our vacation," he wrote. "We had a good time. On the way back we got lost in Indianapolis. My mother was looking at the map upside down. My father got mad. He said 'Oh, hell.'"

A Louisville mother had been forced to correct her 4-year-old daughter for something she had done. So the child decided to bow down to the inevitable and run away from home.

She left the house, but returned in a few minutes to ask a pertinent question.

"Mommy," she wondered, "When you run away from home, do you run up the street or down the street?"

The second grade at the Louisville school where Cindy Masters was enrolled had been studying the human heart.

"Everybody needs a heart," Cindy revealed to her mother.

"Why?"

"Well," came the reply after some meditation, "you've got to have a heart so you can hold your hand over it when you say 'I pledge allegiance to the flag...!'"

Five-year-old David Logsdon of Lexington dug up a worm in his yard.

"Where's his mouth?" he asked his father, A. T. Logsdon.

"He doesn't have any."

"Where are his eyes?" David pressed.

"He doesn't have any eyes."

"I guess," the kid figured, "a worm's not nothing' but a tail!"

Somewhere in Louisville there lives a kindergarten teacher, hiding behind anonymity, who possesses the patience of a prophet, a quality put to test during a snowstorm that hit our town a few winters back.

School was over and the teacher was helping her 4- and

5-year-old charges slip into their boots before they
ventured out into the snow. She came to one tight-lipped
little boy and it took a good five minutes of tugging and
pulling to squeeze his feet into the pair of galoshes he
had picked up.

"These," he said stoically once the operation was over,
"aren't my boots."

The patient teacher reversed the procedure and
struggled another five minutes in disengaging the skin-
tight galoshes from his feet. No sooner was that done than
he had another announcement.

"These belong to my brother," he said, "but my mother
lets me wear them!"

Mrs. Marge Williams, a second-grade teacher at Elizabethtown, was writing common words on the blackboard and
asking her class to break them down and make shorter
words from the letters therein.

"I want you to study this word," she said, writing
"kitten" on the board, "and find as many other words as
you can in it. I see 'it' and 'ten.' What words do you see?"

A little girl stuck up her hand.

"I've found 'itten,'" she announced.

"You found 'itten,'" the teacher said. "How would you
use it in a sentence?"

"Well," came the reasoned answer, "itten this a lovely
day?"

The late Carroll Gullion, in his booklet "Small Town
Tales," related dozens of true-life stories from the Henry-
Carroll County area. One concerned a teacher in Ghent
years ago who set out to change the speech habit of a
first-grade boy who forever was using the phrase "I ain't
got no."

This day she'd told her class to get their pencils ready.

"I ain't got no pencil," the little fellow reported.

"No, dear," the teacher corrected him. "I have no pencil,
you have no pencil, he has no pencil."

"Then," the kid retorted, "who in hell has got all them pencils?"

A sixth-grade class at Hartford Junior High School was well up on modern country music if not ancient Greek poetry. In a review before exams, teacher Roger Frizzell asked, "Who was Homer?"

"He's," one student replied, "a cousin of Jethro!"

You'd think that any woman who taught a Sunday School class of 5- and 6-year-olds for more than 30 years, as Mrs. Gladys Sparkman of Kenton County did, would find it impossible to nominate one experience that stands out from the many others. But Mrs. Sparkman is convinced she experienced the topper one Sunday when her pupils were dabbling in water colors.

"I'm painting a picture of God," one little girl announced.

"That's sweet," Mrs. Sparkman said, "but nobody ever saw God so nobody knows what He looks like."

"Well," replied the kid seriously as she painted away, "now they'll know!"

Dr. Paul Sparks, an assistant superintendent of Louisville schools, heard about a naturally shy and bashful second-grade girl who transferred to a modern consolidated school after having spent her first year in a run-down, one-room rural school in the mountains.

Thrust suddenly into such a strange setting, the change was almost too much for the child and her school work suffered. After several days of patient effort, her teacher began to dent the shell of shyness.

"Would you like to stay after school and let me help you?" the teacher suggested.

The little girl would and that afternoon they were hard

at it when the teacher was summoned by the principal.

"You go on working and I'll be back," she told the child.

However, it soon became apparent that her stay in the office would take longer than expected and she felt she should let the child know she hadn't forgotten her. So she switched on the intercom system.

"Nancy, Nancy," she said. "Are you there?"

There was a prolonged silence from the classroom, but finally a timid, faltering voice spoke up: "Yes, Lord!"

To the 5-year-old boy with an injured arm who came into the office of Dr. V. A. Jackson, a Lexington doctor then practicing in Clinton, a picture was a picture.

The doctor looked at the bad wing while the kid grimaced in pain.

"Well, now," the doctor said, "we'll just have to take a picture of that arm."

"Doctor," asked the kid, holding back the tears, "do I have to smile?"

The innate honesty of her 5-year-old daughter Cindy came home to Mrs. Walker F. Murray of Covington with a jolt when a rather stout (well, fat) lady was talking to the little girl.

"And what will you do," the woman asked Cindy, "when you get to be a big girl like me?"

"I'll reduce," replied Cindy.

Until it closed a few years back, Fontaine Ferry was a popular amusement park in Louisville. One of the busiest concessions at the place was a track on which children could drive miniature cars. The only restriction was that drivers must be as tall as a mark attached to a nearby tree.

Joe Read, then 9, wasn't in any mood to be consoled

when he found he couldn't drive because he didn't reach the mark.

"Don't worry," his dad, Lee S. Read, said, "you'll grow and by next year you'll be as tall as that mark."

"Nope," moped Joe. "It's nailed to that tree and the tree will grow, too."

Clay, the then-6-year-old son of Pat and Mae Warren of Benton, was an ardent Sunday School goer. The class had been studying the story of little Moses and how he was placed in a basket and hidden in the bulrushes to conceal him from Pharoah's men. One Sunday morning, while this course of study was going on, Clay told his father he didn't want to go to Sunday School that day.

"Don't you want to find out what happened to little Moses?"

"You mean to tell me," Clay said seriously, "that child hasn't drowned yet?"

Since her sister, 12, played the violin, Clara Terrell, 4, was familiar with the main component of fiddle strings.

"Do cats go to heaven?" she asked her mother, Mrs. Edmund Terrell.

"I doubt they do," came the answer.

"Then," asked Clara, "where do the angels get strings for their harps?"

Speaking of Sunday School and heaven and such, when he was 4, David Huter asked his parents, Mr. and Mrs. Roger Huter of Louisville, a question they never quite answered satisfactorily.

"What," he wondered, "is God's last name?"

Arthur E. Elden, Frankfort, was having more than just a little trouble in impressing proper table manners upon the 5-year-old son of his household. One night when the kid was wolfing down his food in a style not recommended by the late Miss Emily Post, Elden called a halt to the display in order to deliver a lecture.

"You're a regular pig," he chided. "Do you know what a pig is?"

"I think," came the reply, "a pig is a hog's little boy!"

A mother in Breathitt County almost went into nervous prostration when her 9-year-old daughter came home and reported an incident that had arisen on the school bus she rides.

"A boy asked me if I was a boy or a girl," she said innocently.

"And what did you say?" her mother asked.

"I told him I was a girl."

"And what did he say then?"

"He said prove it."

"How," asked the mother, breaking into a cold sweat, "did you prove it?"

"Why," she answered logically, "I showed him my Girl Scout card!"

The main employment in the Bardstown area comes from the dozen or more distilleries located in Nelson County. Consequently, distilling brand names are familiar even to the very young, as a priest learned when he visited a parochial grade school.

"There are many Biblical names in this area," he said to the class. "There's Bethlehem, Calvary, Holy Cross, Gethsemane, and Loretto. Can any of you think of another Biblical name found here.

"Yes, Father," replied a 10-year-old boy. "Heaven Hill."

Mrs. James Allen, then a teacher at Shawnee High School, received a telephone call at school.

"Willie — — —," the voice on the other end of the line said, "won't be at school today."

"Who is this speaking?" asked Mrs. Allen.

"This," the caller replied, "is my father."

The 10-year-old daughter of a Louisville friend was visiting in the home of another little girl wher she happened into the kitchen and found the man of the house pouring some amber liquid from a bottle into a glass.

"What are you doing?" she asked.

"I'm fixing myself a before-dinner drink," came the reply.

"My daddy," the visitor announced, "just drinks ice water with olives!"

Charley Booe of Frankfort always has had the ability to express himself in a way that is different. For instance, when he was just 4 he came running in from play.

"I beated a snake, I beated a snake!" he shouted excitedly.

"Did you beat it with a rock or a stick?" he was asked.

"No," Charley replied, "I beated it running!"

Kevin Pogue, 5, was returning in the car with his father from the store and holding the candy bars that he had bought for himself and his sister, Phyllis. Accidentally, he dropped one of the bars out the car window.

"Poor Phyllis," he gasped, "I just dropped her candy bar!"

A Louisville friend well remembers the remark made by one of his sons the first time the kid saw the Atlantic Ocean. The family had driven all day and everyone was anxious to reach Myrtle Beach, S.C. As soon as they hit the coast, they drove straight to the beach.

The little boy, who had been raised in close proximity to a swimming pool, sat for several minutes gazing through the car window at all that water spreading out to infinity. Then he turned to his father with a reasonable question for one whose experience was limited to pools.

"Which," he asked, "is the shallow end?"

Students in a southwestern Kentucky kindergarten class were talking about the telephone, its value and how the parents of the children used the implement.

"What does your father use the telephone for?" one little boy was asked.

"He," came the answer, "uses it to call his friends to play poker!"

The first-grade class at Beaver Dam in which Beth Ann McBride is enrolled had been talking about birds.

"Can any one give a bird call?" the teacher wondered.

"Yes, ma'am," Beth Ann replied. " 'Here, birdy!' "

St. Francis School at Loretto was one of the many places were the Head Start program for preschool children was conducted. One day during a play break, Sister Joseph Benjamin, who administered the program, had the boys contest each other in a foot race.

"Me won, me won," shouted the little fellow who finished first.

"Don't say 'Me won,'" the sister corrected. "Say 'I won.'"

"I'll be damned if you did," the boy shot back, "you wasn't even in the race!"

Times do change and so do children, a fact pointed up in an incident reported by Bob T. Long, Benton. Seems a first-grader slipped in the hall at his school and skinned his knee.

"Remember," the teacher consoled him as she examined the wound, "big boys don't cry."

"I'm not gonna cry," the kid replied, "I'm gonna sue!"

The passion of children for telling it the way it is cuts through a lot of flab and gets straight to the heart of a matter.

John E. Heer, Jr., chairman of the University of Louisville's Speed Scientific School department of civil engineering, came eyeball to eyeball on the uninhibited truth of that fact when he was asked to judge an essay contest on pollution for fifth-graders at Holy Trinity School.

"Noise pollution," one child wrote, "is from all the people who talk and don't have a nice thing to say. All they do is gossip."

"Pollution," another figured, "is an ever growing thing which people read about and usually hope other people will do something about."

You can't tell it much plainer than that.

As an example of how children may be doing some serious, free-lance thinking adults wouldn't suspect, consider the how-do-I-answer-that-one-question laid on Mrs. Lloyd Parsons, a teacher at Bridgeport Elementary School in Franklin County, by a 10-year-old girl.

The child came to Mrs. Parson's desk with a query that would have sent even a theological expert scurrying for the Good Book.

"Adam and Eve were the first two people on earth, weren't they?" she whispered.

"That's what the Bible tells us," Mrs. Parsons replied.

"They just had two boys, didn't they?" the child pressed.

"As far as we know, that is correct."

"Well, then," the little girl went on, ending the question and answer period temporarily, "if boys can't have any children, where did the rest of us come from?"

The abiding ambition of the early-teen-age daughter of Louisville friends had been to have a private phone of her very own with an unlisted number. Finally her dream was realized.

Shortly after the phone was installed, her parents heard her scream and rushed to her room to see what was wrong.

"Golly," she sighed with sheer ecstasy, "I just got my first wrong number!"

Mrs. Robert V. Shane, Jr., Danville, had direct contact in a most unusual way with the blunt honesty of children.

The Shanes have two sons — Mike, 9 at the time, and Mark, then 6. Mrs. Shane also had a pair of artificial eyelashes, her first venture into that area of beauty deception.

She had one eyelash in place and, holding the other in her hand, she stepped back from the mirror to admire herself when son Mike walked into the room. The boy's mouth sagged open and a look of frightened surprise flashed over his face as he stared at her.

"Don't tell Mark, Mother," he said finally in a quavering voice. "Slip out and scare him!"

And don't ever overlook the ability of children to improvise on the spot.

Mrs. Nina K. Flint, a Magoffin County teacher, was discussing the proper use of the verbs "setting" and "sitting" with her fourth-grade class one day. After going over the rules of grammar that govern the words, she asked one of the boys to compose a sentence with "setting" in it.

"The man is setting in the chair," he replied after due deliberation.

"No, you've forgotten the rule," Mrs. Flint corrected. "Things that have life sit, things that do not have life set. Try again to give me a sentence using the verb setting."

The boy wrinkled his foreheat in deep thought, then his eyes lit and he spoke up in a voice of triumph:

"The dead man is setting in the chair!"

Among the children of a Louisville family I once knew, the two youngest were pre-school girls only a year and a half apart in age. Needless to say, clothing was passed down from the older child to her younger sister.

Their mother hadn't thought much about that procedure until she bought the youngest child a brand-new dress. She ripped open the package, held the dress lovingly in her arms, then looked at her older sister.

"And," she said proudly, "it never was yours, either!"

Four-year-old Mary Helen Bray of Fountain Run went to church with her parents, Mr. and Mrs. George Bray, on a Sunday when four new members were baptized. Later she was describing the experience to her aunt, Mrs. Emma McDonald.

"The preacher preached," she said, "then he put on another suit and went down some steps into a big tub of water and rinsed out four people!"

Mrs. Edward Murphy, who then was a teacher at an
elementary school in northern Kentucky, asked one of
her second-graders to describe a set of scales.

"All I know," the kid said, "is that scales is something
my mother stands on and it makes her mad."

If she wasn't before, Mrs. Nancy Hughes, a second-grade
teacher at Bowling Green, became a firm believer in the
old cliché about laughter being the best medicine after
she had missed several days of school because of a cold.
While she was away, her pupils wrote her get-well-quick
letters.

One note went this way: "Dear Mrs. Hughes: Being
sick is bad for your health. Get well soon. Love,
Alice Cook."

All parents who have found it suddenly quiet — and dull
— around the house once the children have grown up and
gone can appreciate the memories Mr. and Mrs. Raymond
McFarland, Albany, have of life with their two sons.

Because the things they remember about their boys,
Phillip and David, will be familiar to so many others
who have survived a brace of imaginative, sometimes
obstinate boys, two incidents involving their youngsters
are worthy of repeating.

One day when David was 4, a violent thunderstorm
developed. When the lightning began to flash near the
house and the thunder actually rattled the windows, he
became afraid.

"Don't be afraid, the storm is God's work," Mrs.
McFarland reassured him.

"Well," David replied quickly, "if God's not careful,
He's gonna fool around and get somebody killed!"

Not long afterwards, David developed a habit of
making ugly faces when he was told to do something.
After being warned not to do it again, he turned to his
mother and gave her the same tongue-out, screwed-up-

face look. She immediately spanked him and made him sit in a corner.

While he was sitting there crying, his brother came into the room.

"Phillip," he said to him between sobs, pointing to his mother, "make a face at her!"

As one who has been through the routine, I know the deep truth in an observation made by Mrs. Barry Bacon of Owensboro after she and her husband returned with their four small children from visiting family and friends in Barbourville over a Christmas holiday.

"We made everybody we visited happy twice," she reckoned. "When we arrived and when we left!"

The American Dental Association should have gotten in touch with Miss Angie Doll of Louisville about the possibility of her doing one of those see-your-dentist-twice-a-year-at-least testimonials after an incident in which she was involved. For Angie could have provided them with evidence far more convincing than that "Hey, Dad, no cavities this time" TV plug about how a visit to your molar manipulator can pay off in side benefits.

Angie, you see, was center fielder for the Belles, a girls 11 to 13-year-old softball team in the Lyndon Recreation League. This day an opposing batter lined a blue darter straight at Angie. The ball was coming so fast that it zipped between her glove and outstretched hand and smacked her flush in the mouth.

"Are you hurt?" the coach shouted as he rushed from the sideline.

"I'm all right," she assured him.

"But didn't that ball hit you in the mouth?" he pressed.

"Yeah, but it didn't hurt a bit," Angie insisted. "I've been to the dentist today and the novacaine hasn't worn off yet!"

Ah, yes, the unmistakable signs and smells of spring!
Mrs. L. J. Yancey of Finchville tells about a 4-year-old
girl she knew who was playing near a field where a farmer
was spreading fertilizer.

"Mamma," the little girl shouted running into the
house, "spring is here because I can smell it!"

A Louisville mother who shall remain forever anonymous
for obvious reasons was looking through a box of family
photographs when her 5-year-old son came up to see
what she was doing. The kid picked one snapshot from
the lot and asked her who it was.

"Oh, that's me," the mother said. "The picture was
taken 25 years ago."

"Why," asked the small fry, squinting at the girl in the
picture, "didn't you keep the face you had?"

None of the visitors at her home on Christmas Day had
noticed the honest-to-goodness real wrist watch, her first,
being worn by Donna Evans, 6, of Louisville. As the day
wore on, the child could stand the oversight no longer.

"Oh, my," she exclaimed finally in a loud voice, "it's so
hot in my new wrist watch!"

Once, at least, in the career of every parent an inquisitive
young son or daughter is sure to ask THAT question.
And when asked, the combined wisdom of Dr. Spock and
Dear Abby is needed to compose a passing fair answer.

Take the experience of a Louisville mother when her
time came to answer up. Her 5-year-old son, who had
been outside, came bursting into the house, his face
flushed with excitement.

"Mother, mother," he shouted, urgently piling words together into one breathless sentence, "Tommy-is-going-to-get-a-baby-for-Christmas-and-I-want-one-too-where-do-babies-come-from-anyway?"

The mother took the child on her lap with fear and trembling and, carefully selecting each word, launched into a somewhat halting — if honest — answer to the latter part of the question.

The kid sat quietly for a second after she'd finished, then turned to her with a questioning, yet still trusting, look in his eyes.

"Mother," he said as he climbed down and rushed outside to resume play, "you gotta be kidding!"

Children may resist turning loose such traditional legends as Santa Claus and the Easter Bunny, but they seldom fail to be practical in all matters. Consider Mary Louis Read, 10 at the time.

She had lost a tooth and she and her mother, Madelyn, were discussing the possibility of the Tooth Fairy leaving a coin under her pillow to compensate for the molar.

"I hope the Tooth Fairy doesn't forget," Mary Louis worried.

"She won't," she was reassured.

"I hope," she added, "she remembers the sales tax, too."

The members of a seventh-grade class at a Louisville school were told to write an essay on what they wanted to be when they grew up and why. Among the students was the son of a dentist, and his essay went straight to the point.

"I want to be a dentist, like my father, when I grow up," he wrote, "because I figure by then he will have all the equipment paid for."

I doubt that many people, adults or children, will ever
set down a much longer or complete list of blessings
than did Mary Ann Curran, then 9, when she wrote her
grandfather, John L. Hargan, a pre-Thanksgiving letter
entitled "What Am I Thankful For."

In one breathless sentence, she wrote:

"I am thankful for my mother, father, sisters and
brother, grandfather, grandmother and my good Catholic
religion, priests, sisters and lay teachers, for food, water
and other drinks, for books, pencils, pens, rings, shoes,
socks, for hats and coats, dogs, rabbits, sweaters, skirts,
cats and other animals and for grass, flowers, balls, bats,
boots, car, bus, land, house, churches, tables, for apples
and other fruits, trees, songs, angels, for blessed Mary
and for not letting my grandmother suffer and for the
ABC, for aunts, uncles, lights and the Pope, and I am
glad that I have you and for my desk, horses, cows, pills,
prayer books, for my name, ears, nose, mouth and
hands, trains, airplanes, glasses, the sun, moon, stars,
bricks, stone, wood, doors, clocks, basketballs,
beachballs, hair, hikes, dresses, turkey, heat, chickens,
for the butterflies, and for our Father and Hail Mary, and
for my classmates and friends, for holy water, teeth,
and for the color of my hair, and for peace, and help
me win a prize."

Don't try to tell me that love for all things that are labeled
good — the high and the low, the humble and the
sophisticated — isn't one of the strongest instincts of
any normal child.

Let me tell you a simple little story to underscore the
point.

Jay Paxton of Louisville was digging in the garden and
his two daughters, Laurie, then 4, and Lucy, a year
younger, were being helpfully in the way. In one clod of
dirt he turned over, there were several plump earth worms.

"These are worms," he said to the little girls. "Worms
are good for the soil and you can use them when you go
fishing. Worms are nice."

"Yes, daddy," they replied in perfect unison.

"But there are lots of bugs and spiders around and they aren't so nice," the horticultural lecture continued. "Bugs sometimes sting you and spiders can bite you and make you sick."

"Yes, daddy," Lucy, the youngest cut in, "bugs and spiders are bad, but worms are nice — even if you can't hug them!"

The way children seldom miss a trick is pointed up in a conversation Mrs. George Wombwell of Louisville overheard between Ward Deters and her own son, Andy, both 4. The boys were looking at the sky through a pair of binoculars that belonged to one of Andy's older brothers.

"I see God," Ward announced as he stared upward.

"I," Andy topped him when his turn came to look, "see God and Jesus and the Godfather!"

Mrs. Daniel M. Burlew, II, took her twin sons Jeff and Marshall, age 5, with her to the Middletown post office to mail a sympathy card to a friend whose mother had died. The twins were anxious to drop the card in the box but, upon finding there were several slots, one of the boys had a reasonable question.

"Is this the one," he asked, pointing to one of the slots, "that goes to heaven?"

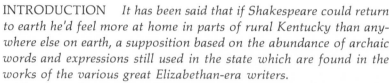

INTRODUCTION   *It has been said that if Shakespeare could return to earth he'd feel more at home in parts of rural Kentucky than anywhere else on earth, a supposition based on the abundance of archaic words and expressions still used in the state which are found in the works of the various great Elizabethan-era writers.*

These speech patterns, and pronunciations, prove — if any proof is needed — the direct geneological ties present-day Kentucky has retained with the Anglo-Saxon people who were most prominent in the settlement of the state.

From the Big Sandy River on the east to the Mississippi on the west, many a Kentuckian, like Ariel in Shakespeare's "The Tempest," will allow after a substantial meal that he has "et a big bate;" like Puck in "A Midsummer Night's Dream," he may describe an active person as "a right peart and nible feller;" like Lady Macbeth, he may say he "gits a-feered" when he is frightened.

A common greeting off the paved roads is for the stranger to "come in and set a spell," the same greeting Spenser used in his poem "The Faerie Queene"; like Sidney, many a Kentuckian will say "fur" instead of far; like Milton, he may say someone is "pied" when they act strangely; like Bacon, he may describe an excited person as being in "a near franzied state."

Shakespeare would have appreciated fully the words of an old man in Pike County who, in speaking of his sister, said "I hain't seed her in 20 year and now I cain't hardly memorize her." Spenser might have used the same words as a woman in Spencer County, 200 miles west, who mused, "When I was a-raisin' we didn't have no fotched on clothes."

The following pages are devoted to real-life stories told in the style and language that had its origin in the days of Elizabeth in England nearly four centuries ago.

CHAPTER 5

THE WAY WE TALK

George Brown of Prestonsburg tells about two mountain men — one a Brown ancestor of his, the other named Jones — who were trading tall tales about the prowess of their heroic ancestors. To hear them top each other, you'd think their kinsmen alone had fought off the Indians and opened the way into Kentucky for the pioneers.

The exchange so whetted their curiosity that they decided to do deeper family research and to meet later and further astound each other.

"I follered my kin back a considerable piece and then I plum quit," Jones announced the next time they met.

"Why'd you do that?" Brown asked.

"Because," Jones answered, applying the needle rather bluntly, "I follered 'em back nearly 200 years to old Virginny and I learnt that a man by the name of Jones onct had stole a horse, skipped over into Kentucky and changed his name to Brown."

"I guess maybe we had better drop the whole thing 'cause we just might be kin to each other," mused Brown. "I follered my kin back to the same time and the same place in old Virginny and, you know, I learnt my great great grandpappy onct had a horse that was stole!"

The next time you get to feeling things are snafued beyond all recall and there just aren't enough hours in the day to do everything expected of you, keep this old Kentucky mountain saying in mind: "They's a whole new day tomorrow that ain't never been tetched yet."

Although the sentence structure often used by some Kentuckians is quaint and sometimes loaded with ancient words, fractured tenses and such, what the person speaking had in mind usually comes across crystal clear.

As in the highly original way John Campbell, an old Leslie County farmer, expressed his philosophy of life.

"When I works, I works hard," he said simply, "and when I sets, I sets loose and when I think, I go to sleep!"

Then there was the brand-new but highly descriptive manner in which a loafer seated outside the Grayson County courthouse at Leitchfield pointed up the fact he hadn't gotten enough sleep the night before.

"I ain't got no idea of how long I was a-bed last night," he yawned as he whittled half-heartedly on an aromatic piece of cedar, "but I threw my pants on a rocker when I got in and when the alarm clock went off this mornin' that chair still was a-rockin'!"

Again drawing heavily on the language style of the great Elizabethan-era writers so admired by the British Islanders who were most prominent in their lineage, many a Kentuckian in mountain or rural regions will give the past tense to a verb simply by adding "ed" to the root word.

Thus, the past tense of know isn't knew, but "knowed;" the past tense of throw isn't threw, but "throwed;" the past tense of grow isn't grew, but "growed" and so on.

Mike Rowady, a Winchester attorney, recounts an experience as told to him by an aged man from the mountains which illustrates that characteristic.

The man, it seems, had spent all his life in the hills of Wolfe County until, when he was past 80, his wife had died and a daughter who lived in Winchester finally convinced him to come and live with her. He had left the mountains in body but not in spirit and he longed to see familiar faces. So finally, he told Rowady, "I gotten all I could take and I gotten me on a bus" and he went back to Campton, the seat of Wolfe County, for a visit.

"I gotten off that bus," he said, "and mosied over to the courthouse. They was these wooden bainches on both sides of the walk and I taken myself a seat on one of them bainches. Directly here come a feller who set hisself down on the bainch opposite of me. Soon as I cast my eyes on him I thought to myself I knowed him. And from the way he looked at me, I knowed he thought he knowed me. The longer I looked at him, the certainer I was I knowed I knowed him. And the longer he looked at me, the certainer I was that he knowed he knowed me. 'Fore long we quit lookin' and we got up at the same time and started toward one another. We met between them bainches and we shaked hands and slapped one another on the back and you never seen such talkin' over old times in all your life."

"And, you know," the old man concluded, "we come to find out it warn't either one of us!"

Perhaps the briefest, but most adequate, health report ever delivered was made by a 90-year-old farmer in Hickman County who still had all his own teeth, who could hear a pin drop, and who could see without glasses.

"Let me tell you," he summarized the situation, "I ain't never had to go to a tooth dentist or a eye-ball doctor in my life!"

One of the most difficult things a person can be called upon to do for another is to give him directions that can be understood. Under such circumstances, the average party will start pointing in all directions and will wind up using 10 words for every one that is essential. And the stranger still will get lost.

That being true, the clearest set of direction I've ever come by was provided by a young boy I stopped at a crossroads in the remote back country of Martin County to ask how to get to the home of a certain man.

"You take the road down the left-hand holler as fur as

you kin," the boy said, never once pointing, "and you turn around. His place is the first one on the right-hand side comin' back out!"

Edwin W. Horne of Frankfort tells about an old man he knew many years ago who claimed he remembered having seen Abraham Lincoln splitting rails. By using basic arithmetic, that would have made him at least 115 years of age.

"If you're that old," some skeptic kidded him, "maybe you remember the fall of Rome, too."

"'Pears to me," the old fellow mused, "I did hear somethin' drap."

After much persuasion, and considerably against his better judgment, an ancient gent from western Kentucky finally went to visit relatives in Louisville. Since he'd never been any farther away from home than the county seat, cronies back home were anxious for a report on his trip.

"Wasn't you afraid you'd get lost?" he was asked.

"How could I of got lost," he almost spat, "when I didn't even care where I was at?"

Some years back when the Western Kentucky University basketball team was playing in the Holiday Tournament at Madison Square Garden in New York, a man called a Bowling Green radio station to ask when the game would be broadcast.

"Air time is 7:30," he was told.

"I know it air 7:30," he fussed, "but when will that game come on?"

The commendable way some people just never will say anything bad about anybody was being discussed by Norman Allen, the Prestonsburg editor. When pushed to take a stand, he allowed, this type of person would even say the devil has his good points — he's industrious, for instance.

To prove his point, Allen went on to tell about a man in his part of eastern Kentucky who was a notorious wife-beater, a thief, a drunkard, a liar, and general no-good. When he died, it was generally conceded that even the old man in the area who was known never to have uttered a derogatory word in his life would be hard pressed to say something good about him.

"Well, what do you say about him?" the loafers at the general store baited him.

The old codger meditated for a few seconds.

"Come to think of it, boys," he said finally, "he was as good a whistler as ever I saw pucker a lip!"

The way people express themselves in normal conversation always has fascinated me. The same goes for O. G. Wilhite, a Monticello banker, who overheard two women talking outside his place.

"Well," one said to the other, "have you saw airy a sight or heered airy a wonder this week?"

Long before the days of school consolidation, one rural county in western Kentucky had 12 high schools. With so many schools in one sparsely populated county, it meant that most of them were very small — one, in fact, had only 30 students and a faculty of three teachers.

With only three teachers, each of the lot had to wear several hats. The basketball coach taught vocational agriculture, civics, geography, and unfortunately, also English. I use the word unfortunately, because this poor fellow could do everything with the English language except use it correctly. He was an especial terror at verb tenses, particularly the verbs "seen" and "saw" and he forever was using them interchangeably.

This eventually led some parents to worry about their children and so they referred the matter to the board of trustees, all of them elected from the narrow limits of the school district. Two of the trustees were in favor of dismissing the teacher immediately, but the third trustee, not exactly Phi Beta Kappa material perhaps, defended the grammar-fracturer in impassioned words.

"Let me tell you this," he summarized his defense, "I'd a heap druther have myself a man who says I seen when he seen somethin' than one who says I saw when he ain't saw nothin'!"

"Uncle" George Henson, who lived in the steep hills that spread out from the North Fork of the Kentucky River in Breathitt County, was an honest-to-goodness Kentucky mountain storyteller. I have spent many an afternoon listening to him spin one tale after another, using the quaint speech pattern of his Anglo-Saxon forefathers, about the hills and the people he knew so well.

"Let me tell you about 'Preacher' Sam Combs and the wildcat," Uncle George started one of his tales as he rolled his ambitious chew of tobacco to the other side of his mouth.

"Now Preacher Sam, he warn't much on recognizin' varmints and one day him and this other feller set out in the woods to go on a hunt. After a while they seen a big wildcat run in a holler log.

" 'Them things make good pets,' the other feller kidded Preacher Sam, 'and if you want me to, I'll poke it out of that log and you can catch it and take it home fer your kids.'

"The other feller, he got a pole and after he'd poked it a few times, the ol' wildcat come a-scratchin' out at Preacher Sam's end of the log, mad as a hornet, and Preacher Sam, he grabbed hold of it.

"There was the awfulest 'rasslin' around you ever heard tell of.

" 'You want me to come and help you hold it?' " the
other feller yelled.

" 'Naw,' Preacher Sam yelled back, "but you might
come and help me let go of it!' "

Don Whitehead, the Harlan County native who is one of
only 25 persons to win two Pulitzer Prizes in journalism,
tells about a New Yorker who came into eastern Kentucky
and was appalled at the thin, stingy land from which so
many mountain farmers scratch a living.

"You say this land is pore and rocky," a farmer told
him. "Stranger, this land will fool you — it's a helluva lot
worser than it looks!"

Years ago a favorite meeting place in the Tar Hill section
of Grayson County was John Tully's general store. Farmers
coming to the store had to cross Meeting Creek and one
day a heavy rain had sent it boiling out of its banks.

A group of men who had made it across were arguing
about how high the water had risen. Finally the eldest of
the lot was called upon to settle the matter.

"That there creek's the highest ever it was," he allowed.
"I looked at it this mornin' and it was so high I could
see clean under it!"

A few years back I was having coffee with banker James
Carpenter and merchant Oakley Arnett in Salyersville
and the conversation turned to an old man they knew.
Seems he had seven daughters and as each neared
marrying age he'd called them in for a heart-to-heart talk.

"Now, gal," he would say, "I don't never want you
marryin' no man just 'cause he's got money. But if he has
got it, remember it ain't no bad fault!"

Another time in Salyersville I heard about "Goosebite" Arnett, once jailer of Magoffin County and surely one of eastern Kentucky's most colorful men. Once, I was told, he got mad at various church groups in the county.

"If the avenging angel come through here killin' all the real Christians," he fumed, "he'd never cock his pistol at any of them folks."

The use of double and even triple negatives, a grammar form pioneered by an English gentleman by the name of Geoffrey Chaucer in a poem called *The Canterbury Tales*, is common in some parts of Kentucky to this day.

Joe R. Johnson of Frankfort recalls a quadruple — maybe it even was a quintuple — negative he once heard down in Clinton, his old home town in the far western tip of the state. A new funeral home had been opened and potential customers were invited to inspect the establishment.

"Ain't this purty?" a woman marveled. "With a place like this, ain't no use of nobody havin' no funeral in no church no more."

It's always good to hear a new way to express a lot of education, and in Nicholasville I heard just such a way. Seems this young woman had become the first in her family ever to graduate from college and someone asked her father if she was going to continue in school.

"Lordy, no," he said, "why, she's educated through to the yon side of nowhur now!"

From what I've seen, real, old-time Kentucky mountain men (and today there aren't many of them left) were an independent breed who possessed many admirable traits, one of which I wish I had enough courage to copy.

For they knew how to handle their women.

Because of their Old World background, they grew up naturally convinced that females should be subservient and kept in their places, which assuredly wasn't at the head of the parade. Many a time I've seen a mountain man walking along a path with his "old woman" trailing several paces to the rear.

George Armstrong of Quicksand, Breathitt County, tells a story which points up this spoke-only-when-spoken-to status of women. He knew an old mountain man who once a week would come down from out of the hills with his wife on their way to Jackson, the county seat. Always he would be riding a sway-back old mule while she walked behind at a respectable distance.

"Don't you think your wife ought to ride?" Armstrong asked him one day.

"Yep," the man answered, "but she ain't got no mule!"

Another story from Norman Allen of Prestonsburg concerns the speaker who was addressing an elderly audience in Floyd County on how the United States should take firm steps to get rid of communism, socialism, and assorted other isms. After he'd orated for what seemed an eternity, one of his long-suffering listeners struggled laboriously to his feet.

"I'm on yore side, fer certain, mister, and the givverment ought to sure get rid of all them isms," he said, leaning heavily on his walking stick. "But the ism I'm fer gittin' rid of first is my rheumatism!"

The matter of survival, whether it's weathering a hard winter or something else, brings to mind an article I once did on a man in Green County who was 102. Being the penetrating young reporter that I was then, I asked him THAT question: How do you account for your long life?

"Well," he replied matter of factly, "I guess it's 'cause I never stole a horse or called a man a liar to his face."

111

Since life was real and earnest in every respect,
Kentuckians of the pioneer period had to be more
stoic and fatalistic than today. An example of these
characteristics is pointed up in a bit of rationalization
Wyatt Shely, Lawrenceburg historian, uncovered in
examining some records dating back to the late 1780's.

Upon being told that her husband had been ambushed
and killed by Indians, Mrs. Jacob Coffman is reported to
have remarked simply:

"I always told my old man the Indians was gonna get
him, and I'd druther have lost my best cow at the pail
than to have lost that old man."

Up along the headwaters of the Middle Fork of the
Kentucky River they still tell about Phil Wilson, a
mountain man who years ago rafted logs down the
stream nearly 300 miles to Frankfort each spring when
the "spring tides" (flood) swept down the stream. He was
just a boy when he made his initial trip, and it marked
the first time he ever had been away from the hill country.

After the logs had been sold, Wilson went with the
older men who made up the rafting crew to have supper
in a Frankfort hotel. The men ordered steak and, since
he'd never been in such a place before, he followed suit.
But when his steak arrived, it turned out to be pretty
much on the rare side.

"What's wrong with this here meat?" he asked.

"Nothing," the waiter almost sneered, "it's good rare
beef."

"Then take 'er back to the cook-stove," Wilson
requested, "and rare 'er some more!"

George Trotter, Lebanon, tells about a man who once ran
a saloon in his town. The customers in the place were
forever inviting him to join them in a drink, but he had a
stock refusal ready.

"Nope," he would say, "whiskey is fer sellin', not fer drinkin'."

Perry Cross, a former state representative and now an auto dealer in Albany, tells stories that have the distinct flavor of the foothills country. One of his took place in the early Depression days when many of the coal mines in the eastern part of his county, Clinton, were shut down.

With work at home impossible to find, a lot of men from the area, among them former coal miners, went north to take seasonal jobs on large farms in Indiana. A sizeable settlement of them located in the central part of the state where hands were needed to pick tomatoes.

One summer two brothers who had migrated to Indiana to pick tomatoes sent for their younger brother, a boy of about 17 who wasn't exactly the sharpest kid on the block. He found his way to the town where his brothers were living, and on his first night they all went to join others from back home in hoisting a few beers at a local tavern.

When the proprietor saw the younger brother, he balked.

"I can't serve you," he said, "you're a minor."

"No, I ain't," the boy bristled, "I'm a 'mater picker!"

Two old gents were sitting in the sun outside the Perry County courthouse in Hazard, passing the time of day and talking about first one thing and then another. Eventually the conversation turned to the health of the wife of one of the men who, as he put it, "had been punyin' around and barely able to take vittles" for some time.

"How's she gettin' on now?" his friend asked.

"Oh," came the answer, "she complains of feelin' better."

In western Kentucky, my sister-in-law, Peggy Creason, heard about a young woman who was corrected by a friend for her persistent use of the word "ain't."

"Don't say 'ain't,'" the friend chided. "It isn't good English."

"Aw, I know English," the user replied. "I can write it real good, but I ain't much good at sayin' it."

Dr. Ernest Foley, a Louisville dentist, recalled overhearing two old gents talk about a mutual acquaintance while they were seated around the pot-bellied stove in a crossroads store.

"You know," one said, "he shore ain't the man he used to be."

"No," the other agreed, "and he never was, neither!"

If backed into a tight corner, I guess I'd have to say John Wooton, a Leslie County mountain farmer who died at age 102, was one of the smartest men I ever knew. Not smart in the usual college-degree meaning of the word, since he never had a chance to go to school and could neither read nor write; but smart in his practical ability to have been able to make out for himself under the most difficult of circumstances, and in his clear comprehension of things happening about him. Any man who had been on his own for more than 90 years, as John Wooton had, and who had scratched a living from the poor, almost perpendicular mountain land, certainly stands apart in initiative, native intelligence, and self-reliance.

I first met John Wooton when he was a mere lad of 90. Although at that time the massive federal programs to retrain mountain area unemployed workers, most of them coal miners, still hadn't been dreamed up, he could see the handwriting on the wall. By contrasting the situation even then with the way things once had been in the hill country, he could see trouble ahead. For when he had settled on his 100 acres on Rockhouse Creek, near Hyden, the county seat, in 1891, he pointed out, the man of nearly every house was a farmer. There were no commercial coal mines, and patches of corn and pumpkins and beans were planted in clearings along every creek and up the steep hillsides.

"But," he said, "there ain't a tenth of the corn growed in Leslie County now that was growed then. Folks has been backin' off from farming ever year. Money has got more plentifuler, coal is runnin' good and folks has gone to lookin' fer a big time.

"They don't realize what will happen when all this coal plays out," he continued, proving at heart that he was a prophet. "Why, they'll have to hire people to learn them how to do things."

With more and more storage dams being built by the U.S. Corps of Engineers on Kentucky rivers to provide a backup water supply in dry times, there's a touch of deep logic in a story told by Dick Morris of Columbia. During one especially arid stretch in late August, he was talking to a man from Knifley, near where a dam was being completed on the Green River.

"Had any water up your way lately?" Morris asked.

"Do you mean," the man countered, "water from the Lord or the givverment?"

Sure enough, many Kentuckians have retained the ability of their Old English ancestors to say a lot in a few well-chosen words. Like, for instance, a man who lived on the outskirts of Leitchfield in a tumble-down, unpainted, tarpapered shack that was a real eyesore.

Since it looked so bad, he was asked by neighbors why he didn't at least splash on a little paint to make it less trashy looking.

"Because," he said, getting straight to the point, "I'm too poor to paint and too proud to whitewash."

And then there's the experience of a man who worked in the government-subsidized poverty program in eastern

Kentucky who ran into a native who had the talent for speaking volumes without being wordy.

When he first started going to the mountains, the poverty worker drove a foreign compact car. Soon, however, he traded it in for a larger, new American-made model.

A few days later he stopped at a crossroads store in the hills and an old man asked him what work he did.

"Oh," he replied jokingly, "I fight poverty."

"Well," the old man mused as he eyed the new car, "it shore does look like you're winnin' the fight!"

George Wooton, who really comes from Hell for Certain, is judge of Leslie County and in the courthouse at Hyden he has installed a novel bench for the benefit of a very special group of his constituents. It's called the "Widow's Bench," and it is reserved for those — not just widows, but widowers as well — who are alone and maybe looking for a new partner.

One Friday morning, Wooton vows, he noticed an aged couple seated on the bench engaged in serious conversation. Some time later the man, who turned out to be a mere lad of 82, came into the judge's office and said he wanted to marry the woman, who was just 69.

"But, Judge," he lamented, "we done run smack into a problem."

Seems that when they had gone into the clerk's office to get a license, they were told that a blood test and a wait of three days for the result was required before the license could be issued.

"Judge," the old man said seriously, "you know that I've voted fer you ever time you've ever run and I ain't never asked a thing from you before.

"But," he went on, "ain't they somethin' you can do, or some words you can say, to bind us over 'til Monday morning?"

The way Kentuckians, more than the residents of any other state, still lean on Old English words and pronunci-

ations is pointed up in a conversation David Harlow,
who now lives in Louisville, overheard in a rural section
some years back when airplanes still were a comparative
novelty.

"You know," an old gent mused to a group of
courthouse yard loafers, "a body wouldn't believe
they air men flyin' around up there in the air, but they
air!"

During the month of January, all aliens in the United
States must stop by the nearest post office to pick up
cards on which they list their present address for benefit
of the Immigration Service. A reminder that this must be
done is broadcast repeatedly over radio and television
stations as a public service.

Apparently some people hear the reminder without
understanding it. Workers at the stamp windows at the
main Louisville post office report that every day while
the reminders are being broadcast two or three people will
stop to say they've been sick and to ask, "Is this where
I get my ailin' card?"

T. C. Purdy, Louisville, passes on a story that shows how
a person sometimes can get all snagged up in the mother
tongue. He was driving in eastern Kentucky and had
stopped at a small restaurant where he ordered a cup
of coffee without cream.

"We ain't got no cream," the waitress told him, "so
you'll have to drink your coffee without milk!"

Another example of how you can get wrapped up in an
outburst of words from which you don't seem able to
extricate yourself is a conversation I once overheard
between two women who were having lunch at an
adjacent table. They were talking about some man and

one of the women allowed she didn't know him.

"Oh, you know him," her friend insisted.

"No, I know I don't know him," she shot back. "I know I know who I know and I know I know I don't know him!"

There are, of course, sophisticates who scoff at the quaint language of the mountains and much of rural Kentucky, and who sneeringly refer to it as country and folksy and illiterate. Ironically these same scoffers upon reading the identical words and phrases in Elizabethan-era works lapse into convulsions of praise at the pleasant sound, poetic qualities, and classic descriptiveness.

Radio, TV, good roads, better schools, and greater exposure to the outside have changed most of the life styles in the hills and rural regions where the people of Anglo-Saxon extraction settled. But in spite of changing times, many of the Old World words, phrases, and expressions live on in everyday conversation.

Which proves, perhaps, that scoffers to the contrary, some things have withstood the test of time because, as many a Kentuckian still might say, "they're a heap lot more endurabler."

Because of the differences in accents, dialects, styles of phrasing, and such, there's little more than a sort of second-cousin-by-marriage relationship between the way English is spoken in, say, Brooklyn or Detroit and in parts of Kentucky. For this is, to be sure, a vast country that abounds in various uses of the mother tongue.

Perhaps no area has more unusual speech patterns than the Appalachian Mountains of Kentucky, Virginia, North Carolina, Virginia, and Tennessee. There, far back in the deep hollows and hemmed in by the steep ridges, Anglo-Saxon words and phrases still are spoken in what to many is a pleasant accent that combines the softness of the South with the flat tones of the plains.

All of which may explain why dialecticians and speech students long have regarded the hill country as a happy hunting ground. Any glossary or speech compendium of pure mountain phonetics would include simple words such as these:

Aig — What a hen lays.

Argy — What two people do when they disagree.

Fit — What they did when the disagreement became physical.

Warsh — What you do to dirty clothes.

Arn — What you do to clothing after "warshing."

Ast — How you get directions.

Bile — What you do to water.

Deef — Hard of hearing.

Backer — What some people chew.

Chiny — Kind of fancy dishes some people use.

Frash — Newly produced (as "frash aigs.")

Peart — When you feel better than tolerable.

Drap — What you do when something is too hot.

Spenders — What holds up your pants.

Years — What you hear with.

Jine — What you do when you volunteer for the Army.

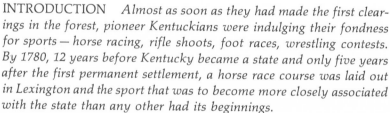

INTRODUCTION   *Almost as soon as they had made the first clear-ings in the forest, pioneer Kentuckians were indulging their fondness for sports — horse racing, rifle shoots, foot races, wrestling contests. By 1780, 12 years before Kentucky became a state and only five years after the first permanent settlement, a horse race course was laid out in Lexington and the sport that was to become more closely associated with the state than any other had its beginnings.*

Sports have remained a part of life in Kentucky to this day and many near-legendary figures — ranging from Mike Fink, the rifle-shooting king of the frontier, to Adolph Rupp, the winningest coach in the history of college basketball — have been associated with the state. Their exploits are a colorful chapter in the history of Kentucky.

But not all Kentucky's mighty sports figures became legends. One who didn't was Lowry Rains, a track coach of sorts who may have been the only man ever to start and also judge the finish of the same 100-yard dash.

Rains, a track buff, taught at a small rural high school in western Kentucky at a time when his favorite sport was unknown there. One year he challenged Murray High School to a track meet and, since he was the only person around who ever had seen such an affair, he was running the show. When he lined up the boys for the 100-yard dash, he was reminded that he had not appointed a judge at the finish line.

"That's all right," he said calmly. "After the boys start up here, I'll just jog down there and judge the finish myself."

Which he did. He set them off, then comfortably outran the field and was waiting for them at the finish line.

So, pick your sport. You'll find it, as life itself, is uniquely different in Kentucky.

CHAPTER 6

T HE SPORTING SET

Perhaps the most often-asked question in all of horse racing has to do with why Man O' War, the thoroughbred of the century in the opinion of sports writers, didn't run in the Kentucky Derby.

He didn't because he wasn't nominated in 1920, the year he would have been eligible. His owner, Samuel D. Riddle, decided to skip the Derby, then only a $30,000-added race struggling for recognition, in order to save him for the Preakness, which he won. He later also won the Belmont, and by 20 lengths.

It was a shame Man O' War, Kentucky bred that he was, didn't get a shot at the Derby because it was the only major race he didn't win in his two years of competition. He was retired after two seasons because the handicappers were putting too much weight on him, including the 138 pounds he toted in the *Potomac Handicap* when he beat the 1920 Derby winner Paul Jones, which carried only 114 pounds.

In all, Man O' War won 20 or 21 races, one by an unbelievable 100 lengths. His total earnings for his brief career was $249,465, an amazing sum when it is realized that purses then amounted only to a fraction of those offered today. Later retired to stud at Faraway Farm near Lexington, Man O' War became racing's greatest sire, with two of his sons, Clyde Van Deusen (1929) and War Admiral (1938), winning the Derby.

His only loss was when he was caught sideways at the post and then was blocked off and was 10 lengths behind before finding room to run. Ironically and appropriately, the name of the horse that edged him that day was Upset.

When he retired after 42 years as head basketball coach
at the University of Kentucky in 1972, Adolph Rupp held
nearly every record for winning at the college level. His
retirement brought on an outburst of Rupp recollections
from players who had performed on his teams. In the
main, they recalled his demand for absolute discipline
from his players; his striving for perfection always; his
precisely-timed, no-nonsense practices; his scathing
halftime lectures.

At practice, Frank Ramsey, an All-America guard under
Rupp, recalled, "you never spoke unless you could
improve on the silence."

And Dale Barnstable, another Rupp star performer,
remembered a classic halftime lecture that was repeated to
him as an example of what to expect when he came to
UK after World War II.

In 1944, he was told, Kentucky was playing Arkansas
State in Lexington and led 34-4 at intermission. One
player had scored all four points racked up by the visitors
and Rupp took note of that in the dressing room.

"Who's supposed to be guarding No. 12?" he asked.

"I am, coach," confessed All-American Jack Parkinson.

"Well, then," Rupp fired back. "get on him — he's
running wild!"

Because of his success, Rupp's name became almost a
household word in Kentucky. Nevertheless, some
Kentuckians never heard of him.

The story is told that one time he stopped at a crossroads store in western Kentucky and decided to buy a
luscious country ham displayed. When he reached into
his pocket, he found he didn't have enough cash, so he
proposed giving a check, and the storekeeper was
agreeable.

"Know who that is?" Rupp asked, pointing to the
signature on the check.

"Well," the merchant replied, looking closely at the
name, "I hope it's you!"

When Bill Spivey, Rupp's first 7-foot player, came to
Lexington in the summer of 1948 he weighed a feathery
168 pounds. A short time later Rupp left for Rome as
coach of the U.S. Olympic basketball team, leaving Spivey
in the care of his assistant, Harry Lancaster. Rupp's
parting instructions were for Lancaster to see that Spivey
had a milkshake with an egg in it three times a day in an
effort to put weight on his sparse frame. He also asked
that he keep him informed of any weight progress.

As the summer wore on, Lancaster kept Rupp posted by
letter. "Spivey up to 175," he reported in his first letter.
"He's up to 180," he said in the second. "He's reached
190 . . . He now weighs 200," subsequent messages read.

Finally Rupp was getting fidgety, so he cabled Lancaster:
"I'm convinced Spivey can eat, but can he play basketball?"

Any golf duffer who panics when he steps up for the first
shot with a crowd impatiently waiting can appreciate the
deep sincerity of the statement made by a woman at Owl
Creek Country Club in Anchorage.

"Happiness," she sighed while a crowd of men fidgeted,
"is getting off the first tee!"

The late Bobby Foster of Central City was a fine baseball
player who once pitched professionally. Nevertheless,
says Larry Stone, he gloried in telling stories in which he
was the butt of a joke.

One tale concerns a game he pitched in which, in the
first inning, he was touched by successive batters for a
triple, home run, two doubles, and finally a single. After
the fifth hit, the catcher sauntered out to the mound for
a conference.

"Boy," Foster claimed he said, "we've got 'em licked
now — they're only hitting singles!"

Foot-in-mouth disease is perhaps the most common
malady to which the human animal is addicted. Like in an
incident that took place at Fulton.

A visitor from nearby Martin, Tennessee, was attending
a civic club lunch, and one of the Fulton members was
trying to make him feel welcome. Learning the stranger
was from Martin, he mentioned the football rivalry that
existed between their two high schools.

He'd never forget, the Fulton man added, one game in
which his son, the Fulton center, literally took the ball
away from a Martin runner and dashed for a touchdown.

"I'll never forget that game, either," the Martin visitor
said. "It was my son who had the ball!"

Horse players never really quit betting on the races, they
just think they're going to, the late Harry Roberts of
Louisville contended. And to prove his point he cited the
case of a fellow he knew who had had an especially
disastrous day at the track.

"I'm never going to bet again," the guy moaned.

"I'll bet," Roberts countered, "you place a bet before
the day's gone."

"You're on!" the convert shouted, reaching for his
pocket.

The Kentucky Derby, the oldest continuously run horse
race on the North American continent, has been called the
greatest two minutes in sports. Because of its color,
tradition, and glamor, the Derby attracts more once-a-year
horse players than any other race in the land.

Curiously, few of the Derby Day-only bettors trust
professional handicappers, men whose job requires that
they study horses full time. As a result, dozens of home-
made betting systems are tried at Churchill Downs. While
most are based more on hope than dope, every practitioner
feels his way is the greatest thing to hit racing since the
introduction of the horse.

Any Derby will bring out bettors who follow these, and other, unorthodox systems of picking (hopefully) winners:

Favorite-Name System: The bettor merely scans the program for a name that rings a bell. If he (or she) finds a horse with the name of a favorite aunt, a place that brings back fond memories or the like, then that's the beast that totes his wager.

Pin-Through-the-Eye System: The player needs only a program and a sharp pin to practice this system. He punches the pin through the eye of the horse pictured on the program, then bets on those hay burners whose names are nearest to the hole made by the pin.

Match-the-Colors System: A favorite among women. The girls wait for the horses to appear and then risk a few bob on the nag whose jockey wears an arm band the color of their eyes, dress, or current color of hair.

Balancing-the-Odds System: Some horses picked this way have won; others have finished just ahead of the first frost. Anyway, the player watches the odds as they juggle up and down. At a given time, say, six minutes before official post time, he picks the horse on which the odds aren't too long or too short but just right. This also is known as the Goldilocks system.

One thing about these and the other home-made systems: Horses picked this way usually are the equal of any in the race until it's time to run.

A real Kentucky fox hunter is a sporting purist who doesn't hunt to kill but for the pure pleasure of listening to fine-blooded hounds chase a wily animal that sometimes seems also to enjoy the carrying-on.

In view of this, it's difficult for some persons to understand why fox hunters invest so much time and money in chasing a little beast they really don't want to catch.

A nonhunting farmer-neighbor was visiting Paul E. Carr of Auburn, one of the state's most ardent fox hunters. They were looking at Carr's prize hounds and the farmer was amazed at the cost of feeding them.

"You make any money off these dogs?" he asked.

"No, I guess not," Carr confessed.

"Then wouldn't it make more sense if you spent all that money to feed a bunch of hogs?" the farmer pressed.

"Well, I'll tell you," Carr answered. "Did you ever try to run a fox with a bunch of damn fat hogs?"

One day I was telling Barney Arnold, the radio farm expert, about a man in Winchester who once told me that he tries to "shoot some craps every day because a fellow never can tell it just might be his lucky day." That reminded Arnold of a bit of advice his grandfather passed on to him in teaching him how to play poker years ago.

"Don't ever play for any higher stakes than penny ante," he said. "They'll get your money from you anyway, but it'll take them longer."

Letcher Norton, once one of Kentucky's most successful high school basketball coaches, tells about a memorable golf game he had one day with Arthur W. Corns in Winchester. On the first tee Corns skied his drive and the ball went straight up and almost out of sight.

Corns shaded his eyes, peered into the sky and yelled: "Fore, Lord!"

Most any gathering of University of Kentucky football followers eventually will find the calendar being turned back to other years and the exploits of the heroes of earlier days being recalled. One name that always is sure to crop up during such excursions into the past is that of John Sims "Shipwreck" Kelly, circa 1928-32.

Kelly, who came from Springfield, was as colorful as a circus poster, the type player who naturally attracted attention and who had limitless ability. He also had great confidence in himself, as proven in a story the late S. A. Boles, UK athletic director in the Kelly era, used to tell.

In those days, the UK practice field was surrounded by a board fence which was decorated with signs and posters. One day Kelly came storming into Boles' office and announced that he wouldn't practice until a new sign that had been added to the fence came down.

"It's an insult to me," Kelly fumed, "and it's got to come down."

Boles investigated and discovered that overnight a Lexington auto supply firm had nailed up a sign that read "Kelly Tires."

"I don't see what's so bad about that sign," Boles said.

"It's an insult to me," Kelly repeated, "because Kelly never tires!"

Fisherman are a peculiar breed. Among other traits, those who practice the art are gullible to the degree that when one person catches a fish with a certain lure, all anglers in sight stampede to lay hands on the same bait.

Bob DeBoe, a guide at Kentucky Lake, was fishing one day and catching croppie like they were going out of style when a stranger in another boat pulled up close and asked what he was using.

"He's sprinkling beer on the minnows," the man with DeBoe replied in a confidential tone.

Without saying a word, the stranger raced back to the dock, leaped in his car, drove to Paducah, bought a case of beer, returned to the lake and started dousing his minnows with the suds.

He didn't catch any croppie, but he did have some of the happiest minnows on the entire lake.

One of the most popular of the commercial fishing docks on Lake Cumberland has a stuffed 9½ -pound bass hanging on the wall of the bait shop as an incentive to fishermen. After a long day of fishing without catching anything, a man from Ohio returned to the dock in the late afternoon, came into the shop and spotted the big bass hanging on the wall. He stared at it for a full minute, then delivered himself of an observation which no doubt summarized the thoughts of countless other luckless anglers.

"The man who caught that fish," he said simply, "is a liar!"

It was an exciting moment in the Billy Eades household at Central City when son Tommy, then a freshman, rushed in to announce that he'd made the high school varsity basketball team.

"Will you get to go on road trips?" his mother asked.

"No," he replied.

"Will you get an A team uniform?"

"No."

"What makes you think you've made the A team?" his mother pressed.

"Because," he reasoned, "I got to take the A team flu shots!"

Before it folded in the late 1950's, the Kitty League, a Class D circuit comprised of teams representing towns in Kentucky, Illinois, and Tennessee, was one professional baseball loop where the unexpected always was expected. And with reason. After all, the Kitty teams were staffed almost entirely with young players making their pro debuts, and at one time it was reputed to have started more major league stars on their way than any other circuit in all of baseball.

Since the league hit its peak during the Depression, a time when money was hard indeed to come by, most of the teams were constantly just one step ahead of financial disaster. As a result, the clubs were hoping always to sell promising players to higher leagues for cash on which to keep going.

Like the night when scouts from a Class A league were present to see a right-handed pitcher the Fulton team was hoping to peddle for a good price. With the scouts watching, the pitcher was nervous and walked the first three batters. The next man lashed a line drive back toward the mound and the ball struck the pitcher's left hand.

He ripped off his glove and began to shake the left hand violently.

"Shake your right hand, shake your right hand!" the manager shouted, running toward him.

"But I was hit on the left hand," the pitcher moaned.

"I know, but make out it's your right hand and it hurts awful," the manager rationalized. "I want to get you out of this game gracefully!"

The late Ed Diddle achieved more records than you could shake a statistics chart at during his nearly 45 years as head basketball coach at Western Kentucky University — most years as coach and most games won at the same school being just two of the many. This, plus the way he often coined entirely new words or sort of backed into the phrasing of sentences in moments of excitement, made him a legend in his own time, and stories about him became legion.

I remember once going to Bowling Green to take a series of color pictures of his squad. In all the confusion, Diddle was having trouble telling his players what he wanted them to do. Finally, he did an ear-splitting blast on the whistle he always kept around his neck.

"Now, boys," he lectured them in his distinctive, lispy voice, "I want you all to line up over here alphabetically according to height!"

Bob Laughlin, now athletic director at Morehead State University and a long-time coaching opponent of Diddle, adds his own story to the Diddle collection.

It seems that some years back when Western was due to play Illinois in an NCAA tournament, Diddle was a veritable bundle of nerves from worrying. A few days before the big game, a friend met him on the street.

"Coach," he said, "did you hear that terrific noise?"

"Noise, what noise?" Diddle asked.

"Illinois!" the friend laughed.

Diddle thought the joke was a corker, and allowed he'd save it to pull on his team to break the nervousness the night of the game. As the team huddled in the dressing room before taking the floor, Diddle uncorked his tension-buster.

"Boys," he said suddenly, "did you hear that racket?"

"What racket?" someone asked.

"Why," Diddle hee-hawed, "Illinois!"

It's always refreshing to hear about an honest expert. Buddy Lepping of Louisville was at Churchill Downs one afternoon contributing heavily to the improvement of the breed when he came upon Mike Barry, sports columnist for *The Louisville Times* and self-acknowledged world's leading horse handicapper.

"Mike, Mike," Lepping pleaded, "help me break even!"

"Sure," Barry replied, "how much have you won?"

For the benefit of those who are too young to have been around then or who are so old now they've forgotten, Oliva Dionne was the world's most famous father in the mid-1930's. In fact, his name became a household word in the spring of 1934 when his wife gave birth to the first quintuplets to survive beyond infancy.

Sometime in the late 1930's, recalls J. Earle Bell of Morganfield, a visitor arrived after hours at Faraway Farm, the Lexington thoroughbred nursery where Man O' War, the most famous race horse of the day, was standing at stud. The visitor was told by the farm manager that the place was closed for the day, but that Man O' War and the other great sires could be seen the next day.

"But I've come all the way from Canada to see this

horse," the stranger said. "Maybe I should tell you who I am — my name is Dionne, and I'm the father of the quintuplets."

"Now that makes a difference and I'll make an exception to the rules," the suddenly impressed farm manager said. "It's not so much that I want you to see Man O' War — I want Man O' War to see you!"

None of the countless stories that were composed when Casey Stengel finally retired from baseball in 1965 after 55 years in the sport touched on the fact that he started his illustrious, and fun-filled, pro career in Kentucky.

The year was 1910 and Casey, then 20, had signed with Shelbyville in the Bluegrass League. However, the team ran into financial miseries early ("but not from what they were paying me," he once said) and the franchise was transferred to Maysville.

It was in Maysville that Stengel became a baseball clown. He had his own version of how that came about.

"There was some kind of insane asylum across from the outfield fence," he related, "and the patients, looking through the cracks in the boards, were a swell audience. Everything I did was funny to them. I'd put my cap on backward, make faces and do prat falls and they'd roll over and howl.

"Finally, I got to thinking I was pretty funny myself. But all the time they probably were wondering what I was doing on the wrong side of the fence!"

Every basketball coach in the land dreams about recruiting himself an agile, good-shooting 7-foot player who will make his status as a genius among hardwood mentors undeniably apparent.

But 7-footers with such qualifications aren't a common commodity and when one does come along there still can be many a slip twixt championship cup and lip, so to speak. Peck Hickman, former head mastermind at the

University of Louisville, discovered that when he landed his first real giant in the early 1950's.

This boy was a picture player, a full 7-feet tall and dripping with natural ability. The only trouble was, he had quite a lot of trouble with such distracting things as English, history, and the like. He barely squeezed through his freshman year, but by the time the cloud bumper had appeared in a couple of games as a sophomore — looking like money in the bank in each — he was on the brink of academic disaster. Hoping to inspire him to greater intellectual heights with an old-fashioned father-son type talk, Peck called him into his office and locked the door.

"I think it's time we thought seriously about your future," Peck began. "Nobody in your family ever has graduated from college. Imagine how proud they'll be when they see you walk down the aisle to get your diploma. They'll know you're an educated man, ready to go out and make a good living for yourself. But you've got to make grades to stay in school."

He continued to talk in that vein, and the more he talked the more the boy seemed impressed. His face flushed, he clinched his fists and his jaw took a determined set.

"Now tell me," Peck pressed when he felt the time was just right, "what is it you want now most of all?"

"Coach," the player almost gasp, "I want a motorcycle!"

Since everything is filmed and then carefully edited, there's no chance of a spontaneous, unexpected remark creeping into a TV commercial these days.

But perfection in commercials wasn't always so. There was the day Billy Southworth, then manager of the St. Louis Cardinals, was being interviewed on a program sponsored by a razor blade manufacturer.

"Did you shave with our blade this morning?" he was asked.

"Why," Southworth replied innocently, "you know bloody well I did!"

And then there was the commercial topper that involved

Paul Bryant when he was football coach at the University of Kentucky. At that time Mel Allen had a late night sports show on NBC-TV sponsored by a cigar company. It was Allen's habit to pull out one of the stogies and light it up as part of the commercial message.

After UK had been invited to a post-season bowl game, Allen had Bryant on the show as his special guest. Midway through the program, Allen broke out the cigars, lit one up and then turned unexpectedly to Bryant.

"Coach," he said, "won't you join me in one of our cigars?"

"No," Bryant replied firmly, "that thing would make me sicker than hell!"

William T. Woodson, formerly senior partner in one of the nation's leading patent and copyright law firms in Chicago, is retired now and lives in Morganfield. An ardent golfer, he tells about an equally avid par-chaser who for years had played three afternoons a week with a friend named George. When he started playing with another friend, his wife asked why.

"Would you play with a man who always improves his lie, talks when you're putting, and cheats on his score?" he asked.

"No," replied his wife.

"Well," the golfer shot back, "neither will George!"

The Kentucky Derby, the premier horse race in the world, has its own trademark drink — the mint julep. Like the horse, the julep wasn't invented in Kentucky, but here both achieved their greatest fame.

The mint julep, which has been described as a depth charge with a Southern drawl, by now has become such a part of the tradition of the Derby that the Kentuckian feels that mint and Bourbon whiskey, both nurtured by Kentucky sun, soil, and streams, just naturally were destined to be linked together from the beginning of time.

"Who has not tasted one," wrote humorist Irvin S. Cobb, a Kentuckian, naturally, "has lived in vain."

The true connoisseur follows an exacting formula in manufacturing a mint julep, a formula that calls for a specific blending of the ingredients — mint, cracked ice, granulated sugar, and mellow Bourbon served in a coin-silver goblet. Perhaps it was Henry Watterson, the famed editor of *The Courier-Journal* for 50 years, who produced the classic recipe.

"Take a coin-silver goblet, one that holds a pint," he prescribed, "and dissolve one half teaspoon of granulated sugar in it with not more than a spoonful of branch water. Take one fresh, tender mint leaf, no more, and crush it gently between thumb and forefinger before dropping it into the dissolved sugar. Then fill the goblet to the brim with cracked ice and let it set until beads of moisture gather on the burnished exterior of the goblet. Then take a few sprigs of mint and decorate the rim of the goblet.

"Into another coin-silver goblet pour at least four fingers of mellow Kentucky Bourbon that has aged a minimum of seven years in charred oaken barrels.

"Throw the other stuff away and drink the Bourbon."

The most famous football team ever to represent a Kentucky college was the great Centre team of 1921 that shocked the sports world by defeating mighty Harvard 6-0 in a classic battle. One of the stars of the team was Red Roberts, a great runner who Coach Charley Moran once said was "the only man to make All-America by loafing — but loafing in the right places."

Roberts was a flamboyant fellow who usually played without a helmet and with only a handkerchief tied around his head.

"Red played without a helmet until the UK game in 1921," recalls George Chinn of Harrodsburg, an end on the team. "But in that game he was tackled by the right ear and it was almost pulled off his head.

"After that, you couldn't find a helmet thick enough for him!"

Kentucky fox hunters, as noted earlier, are purists who get their kicks from spending all night sitting around a roaring camp fire and listening to finely-trained hounds "make music" as they chase — but seldom catch — a fox.

Circuit Judge Robert M. Coleman of Bowling Green, former president of the Kentucky Fox Hunters Association, is such a hunter. One early fall night Judge Coleman was in a group that had spent 12 hours in the field. As they returned home in the early dawn, they met a bunch of men going fishing.

"Can you imagine," the judge said, "anybody silly enough to get up this early to go fishing?"

Speaking of fox hunting, Fred Nunn of Edmonton tells about a very talented hound he once owned.

"He was the fastest thing on four legs and could outrun any fox," he vows. "But he'd never kill a fox — he just liked to chase 'em.

"It really was something to see him take out after a fox and race right up on its heels. Every once in a while he'd let out an extra burst of speed and pass the fox.

"You've never seen such frustration in all your life as when the fox suddenly would discover he was running behind, not ahead of, that hound!"

Because he is so addicted to fox and raccoon hunting, the Kentuckian is notorious for the regard he holds for a good dog. A prize hound is something he treasures above other worldly goods.

One such was a Bath County man, not exactly

prime material for genius status, perhaps, whose
constant companion was a big, rawboned hound. He
might go hungry, but the flop-eared beast always ate.

One hot July day the man was working as a hired hand
in a hay field. The heat was just this side of parboiling
and, as always, the hound lay nearby in the shade. In the
middle of the field, the baler flushed up a rabbit. The
hound roused, but before he could move the man stopped
him with a sharp command. Then he, the man, took off
after the rabbit himself. He came back huffing and puffing,
drenched in perspiration.

"Why didn't you sic your hound on that rabbit?"
he was asked.

"What?" he screeched, "you think I want to run a good
dog in heat like this?"

When Charley Bradshaw was head football coach at the
University of Kentucky, he and Adolph Rupp, then
basketball coach, made numerous appearances together as
speakers on the alumni club circuit. Often they'd warm up
an audience by talking about how they'd grown up in
the country.

"I lived so far out in the country," Rupp, who came
from rural Kansas, said at one meeting, "that we had to
keep our own tom cat."

But Bradshaw, from Alabama, wasn't about to be
outdone.

"I lived so far out in the country," he claimed, "that our
source of entertainment was to go to town on Saturdays
and watch people eating in restaurants!"

Although he never made it to the major leagues, one of
the most talented baseball players ever to perform in
Kentucky was Jay Kirke, an outfielder in the 1920's for
the Louisville Colonels of the American Association.
Since he hadn't received the benefits, if any, of a higher
education, Kirke was somewhat suspicious of all who had.

One year in spring training the Colonels had invited a college outfielder to try out for the team. When the first exhibition game was played, Manager Joe McCarthy started the collegian in Kirke's left field position.

In the first inning, while Kirke sat fuming on the bench, the rookie missed a routine fly ball, the next inning a grounder skipped through his legs, and in the third inning he threw wildly behind a runner for his third error in as many innings.

By then McCarthy had seen enough, and he sent Kirke into the game. The first batter rapped a drive straight at the usually sure-gloved Kirke and he missed the ball cleanly. After the inning was over, McCarthy was chewing him soundly for his mistake.

"Don't ride me," Kirke almost spat. "That damn college boy has got left field in such a helluva shape, nobody could play out there!"

College basketball talent scouts constantly are looking for players who duck when they come through a 7-foot door. Because all teams need at least one big man, pure size often will cause coaches to overlook other shortcomings.

"You take those 6-9 and 6-10 boys," said Sonny Allen, former assistant at Morehead State University. "If they can chew gum and stand up at the same time, they're probably all right!"

The fish hadn't been biting this day in the swirling water below Kentucky Dam and one fisherman's only consolation had come from the beer he'd been guzzling.

Finally, as he was going back to the dock in the late afternoon and feeling no pain, a large fish flopped out of the water and landed in the boat. He immediately leaped upon it and cast it back into the river.

"If you won't bite," he snarled, "you ain't gonna ride!"

Fisherman just naturally don't like to be outdone since they may be among the truly prideful spirits left in our conformity-seeking society today.

At Lake Cumberland a proud angler who returned to one of the docks with a string of about a dozen sardine-sized bluegill had carefully unloaded his catch when another man reported back in with just one fish — a lunker bass that weighed a good 8 pounds.

The fellow who had landed the big one hauled his prize out of the boat and casually placed it beside the string of pee-wees. But the other guy, showing spirit typical of a veteran fisher, refused to go down without a fight.

"Hummm," he mused, looking almost scornfully at the lone big fish. "Caught just the one, eh?"

Two Casey County possum hunters were in the woods when they heard the sound of a distant bell shortly before nightfall.

"That's the church bell," one man said. "This is prayer meeting night."

"Oh, well," the second man oh-welled, "I couldn't have gone anyway, my wife bein' as sick as she is!"

The genius who invented the ancient sport of snipe hunting must also have originated the kind of fox hunting practiced by a group of scarlet-coated horse-riding sportsmen (and women) who gather near Lexington on the first Saturday in November to perform a unique and colorful ritual — the blessing of the hounds.

For the material, take-home rewards of these fox hunters, like others in Kentucky, and of snipers is about the same. Neither group winds up with as much to show for their efforts as the huntsman who trudges all day long and bags only the seat of his pants.

There's a reason. Snipe hunters aren't supposed to get anything; fox hunters don't want to get anything. That's right. Sportsmen like those who gather at Grimes Mill near Lexington for the blessing of the hounds, the traditional ceremony which officially opens the Iroquois Hunt Club season, don't want to bag even that first fox. Their enjoyment, like the hunter who merely sits around a roaring camp fire and listens to the hounds run, is in the chase, not the catch.

The blessing of the hounds is just one part of the picturesque first day of the Iroquois Hunt season. The custom originated centuries ago in France, the native land of St. Hubert, the patron saint of the chase. The Lexington group is one of no more than a half dozen clubs in the United States to carry on the ceremony. It was started in Kentucky in 1931 by the late H. P. Almon Abbott, then bishop of the Episcopal Diocese of Lexington, and it has been continued by his successors ever since.

The purpose is not to praise any mortal creature, but rather to invoke heavenly blessing on all creatures — hounds, horses, foxes and riders — engaged in a thrilling if sometimes perilous sport. The ceremony, which usually is held in the early afternoon, follows a brief sermon given out-of-doors. At the end, each rider — and normally there are 45 to 60 — steps forward and kneels to receive the bishop's blessing and to have the scarlet ribbon holding a St. Hubert's medal placed around his or her neck.

Then they mount and the master of the hounds sends them off in pursuit of a little animal they don't really want to catch.

Some years back I was sitting around one night with Bill Buchanan, the late Oral Bertram, Harry Towles, Ed Adams and a bunch of other fishermen when somebody told about a new bait a friend once had told him about.

Late in the afternoon of a luckless day, the friend claimed to have impulsively dipped the minnow he was using into a jug of moonshine before lowering the line into the water. Almost immediately he felt a strike and pulled in a large bass.

The only thing was: The bass hadn't swallowed the minnow and been hooked. The moonshine-saturated

minnow had the bass by the throat and was choking it
to death!

Still another, shall I say unorthodox, fishing bait was
given to me by Charley Aaron, the Russell Springs expert,
on the solemn promise I'd never reveal it. So what do I
do? Tell about it is what.

Anyway, Aaron claims he baits his hooks with chewing
tobacco.

"The fish snaps up the bait and swims off," he claims.
"Then when he comes up to the surface to spit, I hit him
over the head with the boat paddle!"

Besides being a former retreaded sports writer, I'm also a
long time, and avid, follower of all kinds of athletic
endeavors, ranging from pool to squat tag. Consequently,
I've always fancied myself as knowing which way is south
when it comes to most sports.

But I must admit that I'm a lost ball in the high weeds
when the color commentators who work on the college
and pro TV football games launch into their so-called
"simple" explanation of formations, strategy, pass patterns
and such. This is especially true when the expert positions
himself in front of a blackboard and connects little X's
and O's with lines and arrows as he diagrams what the
viewer either has just seen or may expect to see.

As far as I'm concerned, the end result resembles the
scribbling of a couple of drunken tic-tac-toe players, and
it all throws me for the equivalent of a 15-yard loss.

All that blackboard skull practice is hard enough for
players to understand, much less once-a-week TV
watchers. Which brings to mind a Kentucky high school
coach with a fine player who plain couldn't remember the
maneuvers he always was sketching on the board. In
one game, the boy kept fouling up every play.

"Just think of the way I drew the plays on the
blackboard," the coach reminded him during a time out.

"But, coach," the boy alibied, "I just can't remember whether we're the X's or the O's!"

You might want to add to your collection of strange happenings in sports an odd adventure experienced by a group of Kentuckians who were hunting deer in Canada.

The hunters were trudging through the snowy Canadian wilds when they walked over the brow of a low hill and suddenly came upon another man, dressed in hunting clothes but unarmed, following deer tracks in the snow.

The Kentuckians were understandably puzzled to find a gunless hunter, and he explained his plight as follows:

"About five miles back, I spotted a big buck with the most handsome rack I ever saw. I took careful aim and dropped him in his tracks. I rushed up, tagged him, and began to examine my trophy.

"The more I looked, the more excited I became. 'Now won't this head look great as a gun rack mounted on the wall of my den?' I said to myself.

"Then, in order to get an idea of just how it would look, I placed my gun in the antlers and stepped back a few paces to admire the effect. About then the buck jumped up, shook himself, and took off with my gun still wedged in his horns.

"And that's why I'm following these tracks in the snow!"

Before he became president of Western Kentucky University, a position from which he is now retired, Dr. Kelly Thompson was public relations director of the school. As a matter of fact, he and Coach Ed Diddle were responsible for taking Western into the big-time of college basketball.

Shortly after World War II when Western made its then-annual trip to Madison Square Garden in New York, the team was undefeated and ranked in the top 10 in the nation. The Garden had been sold out for several days prior to the game.

Late in the afternoon of the game, Thompson received a telephone call from a woman who identified herself as a former Western student. She and her husband were anxious to see the game and could he help them?

Thompson scurried around frantically and finally was able to locate two tickets in a choice location and presented them to the woman with the compliments of Western. After the game, Thompson spotted the woman in the hotel where a Western reception was planned and he expected to be smothered in thanks for the favor.

It didn't quite work out that way, however.

"Kelly Thompson, I'm off you for life," the woman fumed when she saw him. "Those tickets you gave us were right next to a woman who had been eating garlic!"

Charles J. "Uncle Charley" Moran is best known to most Kentuckians as the football coach who astounded the college world in 1921 when his Centre College team defeated mighty Harvard 6-0 in a game that still is regarded as one of the classic upsets in all of sports.

But despite his fame as a coach, Uncle Charley perhaps was better known to sports fans nationally as a major league baseball umpire. For 23 years he was an umpire in the National League and late in life, after returning to Horse Cave to live in retirement, he loved nothing more than to recall events from his long career in baseball.

One of his best stories had to do with a stunt Charley Grimm of the Chicago Cubs once pulled on him.

It was during one of those inevitable tie games and in the top of the ninth Moran called a Pittsburg runner safe at home in a slide-in-a-cloud-of-dust play. The whole Chicago team descended upon him, waving their arms and screeching in anger. Grimm stood in the dugout for several minutes before sauntering casually over to the scene of disturbance.

"Boys," he warned his players in a mock-stern voice, lovingly placing his arms around Moran's shoulders, "I'll fine the first man $500 who dares lay a hand on this poor, blind old man!"

Dr. David Lawrence, dean of students at the University of Louisville, tells a story from his days of high school basketball coaching which illustrates clearly how times have changed from then to now.

After finishing at the University of Kentucky, where he was a star player, he went to Sulphur High School in Henry County to coach in 1935. His budget barely was enough to cover the cost of basketballs and one uniform for each of the boys on the squad of 10, but didn't include money for either shoes or athletic socks for the players.

One day, he says, his star player reported that he wouldn't be able to practice that afternoon. Lawrence wanted to know why.

"Because," the boy replied simply, "I wore my Sunday socks today!"

As mentioned previously, W. T. Woodson of Morganfield is a golfer of great zeal himself. He tells about meeting a friend who, if possible, is an even more zealous par chaser.

"Playing much golf these days?" Woodson asked him.

"No, not much," the friend replied, "just in the afternoons!"

INTRODUCTION   *The men and women who went around bestowing names on Kentucky communites many years ago were highly imaginative, to say the least.*

Thus in Kentucky one finds place names that are unique, colorful, bizarre, descriptive, and sometimes unpronounceable. Here communities, large and small, were named for exotic foreign cities (Warsaw), human emotion (Joy), books of the Bible (Job, Mark), birds (Quail), beasts (Wildcat), fish (Sturgeon), and some that defy immediate classification (Helechawa).

Among other place names there is a Spider (Knott County) and a Webbs (Green County), an Alpha (Clinton) and an Omega (Pulaski), a Richelieu (Logan) and a Cardinal (Bell), a Fox (Estill) and a Hunter (Floyd), a Load (Greenup) and a Dice (Perry), a Primrose (Lee) and a Pathway (Calloway), and a Wizard (Martin) and an Oz (McCreary).

And there also are the likes of Nonesuch, Uno, 88, Monkey's Eyebrow, Turkey Neck Bend, Hells Half Acre, Possum Trot, Sweet William, Gravel Switch, Beauty, Black Gnat, Dwarf, Feisty, and on and on.

Sometimes there's a relatively reasonable explanation of how a name was derived; sometimes there is not.

An example of the derivation of a name is Himyar in Knox County. Seems many years ago a resident of the area, which then had no name, lost a promising stallion colt. A search was started and the mountain man who found him shouted, "Him yar!" When the community merited a post office, the horse's stable was converted to that use and the welcome words of the colt's finder became its name.

Oh, yes. There was a Paradise (Muhlenberg County) and there still is a Hell-for-Certain (Leslie County).

FROM PARADISE TO HELL-FOR-CERTAIN

Any list of unusual Kentucky place names begins with
Hell-for-Certain, a remote, isolated, and pinpoint-sized
community located on the stream of the same name in
Leslie County.

The name was coined many years ago when two
pioneer hunters became lost in the steep hills and
wandered for some time before they followed a tiny,
crooked stream that finally led them to the Middle Fork
of the Kentucky River.

"That place was pure hell," one hunter supposedly
editorialized.

"It was hell for certain," the other agreed and a name
for both the stream and the community that followed
was invented.

Today there is considerable dispute as to the exact
spelling and pronunciation of the name. I've heard it
called Hell-for-Certain, Hell-fer-Certain, Hell-fer-Sartin,
Hell-fur-Sartin, and Hell-fur-Certain even by natives of
the region.

It seems no one is certain. Or sartin.

Those who like to play around with Kentucky place
names find such a wide variety abounds that by using
their imaginations a bit, the names can be blended
together to tell simple stories.

As for instance, the story of the first Thanksgiving.

Uno (Hart County) for Ages (Harlan County) I've Said
(McCracken County) that Most (Martin County) any
Story (Marshall) could be Dunn (Carter) by using only

Public (Pulaski) Place (Knox) and Cross Road (Barren) names if one is Sharpe (Marshall) and Does (Knott) Hardy (Pike) Work (Owsley).

We have no Town (Clay) of Thanksgiving, but there are a Million (Madison) or at least a Barnyard (Knox) full of Ordinary (Elliott) Place (Knox) names to Fall (Jackson) Bach (Breathitt) on in writing a Squib (Pulaski) about that Pleasant (Graves) Day (Letcher).

It was in Early Times (Nelson) in the Fall (Clay) before Frost (Green). The Pilgrim (Martin) Farmers (Rowan), despite a Lot (Whitley) of Hazard (Perry), had Knott (Lewis) come a Cropper (Shelby). The Raines (Whitley) had been Wright (Taylor) and the Corn (Whitley) was Plum (Bourbon) Goodin (Knox) Quality (Butler). Everyman (Carroll) was Full (Wayne) of Pride (Union).

To Praise (Pike) Providence (Webster) for the Bounty (Cumberland) and to show the Friendship (Caldwell) they Felt (Clay) for the Redman (Grayson), a Mammoth (Whitley) Summit (Hardin) Meeting (Grayson) and Dinner (Bell) was Wise (Trimble) Lee (Butler) set.

The Pilgrim (Martin) Cook (Wolfe) Said (McCracken) there Wood (Laurel) Bee (Hart) Turkey (Breathitt), Rabbit Hash (Boone), Corn (Whitley) on the Cobb (Caldwell), and Pye (Kenton). A Pig (Edmonson), he Burna (Livingston) to a Cinda (Leslie).

A Little (Jackson) Pilgrim (Martin) Maiden (Bell) Left (Pike) a note on the Lettered Rock (Butler) beside the Indian Trail (Jefferson), Askin (Breckinridge) the Major (Owsley) Redman (Greenup) and his Boyse (Warren) to Meta (Pike) with the Pilgrim (Martin) Peoples (Jackson) and be Fed (Floyd).

Hearin (Webster) of the Prospect (Jefferson) of a big Dinner (Bell), the Chief (Ballard) Said (McCracken):

"Awe (Lewis) Howe (Greenup) Good (Laurel). If by Chance (Adair) you Needmore (Madison), Hunters (Nelson) with Tomahawk (Martin) will get Quail (Rockcastle), Bear (Bell), and Sunfish (Edmonson) to Fry (Green)."

The Memorial (Hart) Day (Letcher) was Helton (Leslie) November 25 in a Pleasant Grove (Washington).

The Peoples (Jackson) Drew (Knott) near to Bow (Cumberland) and say Humble (Russell) Grace (Clay) to

146

the Ault (Elliott) Mighty (Harlan), and White (Warren) and Red (Logan) Lipps (Clay) Said (McCracken) together:

"Grant (Carroll) Uz (Letcher) Goodluck (Metcalfe), Faith (McLean), Freedom (Barren), Unity (Marshall), and Love (Butler). Never Divide (Harlan) Uz (Letcher)."

No Wonder (Floyd) Providence (Butler) had a Smile (Rowan) and Herd (Jackson) the Beauty (Martin) of what was Said (McCracken).

Then the Turkey (Breathitt) Carver (Magoffin) took over. After Dinner (Bell), the Peoples (Jackson) smoked Tobacco (Calloway). One Redman (Grayson), being a Belcher (Pike), had to take a Pinch (Taylor) of Sulphur (Henry) and some Bromo (Rockcastle).

"Mark (Pulaski) this Day (Letcher)," a Pilgrim (Martin) Mann (Rowan) Said (McCracken). "It will Echo (Metcalfe) Long (Madison) through the Pages (Bell) of time. It is the First (Martin) Thanksgiving."

And he was Wright (McCreary).

Those who have traveled in eastern Kentucky surely have come away impressed by the picturesque names that are worn by communities there. To mention only a few, there is Hot Spot, Decoy, Carbon Glow, Boreing, Closplint, Littcar, and Handsome.

Sometimes even the natives become confused by the names. James Still, the gifted writer from Dead Mare Branch in Knott County, tells a story to illustrate the point.

One day Still was riding in an auto with several of his neighbors when they passed one of those roadside signs reading "Litter Barrel ½ Mile."

"Well, dad burn them highway people for always tinkerin' with the names of places," one of the riders fumed. "Why, this neighborhood has been called Kellytown ever since I can rekerlect!"

It isn't an especially unusual name, but Shepherdsville, the seat of Bullitt County, is the only town in the entire country with that particular name. There are Shephardsvilles in Indiana, Massachusetts and Michigan, and a Shepherds in North Carolina, but there's only one Shepherdsville — and Kentucky has it.

Speaking of Kentucky towns that are the only ones of their kind in the country, there's just one Catlettsburg, one Horse Cave, one Kuttawa, one Paint Lick, and one Glen Dean.

As a matter of fact, there are so many Kentucky communities that rate an "only" classification that in just the list of post offices that begin with "A", 30 fall into that category. They range from Aaron to Axtel.

There seems to be no end to the raw logic available to explain the naming of some of Kentucky's uniquely endowed towns.

Take the Hart County community of Uno. Now one just doesn't find a town with a name like that every day, you know — or Uno. But a reasonable explanation is close at hand.

Seems that years ago there was a moonshiner active in the area. He had such a loyal group of clients that, eventually, his customers didn't even have to ask for a bottle of his white lightning when they came to his place. They'd just wink knowingly and say, "You know." In time the community came to be known as Uno, the name it adopted when a post office was established.

Needless to say, Uno has been responsible for many jokes and an occasional misunderstanding. Like the day, before automobiles, when a new drummer for a Louisville hardware firm came into town for the first time driving a team of horses hitched to a buggy.

Being a stranger, he wasn't sure of where he was.

"What's the name of this town?" he asked a man outside a store.

"Uno," came the reply.

"No, I don't know," the drummer shot back, his temper rising. "No need for you to get smart with me. Now I'm gonna ask you one more time the name of this place."

"Dammit," bristled the localite, "I said Uno!"

And that, they say, was when the big fight started.

G. H. Karnes, retired Marion County farm agent, was at a tobacco warehouse in Lebanon when a man came in with his tobacco crop and told the clerk his address was Maple.

"Where in the world is Maple?" Karnes asked.

"Why," the man replied with surprise and disgust, "it's over there close to Crooked Sourwood!"

Some years back Ed Easterly, former Associated Press bureau chief in Louisville, stopped at a roadside stand on U.S. 25 below Livingston in Laurel County. As he was leaving, the proprietor of the place walked up to his car.

"I've been purty much all over Kentucky," he allowed, "but I swear I never heard of that town you're from."

"What town do you mean?" Easterly asked, puzzled.

"Why the town on the sign in front of your car — Explore. Where's that?"

The man was half right. The sign did read: "Explore Kentucky."

Consider these few examples of how even imagination-defying town names can be explained more or less logically:

Bimble (Knox County) — Will Payne, who was largely responsible for the post office being established, owned a yoke of prize oxen named Bim and Bill. The names of the oxen were combined to give the post office its name.

Dwarf (Perry County) — When a post office was set up there in 187ε, it was called Tunnel Hill in honor of an extraordinary engineering feat performed with primitive tools by Sam and Felix Combs in digging a tunnel to divert water from Troublesome Creek to power their grist mill. The post office later was closed but reopened in 1883 and named for another Combs, "Short Jerry," a man of modest stature.

Job (Martin County) — This village was named for the Biblical character of the infinite patience because it took that particular virtue to get a post office established there.

Smile (Rowan County) — When it was learned their petition for a post office had been granted, smile is what the residents of the area did since they no longer would have to walk eight miles for their mail.

Helechawa (Wolfe County) — Although some have said this is a corruption of "hell each way" and was used to describe the road into the community years ago, that isn't the case. The name was invented by W. D. Walbridge, president of the long-abandoned narrow-gauge Ohio & Kentucky Railroad as a name for one of its stations and honored his daughter HELEn CHAse WAlbridge.

Tolu (Crittenden County) — Years ago it was called Hurricane Landing and was an important port on the Ohio River. But one day a group of men were gathered at J. W. Guess' sawmill when someone broke out a jug of cheap whisky called "Tolu Bitters" imported from Santiago deTolu, Chile. Each man took a swig. "You know," someone suggested, "we ought to call this place Tolu from now on." Which they did.

Nevada and Texas may be 1,500 miles apart in reality, but in Kentucky they're separated by only a 30-minute drive. In Washington County there's a town named Texas, while in adjoining Mercer County is the village of Nevada.

Some time back I received an urgent appeal from a University of Kentucky student named Larry Mead that read as follows: "Could you please find out why Monkey's Eyebrow is so named. I would say it is driving me bananas, but I can't stand inane puns." Before he went out of his tree and perhaps was driven to commit an even worse pun (if possible), I was able to answer his question.

Monkey's Eyebrow is a tiny community near the Ohio River in Ballard County. It is just north of Kevil and has as near neighbors such other unimaginatively-named places as Bandana, LaCenter, Ragland, Oscar, and Barlow.

There are at least three versions — two of them facetious — of the origin of the name. One is that around 1900 Harve Yancey was logging with oxen in the area that later became the community when the team bogged down in the mud. The foreman wanted to know where the mishap had taken place.

"Oh, up there by the monkey's eyebrow," Yancey replied flippantly.

"Where in the world is the monkey's eyebrow?" the foreman asked.

"Why," the logger wowed him, "over the monkey's eye!"

Another version holds that at about the same time a big barn dance was held in the area. A teen-age boy kept dropping matches on the floor and had his ears soundly boxed.

"Well, I'll just go back up the hill to Monkey's Eyebrow," he said, making up a name, "where I'm welcome."

The third version of the name origin holds that the crescent shape of Sand Ridge, along which the community once spread, and the grass that grew on it in the old days resembled a monkey's eyebrow.

So you take your pick of the three. Or invent a new version.

Although we sometimes tend to suspect that it just couldn't have been as hot and humid in the old days as today, I have the strong feeling that Kentucky in the summer always has been like a 40,000-square-mile sauna bath. Support for that belief can be found in the names that were given to certain communities.

Specifically, there are more than 150 communities whose names provide a possible clue to Kentucky-style summer. These range from what people look for from June to October — Shade, in Estill County — to the company that gets rich keeping the air-conditioners going — Utility, in Hancock County.

We also have a village named for what seems to be turned up — Furnace (Estill County) — and one named for what most people would like to take — Swim (Rowan County), not to mention one that describes what is felt — Relief (Morgan) — after what breaks a heat wave — Rain (Whitley).

Then, among many others, there are these additional descriptive samples of how the name-bestowers of earlier times must have regarded Kentucky summer: Boiling Springs (Warren), Heater (Livingston), Warm Hollow (Pike), Dry Ridge (Grant), Shady Nook (Henderson), Summersville (Green), and Fryer (Calloway).

And one shouldn't overlook the one town name that points up what most of Kentucky is for five months of the year — Hot Spot (Letcher).

Whether those who named communities had been abroad or merely were name-droppers, numerous Kentucky places bear the names of foreign cities and countries.

The list would include Moscow, Dublin, Cairo, Cuba, Geneva, Rome, Halifax, Bagdad, Bethlehem, Warsaw, Versailles, Florence, Paris, London, Sparta, Newfoundland, Ghent, Petersburg, Bremen, Buena Vista, Mexico, Glasgow, Corinth, Holland, Volga, Bernstadt, Wales, Verona, Utica, Sweden, Sinai, Panama, and Normandy.

Kentucky has a town named 88 and, honest, there's a real and logical reason why it was so named.

For years a school named Shady Grove had existed in the southeastern corner of Barren County and eventually a community, including a store operated by "Uncle" Dabney Nunnally, developed in the vicinity.

After long and arduous effort on the part of residents, Washington finally agreed to establish a post office in the community. The Nunnally store was the logical place for the office and, since he owned the building, it was logical that he should be the postmaster. It also seemed logical that, what with the school and all, it should be named Shady Grove.

However, "Uncle" Dabney, the postmaster to be, had the final say in the matter. He wasn't able to read or spell words too well, he explained, but he was pretty good at figures. So why not name the post office a number, say, 88? Which was done.

Later the name was spelled out and it became present-day Eighty Eight. Nevertheless, to this day much mail still comes to 88, Kentucky.

Every time the size of a small community is discussed, I recall the answer Quentin Bogard, who formerly was associated with Alice Lloyd College, provided when he was asked the size of Pippa Passes, the poetically-named (from the poem by Browning) Knott County village where the school is located.

"Pippa Passes is so small we don't have a village idiot," he would say, with full regard for corn. "We all have to take turns, and this is my day!"

Paradise was (and the past tense is correct) once a pretty little village on the Green River in Muhlenberg County. It was founded in the early 1800's, in the days before the railroads, when it served as the point to which goods bound for Drakesboro, Greenville, and other inland towns were shipped by boat.

The railroads eventually reduced its importance, but it continued, living mainly on past memories, until the Tennessee Valley Authority acquired land a mile upstream in the late 1950's and began construction of the world's largest steam-electric power plant. From then on there was trouble in Paradise.

Once the plant was in operation, smoke, fly ash, and soot from the massive furnaces began to settle so heavily on the village that it was impossible to raise a garden or even put out a Monday wash. In an effort to ease the situation, TVA bought up property in the town. One by one the residents left, the post office was closed and Paradise was no more.

Pollution had destroyed Paradise.

Mrs. Joe Ledbetter is a former Kentuckian who taught school at Talladega, Georgia. Being proud of the state, she always told her third-graders all about Kentucky and its many charms. In so doing, she apparently made quite an impression on a little boy one year.

She was quizzing the class orally in geography.

"Name three continents," she directed this little fellow.

"I think," he replied, "that there is North America, South America, and Kentucky!"

Kentucky has 120 counties and, if indeed there is anything in a name, does it hold that the cleanest of the counties is Bath and the county with the fewest pagans is Christian?

To follow that line of reasoning, is it proper to conclude that, besides merely filling what otherwise would be blank space on license plates, other county names also suggest certain truisms? Or, are the following thoughts concerning county names just examples of guilt-by-word association?

County Louisville Zoo needs most — Lyon.

County that goes best with breakfast — Oldham.

Matt Dillon county — Marshall.
Damnyankee county — Union.
County most familiar with Boy Scouts — Knott.
Liver pill county — Carter
Fruit jar county — Mason
County that tells who committed the murder — Butler.
Credit card county — Owen.
Hot water county — Boyle.
Most desolate county — Barren.
Nemesis of young maidens county — Wolfe.
Deadliest county — Graves.
LB county — Johnson.
How-my-car-sounds county — Knox.
Country bumpkin county — Hickman.

Speaking of the symbolism that can be associated with
the various names of Kentucky counties, Mrs. Ambrose
Dudley, who teaches Kentucky history at East Elementary
School in Frankfort, uses that method in her classroom.
That is, in helping her students remember the county
names she suggests that they match the name with a
familiar object.

"As an example of what I mean," she told her class one
year, "think of a kind of bird for Martin County and a
kind of dirt for Clay County."

The exercise continued, with the students fitting the
county name she had in mind with the symbols she
provided. The names and symbols fitted together properly
until she came to Bath County.

"Give me the name of the county we all have to have
each Saturday night," she directed.

Over 60 per cent of the class gave the same answer:
"Bourbon."

INTRODUCTION   *Before taking up newspaper column writing, for more than 15 years I was a magazine feature writer, a work that took me into each of Kentucky's 120 counties at least once annually.*

All in all, I ground out some 2,000 features, a production figure mentioned only by way of emphasizing the fact that through exposure, if for no other reason, I became fully aware of Kentucky's unique characteristics. I came to appreciate how its location as a state too far north to be south, too far south to be north, too far east to be west and too far west to be east has given it a strong mixture of all the regions of this country.

Perhaps location then explains the many contradictions one finds in Kentucky; why, for instance, this is a state of warm hearts and hot heads; of gentleness and violence; of the most cordial hospitality and the shrewdest kind of horse trading; of great erudition and appalling illiteracy; of hard drinking and tee-totalism; and why it's a state that has produced some of America's great statesmen and, in direct contrast, some of its most notorious ballot box stuffers.

Thus, there never was a shortage of material for feature articles about an endless variety of subjects, ranging from religious cultists who handle poisonous snakes in services to the Old Christmas which still is observed in some parts of the state, and from Welshmen who may have been at the Falls of the Ohio River 325 years before Columbus set foot in the New World to incidents that pointed up Kentucky's unique role in the Civil War.

And, as the chapter title suggests, there was an article explaining why Kentucky is a commonwealth and not a state. Some of these features, and others, are touched on in this chapter.

CHAPTER 8

WHAT'S A COMMONWEALTH, DADDY?

Not too long back I heard a radio announcer say, in
the course of reciting a commercial, that the word
Kentucky is "the name the Shawnee Indians gave to their
home land" and it means "dark and bloody ground."

From all I can gather, that statement was incorrect on at
least two counts. This wasn't the home of the Shawnees
and that "dark and bloody ground" business was just one
of several descriptions different tribes gave the area which
later became Kentucky.

While 20 or more tribes, among them Shawnees, came
here to hunt and fish, modern Indians resided in Kentucky
more or less on a temporary basis. This was because
the region lay between the territory north of the Ohio
occupied by the powerful Iroquois and the home of the
warlike Cherokees to the south. Both of these mighty
nations claimed Kentucky, and their constant conflict
made it dangerous for large permanent villages of other
tribes to be established. It was the warring between the
two strongest Indian nations that led to the "dark and
bloody ground" reputation, Daniel Boone contended.

But in spite of the threat of the Iroquois and the
Cherokees, other tribes did venture into Kentucky, some
to set up small villages, and most of them had their own
name for the region.

John Jackson, an explorer who had come here with the
Shawnees at least 10 years before Boone, held that tribe's
name for Kentucky meant "At the head of the river,"
a name derived, he wrote, from "a deep channeled and
clifty river called by the Shawnees 'Ken-tuck-kee.'"

On the other hand, John Filson, the state's first historian, held that Kentucky was a Delaware word meaning "Place of the meadow." Col. Reuben T. Durrett, another early historian, traced the name back to the Catawaba word meaning "Prairie or barrens," while he also said the Mingoes referred to the region as "The middle ground." Perhaps the most romantic name was the Wyandotte's which translated out to mean "Land of tomorrow."

Even those who haven't seen a stage play during this century or attended a movie since pictures learned to talk no doubt know about a bouncy musical comedy called "Hello, Dolly!" which closed after a record-breaking 2,844 performances on Broadway and then was made into a motion picture.

The show was produced by David Merrick, a theatrical genius whose private life is almost as closely guarded as that of Howard Hughes, the hermit of Las Vegas and other points around the world.

Because of this secrecy, the role a Kentucky mountain girl played in the production of the Broadway show, "Hello, Dolly!," never has been fully revealed. The mountain girl, who might be called the mother of "Dolly," is Knott County native Jeanne Gibson, the second Mrs. David Merrick. The true story of Jeanne Gibson makes the fairy tale of Cinderella almost believable in comparison.

She was born in the heart of the hills on Little Carr Creek at the mouth of Big Doubles where her father, Mallie Gibson, operated a crossroads store. Educated at Hindman Settlement School and Caney (now Alice Lloyd) Junior College, she taught the one-room Wolfpen School in the Dead Mare Branch section of Knott County before blithely setting off for New York to become a model.

From New York, she went to London as press representative for the Claridge Hotel. Later she organized restaurants in Europe for the Diners Club and worked for the Associated Press before returning to America and joining Merrick Enterprises for a couple of years before marrying the boss.

Shortly after their marriage, she met Thornton Wilder, who himself had Kentucky ties, what with having attended Berea College. His straight play "The Merchant of Yonkers," which had been renamed "The Matchmaker," would make a first-rate musical, she convinced Merrick.

And it did. Under a third name — "Hello, Dolly!"

Ever so often, even now, we read about someone being bitten by a poisonous snake during a mountain religious service in which reptiles are handled. Perhaps this causes one to wonder what kind of people will take up and handle rattlesnakes and copperheads as though they were docile house pets.

Let me give you my opinion, arrived at after having attended countless snake-handling gatherings, visiting cultists in their homes and spending hours talking to them.

Almost without exception I have found them to be generally uneducated religious fanatics who live far up the more remote mountain hollows in Harlan, Bell, Letcher, and Knox Counties. Life to these people is real and earnest; they are desperate for something to break the monotony of their drab existence. Snake handling does this to a certain extent by focusing limited attention on them.

This is not to suggest, however, that they're insincere show-offs. Their religion has to be something they can see and touch as well as feel inside. Most of them have seemed deeply religious and base their beliefs upon a literal translation of Biblical passages found in John 14, James 5, Mark 16, and Hebrews 11. These passages, they say, call upon "true believers" to take up serpents as proof of their belief in the power of God to protect his own.

"We've got enough faith in God to believe He can lock the jaws of them serpents and protect us who believe," Oscar Hutton, a leader among Harlan County cultists, told me 20 years ago. "Even unbelievers ain't afraid of a serpent when God locks its jaws."

But from the other side of the room came a comment

from his wife I've never forgotten.

"I," she said simply, "am afraid of 'em any time!"

One of the toughest things this side of the new math is trying to explain the eccentricities of Kentucky geography to a stranger.

For instance, Kentucky has a town named Liberty and another named West Liberty. Which is reasonable enough until it is pointed out that, instead of being west of Liberty, West Liberty actually is 125 miles east and a bit south. Moreover, North Middletown is 90 miles due east of Middletown, South Elkhorn is 150 miles west of Elkhorn City, and East Union is more than 175 miles west of Union, to mention only a few other apparently displaced places.

But the confusion barely starts there. Kentucky has 120 counties and 107 towns bear the same name as a county. However, only 27 of the towns are in the county whose name they wear.

Let me explain. Henderson is in Henderson County, Harlan is in Harlan County, Greenup is in Greenup County and Shelbyville is in Shelby County, as one would expect.

However, Carlisle isn't in Carlisle County — it's the seat of Nicholas County, while Nicholasville is the seat of Jessamine County. Neither is Crittenden in Crittenden County — it's in Grayson County, the seat of which isn't Grayson but Leitchfield. Grayson, in turn, is in Carter County.

And then there's the classic displacement of the towns of Fulton, Hickman, and Clinton in far western Kentucky. Fulton and Hickman Counties adjoin each other and the town of Fulton is properly in Fulton County, but it is not the seat. The town of Hickman is the seat of Fulton County, while the seat of next-door Hickman County is Clinton, but the seat of Clinton County is Albany, 250 miles directly east.

That's why in Kentucky it sometimes seems you just can't get there from here.

In some respects, the deep tragedy of the Civil War was more clearly underscored in Kentucky than in perhaps any other state. For while other states were solidly on one side or the other, Kentucky was the true border state, almost evenly divided in sentiment between North and South. Fathers differed from sons and went forth to fight against them in Kentucky. Brothers parted from brothers over the issues that divided the nation; friends turned against friends.

Because of this house-divided posture, many unusual and ironic incidents arose in Kentucky, including a bizarre, favor-for-a-favor happening that involved Daniel Moneyham, a Confederate, and John Russell, a Union soldier. Although they had grown up in the Adair-Green County section of Kentucky, the two were not acquainted until Moneyham was captured by Union forces early in the war and Russell was assigned to guard him.

"They're likely to shoot you," Russell told Moneyham after a couple of days. "You're a young fellow and I'd hate to see you die that way. You run away and I'll fire over your head and you can try to escape."

The plot worked. Moneyham fled and eventually rejoined his outfit.

Some months later, during a battle in Tennessee, a large number of Union troops were captured by Moneyham's unit. Among the prisoners was Russell. As soon as Moneyham recognized Russell, he went to his captain and told him how the Yankee had saved his life. Russell was set free.

The magnitude of the favor wasn't known until later. The other Union soldiers captured with Russell were sent to the notorious Andersonville Prison, where more than half of the 35,000 men confined died of disease and malnutrition.

Always on the day after an election losing candidates are said to be ready to take the long and bitter voyage "up Salt River" to the legendary land of defeated politicians.

The phrase "up Salt River" originated in Kentucky and had a basis in fact. But over the years it has come to

stand for the place where all those defeated for office go
to lick their wounds and regain their composure. The
term originated, supposedly, in 1844 when Henry Clay,
the Whig, was running against James K. Polk, the
Democrat, for president.

One day during the campaign, Clay was due to speak at
Brandenburg. He left Louisville by steamboat in plenty
of time to arrive for the speech, but the river was low and
the steamer grounded some distance downstream. Clay
then hired a man who lived near the river to row him the
rest of the way to Brandenburg in a john-boat.

When the trip resumed, Clay busied himself with his
speech and paid no attention to where they were heading.
Bending his back to the task of rowing, the oarsman,
who only incidentally happened to be a Democrat, took
the wrong turn to the left at West Point and headed up
Salt River, which flows into the Ohio there.

By the time Clay noticed they were going up the wrong
river, it was too late to get to Brandenburg for the
engagement. Soon the whole country knew about the
man who wanted to guide the ship of state getting lost up
Salt River in a john-boat.

When Clay was defeated in the election, some wit
pointed out that he "was heading up Salt River," and the
expression has been tagged onto losing candidates ever
since.

If all the explorers who may have preceded Columbus to
the New World could be called from beyond this vale of
tears into solemn convention, they'd undoubtedly swamp
Rhode Island.

For some historians today believe that assorted groups
of Phoenicians had come here long before the time of
Christ. They, in turn, were followed by Christian, Irish,
Icelandic, Viking, Welsh, and Portuguese explorers, all of
whom nosed out old Chris for first place honors.

The Kentucky-Southern Indiana area is deeply involved
in a tantalizing legend concerning Welshmen who not
only may have landed in America three centuries before
Columbus, but who even may have pressed as far inland

as the Falls of the Ohio River, now present day Louisville.

The story, based both on fact and supposition, goes like this:

In 1167, Welsh sailors, commanded by Madoc, one of the 17 sons of the Prince of Wales, sailed to this continent and landed along the Gulf Coast of Alabama. Moving north, they eventually reached the Falls of the Ohio and 14 miles upstream, atop a steep ridge that rises from the river on the Indiana side, they built a stone fort.

Native Indians in time overpowered the Welshmen in a battle that raged down river to the Falls. Many Welsh were killed; others were captured and released when they agreed to leave the region. According to old wives' tales, they went eastward and intermarried with the Indians, a fact supported in the papers of Captain John Smith, who told of the Pilgrims finding "white Indians who spoke almost pure Welsh."

Did Madoc's men really reach what today is the Louisville area?

Reuben T. Durrett, an early historian, told of skeletons in armor that were reputed to have been found near the Falls. Ancient pickaxes, not of Indian design, also were supposed to have been found by early settlers.

But perhaps the most solid fact to support the belief that Welshmen were in this area long before any other settlers was the stone fort on the ridge upstream from the Falls and which later was called Fern Grove. Many pioneers used stones from the fort to build houses. But before all traces of it were gone, Indiana University sent geologists to survey the ruins.

A report they filed in 1873 read in part: "The stone fortress occupies a narrow ridge facing the Ohio in the east and Fourteen Mile Creek on the west . . . Around the sloping sides, a wall some 150 feet above the river has been made by piling stones mason fashion . . . Within the walls are stone mounds, evidently for lookout posts . . . On top of the enclosed ridge was a place for cultivation and a large indentation for collecting water in time of siege . . ."

Early this century Fern Grove became Rose Island, once a noted pleasure resort. The area now is owned by the federal government.

Were Welshmen in the area long before Columbus?

The answer to that mystery is locked forever somewhere in the tangle of vines and underbrush that now covers Fern Grove and the rock escarpment that towers above it.

The tight little rectangle of real estate in Frankfort enclosed by Wapping, Wilkinson, Washington, and Main Streets is known as "The Corner of Celebrities." And for good reason since over the years the classic old mansions located within the tree-fringed block have been home to an astonishing number of national personalities in the fields of law, politics, and diplomacy.

John Brown, the first U.S. Senator from Kentucky, once owned the entire block and started it all by erecting his famous home, Liberty Hall, at the corner of Wilkinson and Main in 1796, from plans drawn up by his good friend, Thomas Jefferson.

Since that time, the neighborhood has been the birthplace or home of two justices of the Supreme Court, nine Senators, six Congressmen, seven ambassadors, two Cabinet members, and six admirals. Two of the houses in the block — Liberty Hall and the mansion Senator Brown built for his son, Orlando — today are house museums open to the public.

Liberty Hall set the pattern for other homes in the area. Perhaps no place in Kentucky entertained more important guests. At one time in 1819, overnight guests included President James Monroe and two of his aides, both of whom later became president — Andrew Jackson and Zachary Taylor.

As the fame of Liberty Hall spread, other prominent families bought plots from Senator Brown and built substantial mansions of their own. Needless to say, an address within the block came to be a sure sign of station and affluence. Eventually a segment of society almost as rigid and unbending as royalty in its social conduct resided within the square.

A story is told in Frankfort which illustrates the nature of the society in the neighborhood. One morning shortly before the Civil War a lady who lived on the block was out for a stroll when she met a gentleman. Since they had been formally introduced, she felt she could reveal a bit of startling news to him.

"I have just seen smoke pouring from the roof of a house across the street from mine," she said. "I believe it must be on fire."

"Did you warn the residents?" the gentleman asked.

"I most certainly did not," she answered haughtily. "I have never been introduced to them!"

Just as instinct compels salmon to return to the stream where they were hatched to spawn and the swallows to return to Capistrano, so does a deep-inside urge drive me to return at least in thought on the first Monday in every April to Benton, the only town in Kentucky where I was born.

For the first Monday in April in Benton is Tater Day, a unique trade-court day that has been observed annually since 1843. Actually, Tater Day — and it's "Tater" and not "Potato" — is far more than that. It's the only monument ever dedicated to that otherwise humble and unsung farm product, the sweet potato. Thus the day is a pure slice of small-town Americana that has survived the sophistication of modern times.

Started as a day when farmers came to town for the opening of court and to buy and sell seed sweet potatoes, Tater Day now is an area event that attracts up to 10,000 traders, peddlers, buyers, and plain spectators from a 100-mile radius.

Many a story has had its roots in Tater Day. C. K. Reid of Madisonville tells one about an old German farmer who, years ago, always parked his wagon loaded with fine potatoes in the same spot on the court square.

One year, however, he didn't get to town until after noon. Then he came limping in, his clothes dusty and dirty and torn in several places. He had loaded his wagon the night before, he explained, and started out early, driving his best team of young mules. On the edge of town a pack of hounds chased a fox across the road and under the wagon. The unexpected activity spooked the mules and they took off up the road. He was thrown from the wagon; potatoes flew everywhere; but the mules kept running.

"Did you catch 'em?" he was asked.

"Hell, no," he replied in his thick German accent. "It seemed the faster dem mules voud run, de fudder avay they vould got!"

By the time Christmas is far enough past for most of us that the bills already have started pouring in, only then is Christmas Day being celebrated by a mere handful of Kentucky mountain people. These are the people of Anglo-Saxon or German lineage who still hold to the traditional "Old Christmas."

The observance is based on the fact that, since the exact date of Christ's birth long has been debated, January 6 is one of several days that have been celebrated in different parts of the world. It wasn't until about 350 A.D., in fact, that Pope Julius decreed December 25 as Christmas, a date given widespread, if not universal, acceptance.

At one time many in the remote hollows of eastern Kentucky, where people of Scotch, Scotch-Irish, and English ancestry mainly settled, observed "Old Christmas." I'm not sure if any are left today.

I attended an "Old Christmas" party shortly after World War II at the home of an aged couple on Hell-for-Certain Creek in Leslie County.

Many details now are somewhat hazy in my mind, but I recall 30 or 40 persons being present. In one corner of the large room was a cedar tree decorated with strings of popcorn and apples. On a table was a wassail bowl filled with applejack. After one of the men read the Christmas story from the Bible, simple gifts were solemnly exchanged.

But most of all I recall the men, their leathery faces softened by the flickering glow of the kerosene lamps and the open fire, telling Old World Christmas tales that were centuries old when their ancestors had come to this country: How at the stroke of midnight a deep hush would fall over all the world and the cattle would softly low and fall to their knees, just as they had done on that long-ago night in Bethlehem, and for a brief moment they would have the power of speech.

It may have been my imagination, but the hills did seem strangely quiet when the clock bonged out midnight. I can't testify what the cattle did, but that one "Old Christmas" observance impressed itself so vividly in my mind that I've never forgotten the simplicity and reverence of the occasion.

The case of Jesse Stuart, Kentucky's most prolific author, is proof that, contrary to what the old saying holds, a prophet isn't always without honor in his own country.

For in the case of Stuart, it was local people who requested that the new posh lodge at Greenbo State Park be named in his honor. The gesture shows the high esteem held for Stuart, who was born and still lives less than 10 miles from the park and who has based most of his 40 or so books and 1,500-plus short stories on events and legends that originated in the low mountains surrounding the park area.

But Stuart wasn't always held in such high regard. There was a time when he was a prophet with practically no honor on his home grounds.

Nearly 40 years ago when Stuart, then a Greenup County teacher, had advocated changes in education — consolidation, elimination of the trustee system — he was branded a troublemaker out to wreck the very school system that had educated him. He was forced to back his convictions with his fists on numerous occasions.

On top of that, his stories, which were just beginning to attract national attention, were so vivid and detailed that folks in the area often could detect themselves in his assorted writing. The idea arose that he was making light of the people among whom he was born and always had lived. Residents would turn their backs when he walked down the street.

Then, to the eternal credit of the area, starting around 1950, the situation changed. It was almost as though for the first time home folks began to realize that, far from making fun of them, Jesse Stuart had put on paper the real heartbeat of the hill people, had pictured them as they truly are. They began to chuckle over such hilarious short stories as *The Frog Trouncing Contest;* they spotted the beauty expressed in the poetry volume *Kentucky Is My Land,* and they felt a lump in their throats as they read the touching legend they all knew and which Stuart turned into his book *The Friendly Spirit of Laurel Ridge.*

The prophet suddenly was with honor in his home country. Jesse Stuart Day was held in Greenup and a marker in his honor was erected on the courthouse lawn.

And in time they named a state park lodge for him.

"If" has been called the largest word in the English language, but in few instances is its historical immensity more clearly underlined than in the case of two famous Kentuckians — Abraham Lincoln and Jefferson Davis.

As every school child knows, Lincoln was born in a Kentucky backwoods log cabin near Hodgenville, while Davis, who 52 years later was to be his Civil War adversary, was born only eight months earlier and 100 miles west in another Kentucky frontier log cabin at Fairview.

The fathers of both were roamers to whom the next step always loomed as the promised land, and so their families were constantly on the move. Consequently, both left Kentucky at an early age with their parents — the Lincolns going north to Indiana and Illinois, the Davises going south to Mississippi. The two boys grew to manhood in radically different social, economic, and political environments.

But what if the migratory routes of the two families had been reversed? If the Lincolns had gone south and the Davises north, what might have been the destiny of their sons?

If the families had turned 180 degrees in leaving Kentucky, would the two sons have been as they were or would they have been as different as the sections where they grew up? Might Davis have been elected 16th president of the Union and Lincoln the only president of the Confederate states?

If these two Kentuckians actually had gone in opposite directions from the state of their birth, what would have been the affect on the nation? Would there have been a blood-bath to brand slavery as intolerable and change the emphasis in the name "United States" from "states" to "united?"

If . . . What a mountain of questions one two-letter word can pose!

One day at lunch the conversation somehow got sidetracked and turned from inflation, mini-skirts, taxes, and such timely topics to the most unforgettable characters those of us around the table had known.

My spur-of-the-moment nominees included the likes of politician Alben W. Barkley, author Jesse Stuart, coach Ed Diddle, historian Dr. Thomas D. Clark, lawyer William H. Townsend, and Senator John Sherman Cooper, all men I have known, and one I never knew — "Bad" John Wright.

All I know of John Wright is what I've heard in southeastern Kentucky, his domain, but I have the feeling he just may have been the most unusual Kentuckian of all.

John Wright lived in a remote corner of Letcher County in what today is the town of Jenkins and his time spanned from before the Civil War in which he fought — on both sides, some say — to well into this century. It was he that author John Fox, Jr. used as a model for his character "Devil" Jud Tolliver in the book *Trail of the Lonesome Pine*.

The mountainous area around Jenkins still abounds in John Wright tales, most of which no doubt really happened. After the Civil War, one hears, he served as a peace officer and later worked as land agent when

John C. C. Mayo was acquiring the acreage which in time became the vast holdings of Consolidation Coal Company.

As a peace officer, Wright engaged in many a shootout. As a matter of fact, one story holds that his greatest regret was that he never quite broke even in this life, what with having sired 27 children but having dispatched 28 men in gun battles.

Old timers recall hearing him tell about going once to serve a warrant on a notorious man who vowed he'd never be arrested alive.

"He was settin' in the front room," they recall Wright saying, "and when I walked in he didn't say nothin', just whipped out his pistol and snapped the hammer down on an empty chamber.

"I said 'I don't want no trouble,' but all he done was pull the hammer down on another empty chamber. By then I was gettin' kinda nervous, of course, so I yanked out my pistol and I shot him.

"If that taught me anything, it were to never let no man git the draw on me again!"

One of the several robberies staged in Kentucky by Jesse James and various members of his Middle Border raiders occurred on September 3, 1880, when he and one accomplice held up the Mammoth Cave stagecoach. However, there was a bizarre aftermath to that event which happened months later in Missouri.

The Kentucky robbery took place near the appropriately-named Little Hope Baptist Church when the stage, carrying passengers from the cave to the railroad at Cave City, was stopped by two men on horseback. The seven passengers were made to step outside. While the larger of the two robbers had them empty their purses into a wheat sack, his smaller companion, a stoop-shouldered fellow with watery blue eyes, carefully examined each of the passengers for watches and jewelry that might catch his fancy.

One passenger, Judge R. H. Rountree of Lebanon, a leading Kentucky political figure, was wearing a gold watch that drew the eye of the bandit. He inspected it closely, then turned it over and read aloud the inscription on the back:

"To Judge Rountree, with best wishes from Gov. J. Proctor Knott."

"This is one watch I'll always be proud to wear," the stoop-shouldered bandit bragged as he rode off.

Two years later, on April 3, 1882, in St. Joseph, Missouri, when authorities were called to investigate the murder of a Mr. Howard, who had been shot in the back, their findings proved he really was Jesse James.

But that isn't the strangest part of the story.

When James had fallen to the floor, a gold watch had partially slipped from his pocket. On the back of the watch was this inscription:

"To Judge Rountree, with best wishes from Gov. J. Proctor Knott."

From the late 1870's until shortly before World War I, the finest hardwood in the world was harvested in the mountainous area of eastern Kentucky that is veined by the various branches of the Big Sandy River.

Oak, beech, maple, hickory, and tulipwood from the region brought premium prices in France for wine casks, in England for ship beams, and in Italy for fine furniture.

Since there were no year-around roads, and rails had barely touched the upper tip of the region, the Big Sandy and its Tug and Levisa Forks provided the avenue in and out for commerce as well as residents.

Trees would be felled in the hills, snaked by oxen to the streams, banded into rafts, and floated downstream on the spring "tides" to Catlettsburg, the town at the point where the Big Sandy empties into the Ohio. Catlettsburg eventually became the world's largest hardwood market center.

At times, rafts of logs, jammed so tightly together that it was possible to walk across the river, stretched for miles up the Big Sandy. Often a thousand or more rough-and-tumble rafters and timber buyers would be in town at one time. Most of them came looking for excitement and

Catlettsburg's 21 saloons on Front Street alone provided it in full measure.

Tales of those rip-snorting days still are repeated. One involved a raw-boned Pike County man who bet another raftsman he could swim the river at its mouth carrying him on his back. A spot free of logs was found and the braggart took on his handicap and started dog-paddling across.

Halfway over, he realized the river was wider than he'd reckoned.

"Young feller," he puffed to the man on his back, "if'n I was you, I think I'd help out by kickin' a mite!"

They say there's no more bitter disappointment than being beaten in a political race. In view of that, is it possible that disappointment over losing an election for mayor drove from Central City a man who went on to become a U.S. Senator, candidate for the Republican nomination for president, and head of one of the nation's largest corporations?

The man was T. Coleman du Pont. The story of the man who emerged as an industrial giant and who started his career in Central City, goes like this:

Du Pont was born in Louisville in 1863. His father owned a paper mill and a street railway in Louisville and coal mines in Muhlenberg and Ohio Counties. After graduating from MIT in civil and mining engineering, Du Pont went to Central City in 1883 to handle his father's coal interests. Later he took charge of the Central Coal and Iron Company and expanded into other ventures.

By then Du Pont, a big, friendly man, was one of the most popular figures in Central City; so popular, in fact, friends convinced him to run for mayor in 1892. He was defeated and there still are old-timers who say this so saddened him that he left less than a year later to join a steel company at Johnstown, Pennsylvania.

In 1900, at the urging of his two cousins, Alfred I. and Pierre du Pont, he became head of E. I. du Pont de Nemours & Company, at that time valued at $600 million.

After serving as U.S. Senator from Delaware, the man who couldn't get elected mayor of Central City received 13 second-ballot votes for Republican nomination for president in 1916.

But early disappointment or not, Du Pont never forgot Kentucky. He was the donor of the money which enabled the state to buy the land now enclosed in Cumberland Falls State Park, and it is his name that the park lodge bears to this day.

Let me tell you a little off-beat story that touches on the World Series of baseball, and which also illustrates how times change in the life span of just one person. It was told to me by the late William H. Townsend, Lexington lawyer and Lincoln expert. The story directly involved Townsend, the daughter of a Confederate general killed in the Civil War; it also indirectly involved the 16th president of the United States and his Kentucky-born wife. In order to fit those diverse pieces together, the story must be told flashback fashion in three scenes.

Scene one was set in Washington soon after the death at the Battle of Chickamauga in 1863 of Confederate General Ben Hardin Helm, the husband of Emilie Todd, a half-sister of Mrs. Abraham Lincoln. When the Lincolns heard of the general's death, the president arranged for Mrs. Helm and her young family to pass through Union lines and come to live with them at the White House. One of the Helm children was Elodie, a mere baby at the time.

Scene two took place after the Civil War. By then Mrs. Helm had returned to Kentucky and had bought a beautiful house south of Lexington which she renamed Helm Place. Still living with her mother was Elodie, who later was to marry Walter Lewis.

Scene three took place following World War II. Elodie Helm Lewis, then 88 and the last survivor of the family (she died in 1953), had decided to sell Helm Place and Townsend wanted to buy it — and did. It was a warm October afternoon when he went to Helm Place to close the deal.

"Miss Elodie's awful busy and can't be disturbed right

now," the maid told Townsend, "but you might come in and wait."

When he entered the hallway, Townsend could see Mrs. Lewis in an adjoining living room seated in a large chair, bending forward until her head seemed to rest on a table. Tiptoeing into the room, he could tell why she couldn't be disturbed right then.

The woman who had lived with the Lincolns in the White House during the Civil War was listening with undivided attention to the World Series on the radio!

In August of 1946 a Pennsylvanian, who had prospected for gold and had raised cattle in the Old West before coming to personify the Kentucky Colonel, died at his farm on the outskirts of Lexington. The man was Colonel Edward R. Bradley, master of Idle Hour Stock Farm, the picture-postcard property which produced four winning horses in the Kentucky Derby.

Although remembered best as a legendary horse breeder with a soft spot in his heart for charitable causes, Bradley was a professional gambler. His vast fortune came from the Beach Club in Palm Beach, Florida, which he bought in 1898 and turned into the number one casino of the times.

Colonel Bradley never presented himself as anything but a gambler. Testimony he gave before a Senate committee in 1935 made that clear.

"What do you do?" he was asked.

"Gamble," Bradley answered.

"And what do you gamble on?" the questioner pressed.

"Anything," came the simple reply.

Despite being by his own admission a gambler, Bradley's greatest single loss may well have been to his wife. At one race meeting, Mrs. Bradley decided to bet $20 on every horse except the favorite in one event. Feeling it was a foolish bet, he told his betting commissioner to take the money, but to keep it instead of betting it.

The unexpected happened. Wishing Star, a 943-to-1 shot came in first. Rather than tell her what happened,

the colonel simply dug down into his pocket and paid her
in cold cash — $18,860!

Perhaps that's why, despite his love for racing, he used
to offer this advice to horse players:

"Betting the races will break any man in time,"

Because it is filled with the optimism that Christmas
brings and also because it illustrates the stoicism and
depth of character that is a trademark of Kentucky
mountain people, let me tell you a story that originated
with Mrs. Mary Breckinridge.

Mrs. Breckinridge was founder of the Frontier Nursing
Service, an organization that for more than 40 years has
provided medical service and nursing care for a remote,
doctor-short region of Leslie, Clay, and Perry counties.

But the FNS has done more than just provide medical
needs that otherwise would have gone unmet. It also has
ministered in no small way to the spiritual, cultural,
and educational needs of the people who live far up the
deep hollows carved from the hills by such picturesquely-
named mountain streams as Cutshin, Hell-for-Certain,
Redbird, and Squabble.

Starting in the earliest years, an annual custom at
Wendover, the headquarters of the service, was the staging
at Christmas time of the Nativity Play, with local children
portraying the various characters. As the custom
continued, it became part of the culture of the region and
children for miles around eagerly looked forward to
Christmas and the chance to appear as an angel, a Wise
Man, or some other character in the play.

More than 30 years ago, a little boy named Paul was
one of the angelic host in the play, a role he did with
great enthusiasm. As soon as the play was over, he asked
if he might do the same role the next year, and Mrs.
Breckinridge assured him he could.

Some weeks later, while helping his father, Paul fell
into a grist mill and his right arm literally was torn out
at the socket.

The boy was rushed on muleback to Wendover. When

175

Paul arrived he was in deep shock and Mrs. Breckinridge and another nurse did what they could until the medical director could arrive from the FNS Hospital at Hyden, six rough miles away.

Paul was unconscious for some time and the first thing he saw when he regained his senses was the worried face of Mrs. Breckinridge bending over him. He glanced down at the place where his right arm had been, then slowly lifted his eyes.

"I reckon I wish you'd let me be a Wise Man in the play next Christmas," he said to Mrs. Breckinridge, as a big tear slowly rolled down his cheek. "They don't have to fold their arms!"

Although I have a violent dislike for those who specialize in embarrassing people with verbal putdowns, I do appreciate parties who have the talent for delivering a squelch when no other conversational form will suffice. For the perfect squelch is a many splendored thing that sometimes can be as blunt as a punch in the nose and sometimes as gentle as a drop of dew.

An example of the gentle squelch concerns a cloak room attendant who worked years ago at the famous old Latham Hotel in Hopkinsville. While he never used checks, he had the reputation for never making a mistake in returning the wrong hat or coat to a customer. One day a man tried to needle him about his great memory.

"How do you know this is my coat?" he asked when a wrap was handed to him.

"I don't know it's your coat, boss," came the gentle answer. "I just know it's the coat you came in with!"

Those familiar with the eastern quarter of Kentucky know that it is a region where the scenery is filled with high, steep hills. Most of the flat land suitable for crops lies in the pinched valleys carved from the encircling ridges by literally hundreds of small streams that bear such picturesque names as Cutshin, Squabble, Lonesome, Troublesome, Quicksand and Hell-for-Certain.

But the creek bottom land wasn't enough for the needs of the people who settled there. So they cleared the precipitous hillsides and used that land too, for cultivation and grazing the family cow and mule.

The steepness of the hillside farms gave rise to many real and fictional stories. Some plots were so steep, I've heard it said, that the seed was stuffed into a shotgun and fired into the ground. By planting potatoes on the slopes, I've also heard, farmers saved labor at harvest time by placing sacks at the bottom of the hill and letting the spuds roll down into them. Horses and mules used for plowing in the mountains had to have legs longer on the downhill side to brace themselves and keep from falling out of the fields, old-timers say.

Some years back a boy appeared before Judge A. M. J. Cochran in Federal Court at Jackson to explain why his father, who had been summoned as a juror, wasn't present.

"Pap can't make it in," the boy said, "'cause he fell out of the upper farm and broke his leg!"

Since the words "Commonwealth of Kentucky" appear on our flag, great seal, and official documents, exactly what is Kentucky — a state or a commonwealth?

Here's the answer:

Commonwealth is used as the official designation of four states — Pennsylvania, Virginia, Massachusetts, and Kentucky. The term goes back to the time of Oliver Cromwell when he created the Commonwealth of States or Colonies of Great Britain. Virginia, Pennsylvania, and Massachusetts, being commonwealths of Great Britain before the Revolutionary War, incorporated the word into their names when they separated from the mother country.

In America, a commonwealth is regarded as a state having its immediate outgrowth from one of the original 13 colonies. However, Kentucky, once a part of Virginia, is the only state to adopt the term commonwealth when it became a separate state.

Clear? As mud?

INTRODUCTION   *There are those who, in light of eye-popping
whopper tales told in the state, have suggested that either all Kentuckians are liars or all liars are Kentuckians.*

*Neither suspicion is correct. Entirely. In truth, Kentuckians appre-
ciate good stories so much they're apt to get carried away and in their
enthusiasm embellish a bit on hard fact.*

*It should be pointed out, however, that Kentuckians aren't alone
when it comes to the type of stories in which the first teller doesn't
have a chance. After all, the Burlington Liar's Club didn't originate in
Kentucky. But it's prize-winning stories are topped every day of the
year by countless unknown Kentuckians in tale-swapping sessions at
the crossroads general store, the courthouse, barber shop, neighborhood tavern, or wherever people gather.*

*To show how Kentucky tale-toppers operate, William Buchanan,
long a district supervisor for the Department of Fish and Wildlife
Resources in eastern Kentucky, tells of an incident that cropped up
one night in the afterglow of a sportsmen's club meeting. The talk
turned to raccoon hunting and the number, and especially the size, of
the animals some of the men had bagged in their time. As the tellers
were heard from, each outdoing the others in order, one old man kept
trying to get the floor. Finally, he interrupted the hunter who
was talking.*

*"Now let me tell you about the hunt I was on," he cut in, his voice
growing more excited as he went on. "The other night I was out in the
woods with my dogs and I caught three coons. And I want you
to know the least one of the lot was the biggest damn coon ever I
saw!"*

*If you aren't afraid your mind will boggle, here is a short roundup
of representative Kentucky tall tales.*

CHAPTER 9

M̲OVE OVER BURLINGTON LIAR'S CLUB

Why the Kentuckian is such a great hand at spinning tall
tales perhaps is summarized succinctly in a statement
made by John Bratcher, Louisville resident from Edmonson
County, who professes great concern for truth in all
matters always.

"Being a Bratcher, I'm naturally concerned about true
facts," he says. "Why, I'll tell the truth four or five
different ways before lying about it!"

Because J. Ed McConnell, a respected businessman and a
former president of the Louisville Chamber of Commerce,
is noted for devotion to fact, and because the leading
character in some of the stories he tells was named
Truthful, only a hardened skeptic would doubt him.

Truthful's last name was Dawkins. He was a barnyard
biologist and keen student of nature, and lived at Forks
of Elkhorn, McConnell's former home base, in Franklin
County. Having grown up hearing so much about him, it
was only natural that McConnell should become
Truthful's biographer.

Anyway, once upon a time, one story goes, Truthful
was crossing a swinging bridge over Elkhorn Creek when
he saw a 5-pound bass about to be consumed by a snake
at least 8 feet long and as big around as a milk bottle.
Truthful killed the snake, thus saving the fish. Since he
was going fishing, he fed some of his bait to the fish, a
process he repeated each time he crossed the bridge in the
next several days.

Eventually the fish began to wait under the bridge for the daily handout from Truthful, and a lasting friendship began. Once during the feeding, the fish flopped out of the water. Thereafter, when Truthful showed up, the fish would come clamoring out of the water onto the bank and remain for progressively longer intervals. In time, the fish even began playing with Truthful's dog.

Then came the day when, as Truthful started walking away after snack time, the fish tried to follow him, flopping around on its tail and front fins. The fish actually followed at his heels all the way home. There Truthful fixed a tub of water for it to lounge in, and the thing became a real pet. In subsequent weeks, it began eating with his dogs and learned to growl like the mutts.

Many neighbors came to see "Fish," the imaginative name bestowed upon the new pet. One man who often "saw things" took the sobriety pledge for life after witnessing Fish eating with the dogs.

In time Fish followed Truthful everywhere, and that led to tragedy. One day as they were crossing the slatted swinging bridge over Elkhorn Creek, Fish slipped between two of the slats, fell into the water and drowned!

Some of the wildest tall tales told in Kentucky involve hoop snakes, a sort of legendary serpent that supposedly puts its deadly-poisonous tail in its mouth and rolls like a hoop in pursuit of its prey.

The Mammoth Cave region is working alive with hoop snake tales. One story is about a hoop snake that supposedly attacked a boy who was hoeing tobacco.

Busy at his job, the boy looked up just in time to see the snake rolling down upon him over the plowed ground. He dodged barely in time but the snake's deadly stinger hit the hoe handle. Immediately the handle began to swell until it burst, throwing a shower of splinters in all directions.

As proof of his near miss, the boy picked up the splinters and, as an old man, still showed them to skeptics.

Paul Camplin, a retired Navy submariner who now lives in Frankfort, once was witness to a submarine that actually ran into a car. Honest. That variation of the old man-bites-dog theme happened shortly before Camplin retired from the Navy and while the submarine on which he was serving was operating out of New London, Connecticut.

One day in returning to port, the sub overshot the landing and rammed into the sea wall at the rear of the piers. The long bow of the craft skidded across the wall and came to rest squarely on top of a car parked near the landing area.

The car came out a decided second best in the encounter. After some time, the owner appeared and asked all witnesses, including crew members, to sign a statement, giving full details of the accident.

"I hate to trouble you," he apologized, "but, after all, what insurance company would possibly believe me if I didn't have a lot of witnesses when I report this car was hit and run over by a submarine?"

A true Kentucky tall tale-teller always has at least one delayed-ending story that's intended solely for the wide-eyed suckers who will bite on anything. And being a fable spinner in the best Kentucky tradition, Charles Aaron, a Russell Springs fisherman-oil distributor-world traveler, has several.

"This was the coldest winter anybody could remember," one of his best stories begins, "and coons were scarce in this part of the country. One day an uncle of mine, who was a great coon hunter, was walking down by the Cumberland River, which was frozen over solid, when he saw a coon track. He followed the track to a hollow tree that literally was packed with coons.

"The tree was too big to chop down, but my uncle had a brainstorm, or at least a pretty good blow. He ran to the house and came back with a bucket of water and a sack of shelled corn. He scattered the corn on the ice of the river around the tree and then covered it with water.

"Next morning he came back and found 99 coons frozen to the ice. They'd come out of the tree after the corn and the water had frozen their feet to the ice."

"Why," some sucker always would bite when he told the story, "don't you just make it an even 100 coons your uncle trapped that way?"

"Do you think," Aaron would retaliate, "that any uncle of mine would tell a lie for one measly little coon?"

Ralph Day of Louisville tells about the pro at a small town golf club who had been relieving members regularly of their cash in matches. However, one day he was stopped on the street by a country bumpkin in bib overalls and yellow shoes who reckoned he'd like to take him on in a match.

"I only play for money," the pro sneered.

When the country boy produced a big wad of high-denomination bills, the sneering turned to open drooling, and a $10-per-hole match was arranged.

Next morning the patsy appeared on the first tee with four rusty clubs and a couple of beat-up balls.

"All I ask," he said, "is that you give me three look-outs for the 18 holes."

Thinking that meant three strokes, the pro agreed greedily and prepared to take his first swing. At the top of his backswing, the bumpkin punched him smartly in the seat of the pants with his putter and yelled "Look out!" The startled pro's ball trickled off the tee perhaps 50 feet.

When the two were coming up the course on 18, a group of club members went out to see how much the pro had won. They found him ashen in color and shaking like a leaf. When they learned he had lost every hole on the round, they wanted to know why.

"Well," he replied in a trembling voice, "did you ever play 18 holes of golf with a guy who had two 'Look-outs!' left?"

J. M. "Blick" Smith, a hunter, fisherman, and tall tale-teller of great renown who lives in Franklin, tells about an ingenious raccoon hunting team that Fred Nunn, a ditto who lives in Edmonton, once put together.

It seems Nunn trained a monkey to work with his best coon hound. When the hound treed, it wasn't necessary for Nunn to shinny up the tree or try to shake out the quarry since he taught the monkey to climb into the branches of the tree with a small caliber pistol and shoot the coon.

The fame of his monkey soon spread beyond the limited environs of Edmonton, and before long Nunn was besieged with attractive offers for the little beast. Finally, he could resist no longer and he sold the monkey and pistol to a persistent bidder.

A few nights later, the new owner took the monkey into the woods with his best dog. Soon the hound treed and up into the branches, pistol in hand, went the monk. After searching for several minutes, and finding no game, he came down and, lo and behold, shot the dog.

The unnerved man rushed back to Nunn to tell him what had happened.

"Oh, yes, there was one thing I forgot to tell you," Nunn explained logically. "That monkey hates a liar!"

Somebody, it seems, always is making slurring remarks that reflect directly upon the honesty of fishermen and the size of catches they report. Like the scoffer who once said that if the fish they land really were as big as in the stories told about them, sardines would have to be sold in garbage cans.

Which in nowise is intended to reflect upon a story told by Carl Wolfe, a fisherman of repute in Edmonson County. For since his tale is substantiated by Charles E. Whittle, Sr., and Thomas J. Moody, two other fishermen with illustrious records for truthfulness, there's no reason to doubt it's absolute authenticity.

Wolfe fishes a lot at Nolin Reservoir, specializing in catching big yellow catfish. Four or five summers ago when he went to check on some nets he'd put out, he came running back to his cabin to get a gig.

Seems an old junked auto had been dumped into the lake and was half submerged near the shore. Through an open window of the car, Wolfe could see a 50 or 60 pound yellow cat wallowing around inside. All he needed to land the prize was a gig.

But he came back empty handed.

"While I was getting my gig," he explained, "that son-of-a-gun rolled up all the windows and latched the door.

"He must have guessed what I was up to," he added reflectively. "Them big yellow cats are smart as hell!"

And why shouldn't they be smart? After all, everyone has heard of schools of fish.

When he was a boy in Central City, reports John Harrelson of Louisville, "Dad" Hunt of nearby Graham was one of the premier storytellers of the area. One day, Harrelson recalls, he got all wrapped up in a big tale about having seen two blacksnakes engaged in mortal combat as each tried to swallow the other whole.

"Finally," he ended the narrative, "neither one of them was there!"

I have previously mentioned in this chapter Fred Nunn and J. M. "Blick" Smith, two tall tale-tellers who more or less work as a team since they spin truth-stretching stories involving each other. As, for instance, the mind-expanding story Nunn tells in which Smith is the central figure.

One day, he vows piously, he was squirrel hunting in Simpson County when he met Smith on a back country road. He was carrying five squirrels but no gun.

"I didn't use a gun," Smith is reputed to have answered in reply to the obvious question. "I killed these squirrels with rocks."

When Nunn appeared skeptical and professed not to believe a word of it, Smith, somewhat crushed that his old hunting friend should doubt his solemn word, offered to give a demonstration. They retired to a nearby patch of woods and waited until a squirrel frisked out on a limb. Then Smith took a golfball-sized rock from his pocket with his left hand and brought it down with a perfect throw.

"I didn't know you were left-handed," Nunn marvelled.

"I'm not," the modest Mr. Smith replied, "it's just that I tear 'em up too bad when I throw with my right hand!"

Some years back I loosed a series of horticultural wonder tales by having quoted Arthur Cary, Louisville, as knowing a friend who once raised a watermelon so big it took two men to thump it.

In the backwash from that tale, Dr. B. W. Kelly, another Louisvillian and long a melon grower of considerable repute, reported that he would not have any of his monster-sized beauties that particular year.

"I planted the seed in ground that was too rich," he said sadly, "and the vines grew so fast the melons were worn out from being dragged around!"

George Brown, Prestonsburg, is a fox hunter and how he views his sport and those who practice it is pointed up in the fact he was one of the jurors who pooled resources and paid the fine of the first man ever found guilty in Floyd County of fox hunting without a license. Being such an ardent fox chaser, it stands to reason that Brown has his own supply of topper tales involving great chases he's been on and talented dogs he has hunted with.

The most durable and best dog he remembers was "Old Blue," a famous hound that belonged to a friend in adjacent Johnson County. While Old Blue was as fleet as the wind and could run for hours without tiring, he had one slight hangup. He plain hated railroad trains and it was his habit to stand in the middle of the tracks and bark defiance at oncoming locomotives until leaping aside to safety at the last split second.

Unfortunately, one day Old Blue miscalculated a locomotive and it clipped off his right front leg. The owner immediately applied splints and potions and in no time the dog was back on the chase, running on three legs.

Later the owner decided to whittle a wooden leg for Old Blue. The first time out on his new peg, he outran all the other dogs in a big hunt by a full half mile. And, as if not satisfied with that feat, the very next day Old Blue raced the high-balling Jenny's Creek train through Hager Hill Gap and bested the hated engine by at least three country blocks!

In these crowded-sky days, when just taking off from some airports takes more time than flying to one's destination at faster-than-sound speed, it's difficult for those under the age of 30 to appreciate how air travel has changed in a relatively few years. Yet it wasn't too long ago when even propeller-driven biplanes (or "aeroplanes," as some called them) were so downright uncommon in rural areas that the landing of one of the craft was enough to empty a Kentucky county seat town as the curious flocked to see the strange object.

Coleman Smock, who grew up in Marion County, recalls the arrival of a plane in Lebanon at about the time of World War I. The craft made several slow circles over the town and a throng had gathered at the nearest cow pasture when it came down for a bumpy landing. After a few minutes, the pilot climbed back into the open cockpit, adjusted his goggles and took off while the spectators watched in open-mouth amazement.

"What do you think of that?" someone asked an old man whose eyes were about the size of dinner plates.

"That," he replied, pure awe dripping from his voice, "is the biggest lie ever I saw in my life!"

A lazy man's way of harvesting fish is to use dynamite. The method is both simple and illegal: A stick of dynamite is lit and thrown into the stream and the concussion of the resulting underwater explosion stuns the fish and causes them to rise to the surface where the poacher is able to gather as many as he wants without bothering to dig even one worm.

John Sandlin, an old-time resident of Oneida, Clay County, used to tell about a persistent dynamiter who plagued the South Fork of the Kentucky River country. Since he was known to all the local game and fish wardens on sight, the man never had been caught.

Finally, authorities imported a warden from another section of the state and put him on the trail of the law breaker. In due time, the officer called on the suspected dynamiter on the pretense of wanting to buy a big mess of fresh fish.

"Only way to get 'em this time of year," the warden was told, "is to dynamite for 'em."

Off to the river and out into the middle of a wide, deep hole they went in a small john-boat. There the man pulled a big stick of dynamite from his pocket, lit the fuse, let it burn a few seconds, and then suddenly thrust it into the hand of the undercover agent.

"What am I supposed to do with this?" the startled and nervous warden asked.

"Well," the poacher replied reasonably, "you can hold it or throw it out there in the river, just as you see fit."

Needless to say, he saw fit to heave the dynamite as far out into the stream as possible. There was a mighty explosion, a geyser of water erupted high into the air and stunned fish rose immediately to the surface.

"Now if I was you," the man said to the still-shaking warden in a confidential tone as he set about picking up fish, "I wouldn't tell nobody what I'd done — it's ag'in the law, you know!"

Wallace Thompson, a Metcalfe County hunter-farmer, used to tell a great tale about a man he knew who owned an especially talented coon hound.

"You just never heard of a dog being so smart," Thompson vowed. "This man would take a piece of wood and whittle it to the size of the coon hide he wanted to stretch over it, show it to the dog and he'd hunt until he found one that exact size.

"But one night the man's wife left her ironing board on the back porch. The dog saw it and took off to the woods, and never was seen again.

"The owner finally figured out what had happened," Thompson concluded. "His guess was that the hound just clean run himself out of the country looking for a coon with a hide the size of that ironing board!"

In addition to having a deep sense of humor and an awesome memory, Charles E. Whittle, Sr., previously mentioned, is a teller of sometimes believable sometimes unbelievable tales in the best Kentucky tradition. One of his latter-category tales concerns a lying contest once held in the general store at Bee Springs in Edmonson County.

A group of men were gathered around the pot-bellied stove in the store one winter day and the proprietor offered a pint of whisky to the man who could tell the wildest tale. The fibbing began and finally all except two men, Pete Sanders and Tom Saling, had been heard from.

"You know," said Sanders, a big, rawboned fellow, "the other day I was over on Nolin River opposite Dismal Rock when I saw something you just won't believe. Up on the top of the rock I could barely see the figure of a man. As I watched, he ran up to the edge and jumped off the top of that 300-foot-high rock. He jumped clean across the river, lit on the other side and kept right on running."

Everybody was about to award the prize to Sanders until Saling, a small man, took undisputed possession of the whisky.

"I hadn't meant to say anything about it because I thought nobody would believe me," he said slowly, "but now that I've got a witness, I might as well own up to it — that was me who jumped off that rock!"

Dr. D. K. Wilgus, who did extensive research in folklore at Western Kentucky University in the early 1960's, once heard of an exceptionally intelligent hunting dog, one that could have rated no lower than Phi Beta Kappa in the canine world, named "Razzie" down in Union County.

Among other talents, his proud owner boasted, Razzie would hunt only what he was told to seek out, completely ignoring all other critters. If squirrels were announced as the quarry for the day, Razzie wouldn't so much as sniff his super-sensitive nostrils at the most tempting raccoon, rabbit, or quail.

One morning, the owner went on, he decided to play a trick on old Razzie. He gathered up his fishing equipment and whistled for the dog.

"Razzie," he announced, "we're going fishing today."

Quick as a flash, Razzie disappeared. When he didn't return after several minutes, the owner went looking for him.

"You won't believe this," the owner said, summarizing the situation correctly, "but I finally found Razzie in a damp spot behind the barn, digging up fishing worms and putting them in a can!"

Speaking of smart dogs, as was just the case, in Hopkinsville they tell about a fellow who was bubbling and singing like a happy tea kettle over the raw intellect of his favorite dog. To point up the beast's amazing IQ, he told about the night his home caught on fire.

Everything was confusion, he said. He was able to bundle up his wife and children and get them out of the flaming building.

"At about the time the place was ready to cave in," he vowed, "that dog dashed back into the house and returned, scorched and seared, a few minutes later with — what do you think between his jaws?"

"I give up," someone who was listening surrendered.

"With," the proud owner said, "our fire insurance policy wrapped up in a damp towel!"

Get a genuine Kentucky crossroads storyteller wound up and he'll try to convince you water runs uphill or night is day in disguise if it contributes to a more imaginative tale. Moreover, while his story may defy everything from logic to the law of gravity, this particular breed of narrator will defend to the death its absolute authenticity.

Paul Sparks, an assistant superintendent in the Louisville school system, recalls a story from his boyhood days in Lawrence County that proves the point.

A big bunch of men were sitting around the general store at Blaine one day, each in succession topping the yarns that had been told previously.

"Did I ever tell you all about a beaver chase I had once?" one man said when he finally got the floor. "There just never was such a chase. My dogs picked up this beaver at the creek and chased him until he run up a holler that had steep rock cliffs on three sides.

"With them rock cliffs on the sides and in front and my dogs right on his heels," the man continued, becoming more expansive all the while, "that old beaver seen he was in a lot of trouble. So he climbed up a beech tree and got away."

"Hold on," another of the men interrupted, "beavers can't climb trees."

"I doggie," the teller rebutted, "this one had to!"

Years ago during a slack farm-work season a dozen or so men were huddled close to the potbellied stove in a backroads store in Adair County. Eventually they began regaling each other with truth-stretching stories.

"A year ago last fall," one of the loafers began, "I decided to plant me some turnips and the only ground I had was an acre lot. I sowed it but only one turnip came up and it right in the middle of the patch."

"Well," he went on, "I want you to know that one turnip grew bigger and bigger until finally it pushed down the fences clean around that patch."

"Some turnip, all right," another man agreed, "and it reminds me of a kettle I helped make when I was working for an iron company in Ohio. That kettle was so big you

190

could tap it on one side and it would take an hour for the sound to return to the beginning."

"What did they need such a big kettle for?" the first man asked.

"Why," came the answer, "to cook that turnip of yours in, of course!"

Having teed-off with a Truthful Dawkins tale, what better way to finish this chapter than with another story involving that paragon of fact and reality as recorded by his personal Boswell, J. Ed McConnell?

Some years ago, it seems, Truthful rented some fertile farm land that lay inside a tight bend of Elkhorn Creek not far from the Kentucky River. He planted the field in corn, but when it had come up he noticed that several rows just above the bend in the creek were being knocked down every night.

Investigation uncovered facts too bizarre to have been believable if told by anyone except Truthful: big fish from the river were chasing smaller 10 to 15 pounders up the creek. In trying to get away, the small fish were going so fast they weren't allowing for the curve in the creek and they were sliding out into the field. The corn was knocked down when they flopped around getting back into the water.

Well, Truthful decided to catch one of the big fish that were terrorizing the smaller ones. He borrowed a 100-foot roll of steel cable, made an anchor-sized iron hook and baited it with a live groundhog and cast it out into the creek.

The bait was struck just at the bottom of the curve. Truthful quickly tied the cable to a team of mules he had standing nearby and started them pulling in the opposite direction. Gradually the cable began to move, then it suddenly went slack. Truthful looked back and there was no fish but, believe it or not, the creek was as straight as an arrow.

The fish had thrown the big iron hook; it had caught in the bank and the hard-working mules had pulled the curve right out of the creek!

INTRODUCTION   *They say it's good mental therapy to speak up and bring things that gnaw at you into the open rather than letting them simmer on a low burner in the dark, back recesses of your mind. That being true, I'm sure that I might long ago have been fitted for a straitjacket — belted-back model, of course — if I had not had a column of type at my disposal as a vehicle for relieving myself from time to time of things that irritate or concern me.*

As the years roll by and I mark up five birthdays in every ten, I'm amazed at how college friends I see only infrequently have aged so much they no longer recognize me. At the same time, I grow more conscious of how badly mirrors lie to me.

I'm put out of sorts by guys who listen to my brand-new jokes and then upstage me with, "Now the way I heard that one . . ."; by restaurants where you sit for 30 minutes before getting a glass of water, always without ice; by $3 movies that never are as good this week as the previews promise next week's attraction will be; by parents who so dominate a conversation with nonstop stories about their kids' incredible accomplishments that I never have a chance to tell them about my own remarkable offspring.

And, although I'm probably the worst golfer since cow pasture pool was invented, I'm infuriated by fellow duffers who are so enraptured by the pros on TV that before every putt they fall face down to read the green, à la Jack Nicklaus.

Since I've always considered myself as Everyman Incarnate, the most average of average persons, perhaps you, too, have had your teeth rattled by many of the things that I have confessed to in type, some of which follow.

CHAPTER 10

WHAT BUGS ME . . .

Next only to dreaming of becoming the Tom Mix of Benton, the earliest and strongest of my boyhood ambitions was wanting to learn to whistle. While I eventually did develop an eardrum-shattering whistle that could crack wall plaster at 20 paces, I wasn't born that way; I had to develop it. In fact, I must have been the last in my gang to learn to whistle. All the other guys were making like overalls-wearing canaries at a time when I still was blowing silently. It was a moment of great personal triumph when the first tweet came out, and I was in hog heaven when I honed my budding talent to the point where I could whistle two notes simultaneously. Thereafter, I whistled constantly.

Which background is intended only as a means of emphasizing the fact that back then whistling was a natural thing with boys. And that brings me to a disquieting observation: I don't believe that is true any longer. Not since my own now-grown sons — whom I carefully trained to follow in my shrill but skilled footsteps — were small have I heard 9 or 10-year-old boys whistling as they walk along.

I whistled because I was happy, or at least didn't know I wasn't. I hope the current shortage of whistlers doesn't indicate a sudden inner somberness among the small fry. There's probably a simpler explanation for why I don't hear boys whistling any more. I doubt the kids can whistle today's totally forgettable tunes.

I'm so absent-minded that I often forget to remember the Alamo, not to mention the *Maine*. What is more, I instinctively feel in my pockets for overlooked letters every time I pass a mailbox.

All that is deplorable, I grant, but not as bad as my inability to remember names. Anyone who ever has come up with a complete blank when they have tried to introduce a person they really know quite well can testify how embarrassing that can be.

Because of this memory deficiency, I was interested to read the satin-smooth technique Franklin D. Roosevelt developed for handling the forgotten-name matter among the thousands of minor league politicians with whom he dealt. He would stop in the middle of a conversation, smile broadly and say, "I'm afraid I've forgotten your name."

If the person gave his last name, Mr. Roosevelt would shake his head and laugh, "No, no. I know your last name. It was your first name that slipped my mind."

Mr. Roosevelt was ready, too, if the politico gave his first name. "Of course," he'd say. "I know your first name perfectly well. It's your last name I seem to have forgotten."

Either way he succeeded in getting the person's name without embarrassment and, in the end, perhaps even turned a shortcoming into an advantage.

That's a fine system, to be sure, but I doubt it would work for me when I forget my wife's name.

There are mornings, especially Mondays, when I feel like the symptoms on a bottle of patent medicine and the world seems uphill in both directions.

On these occasions I imagine my innards are being eroded away by nondefinable ailments that would defy the diagnostic talents of Rex Morgan, M.D., and all the brothers Mayo.

One day I trapped a doctor friend (not a psychiatrist) in our front yard and subtly discussed the matter with him, and I came away greatly relieved for at least two

reasons. For one, he didn't charge me for an office call;
for another, he said I probably suffer only from an
overactive phobia of some sort.

That word "phobia" intrigued me and I retired to the
late Mr. Webster's best known invention for further
consultation. A phobia, to paraphrase what I found, is an
exaggerated fear having usually an illogical or symbolic
fear. I learned further that phobias come in assorted
shapes, one or more of which may fit you. Maybe there is
a phobia for your very own in this partial list now
available on the market:

Ochlophobia, fear of crowds; kenophobia, fear of large
empty spaces; triakaideaphobia, fear of the number 13;
gephyrophobia, fear of crossing bridges; dematophobia,
fear of being in a house; harpaxophobia, fear of robbers;
laliophobia, fear of speech; chionophobia, fear of being
snowbound, and so on.

Since I'm pretty much a scairdy-cat myself, only one
phobia seems all-inclusive enough for me — pantrophobia,
fear of everything.

The very early morning, that period of all the calm and
quiet and dew before even the roosters have found much
to crow about, is an inspiring time, to be sure. In fact,
at some time or other just about every poet or philosopher
has been moved to compose stirring lines of praise to the
coming of the dawn.

"Sweet is the breath of morn; her rising sweet with
charms of earliest birds," the poet Milton once wrote.

"The morning steals upon the night, melting the
darkness," Shakespeare extolled.

"The breezy call of incense-breathing morn," Thomas
Gray described it.

"The morning hour," the ever-practical Benjamin
Franklin figured, "has gold in its mouth."

Of course, not all those who have risen by the dawn's
early light have found beauty, inspiration, or poetry in the
experience. Some sleepwalkers have been driven to
downright salty comments.

The most pointed summation of early rising I ever heard

was a reverse-English tribute made by the late Earl Wallace, commissioner of the Kentucky Department of Fish and Wildlife, after arising at 3 a.m.

"Getting up this early," he said, "isn't so bad after you get over the first mad!"

During my rare moments of deep meditation, I can't help wondering how archaeologists might catalogue American women of our time if, in sifting through the ashes of our civilization several centuries from now, they unearthed a capsule containing samples of present-day TV commercials.

Would the intellects of that future day scan the commercials and assume the women of our long-ago era were a sad lot indeed? Or would they be charitable and conclude that no human creature possessed of a brain could possibly have been so inane and addle-pated?

Before rising up in righteous indignation and branding me a male chauvinist pig, I hope the women will review in their minds some of the commercials they see every time the boob tube is on.

There's the woman who lapses into a rapture of ecstacy when she opens a box of detergent and finds a towel inside; the bevy of giggling matrons who gather around a supermarket display to squeeze the bathroom tissue; the weepy bride kind Mrs. Olson saves from divorce court by showing her how to make a decent cup of coffee.

Then there's the woman who seems apt to break out in hives from worrying over what's a mother to do when her family won't take time to eat a fieldhand-sized breakfast, the dancing teacher who may be forced into early retirement because of dandruff that makes it appear she's been in a snowstorm when she wears black leotards, the housewife who lapses into a tizzy of joy when a white tornado cleans her dingy kitchen floor, the pretty young chick who scrubs her teeth with a certain toothpaste and then goes around tattooing the cheek of every man in sight with the lipstick imprint of kisses she blows at them.

There are dozens of other examples, all of which explain why, based on what they could learn of our

196

womenfolk from the TV commercials, the civilization
that follows ours just might try to disclaim any kin.

What ever happened to good old names and addresses?

What happened to good old names and addresses is
they've been swallowed up by computers that are more at
ease with numbers than names. We've lost our need for
personal names and increasingly are being identified by a
mass of impersonal numbers.

A bit of numerical research I undertook points up that
while I may be Joe Cross Creason, Sr. to some, I'm much
better known as a combination of numbers to the
computers that seem to be in control of things today.

To the Social Security Administration, I'm No.
40120519; to the Veterans Administration, I'm 17044751;
to South Central Bell, I'm No. 8960498; to the Navy,
I'm No. 361332; to my employer, I'm No. 18860; to the
Kentucky Department of Public Safety, I'm Nos. K65632
and K65633; to the mortgage company, I'm No. 34864; to
the life insurance company, I'm No. 4242971; to the
sheriff, I'm No. 41129543; to the magazine which promises
great riches as a jackpot winner subscriber, I'm No.
131726769, and to the Library of Congress, I'm Card
Catalog No. 72-88786. Even to the laundry I'm a number
—No. 87F80. The one with the ring around the collars.

The other day a pithy, crossroads commentary of our
inflated times was attached to the menu in a restaurant
where I had lunch. It read: "In the old days, the man who
saved money was a miser; today, he's a wonder."

That set me to meditating upon money in general and
the fox-and-the-grapes attitude many of us take in regard
to the accumulation of coin of the realm in particular.
Because we have so little money ourselves, we try to
rationalize, like the fox when he couldn't reach the grapes,
that we really didn't much want it anyway.

As a result, we've retreated behind a bunch of tired shreds of rationale to cover up our inability to do more than make the money in the bank and the days in the month come out even.

For instance, if a man openly runs after money, we say smugly that he's money mad. If he accumulates and keeps it, we brand him a miser. If he spends it freely after getting it, we call him a playboy. If he never does get it, we call him a ne'er-do-well. If he doesn't try to get it, we make him out to be lazy. If he gets it without working, we sneer that he's a parasite.

And if he finally gets it after long years of hard work, we sigh and allow that he's a fool who really never got much out of life.

Kentucky is a state of small towns, and small towns usually are referred to by sophisticated city dwellers in terms only that are totally unflattering. A small town, say those from the land of concrete canyons, is Squaresville, U.S.A.; the kind of place, man, where the cats really go "meow", and where the only swingers are old women swaying to and fro on the front porch. A small town, they sneer, is Hick Heaven where only three things happen — morning, noon, and night; where everybody knows everybody else's business; where gossip is the leading civic pastime, and where a hot spot is a bench on the sunny side of the courthouse yard.

On the other hand, a small town has certain distinctions (actually virtues) that never are seen by the demeaners who pass through maybe once and then become instant, all-inclusive experts. For a small town also is a place where there are more trees than people; where city slickers go to get outsmarted; where you don't have to count your change; where birthdays are remembered and business is done on a first-name basis; where people go home to lunch; and where the barbershop is the only place you get clipped.

What is more, a small town is a place you leave in order to make enough money to return to live.

I'm an expert on small towns. I came from one.

If Sir Walter Raleigh, he of cloak-over-mudhole fame, could return to earth today he'd no doubt feel that in at least one respect times have changed little in the past three centuries. For he would find that smoking, his best known invention, and tobacco, which he introduced to English society after a visit to the New World, still are being attacked.

Ever since the surgeon general's report, critics of tobacco have been describing smoking as dangerous, loathsome, filthy and/or morals-destroying — almost the exact words that were being used to rap the use of the weed when Sir Walter was still around some 300 years ago.

In some ways, the mean things being said presently about tobacco actually sound like a sugary commercial compared to the attacks that were delivered in Sir Walter's day. There was, for example, the written assault let loose in 1604 by King James I of England in what he titled "A Counter Blaste to Tobacco." About the best thing he could say was that "the unsavorie, filthie, stinking smoake is a vile custome." James' warning to smokers continued: "Have you no reason to bee ashamed and to forebeare this filthie noveltie, so basely grounded . . . a custome loathsome to the eye, hateful to the Nose, harmeful to the Braine, dangerous to the Lungs and the black stinking fume thereof nearest resembling the horrible Stigian smoake of the pit that is bottomless."

There may be some consolation to the present-day producers of Kentucky's primary farm crop in what James did after that. Within a year he'd given up his attacks on smoking as useless, imposed a levy of six shillings and sixpence on every pound of the weed, and reconciled himself to the "filthie custome of tobacco" by dipping deep into the suddenly-bulging tax coffers.

This is the age of the surtax, the devious method of adding an additional bite to levies already in effect that politicians who have been elected on the promise of no new taxes use to solve their eternal need for more money. Thus, in a very loose sense, their "no new taxes" pledge is kept; old taxes simply are given more wallop.

Which is mentioned here only by way of introducing a revolutionary plan I have in mind. I propose to use the surtax concept as a vehicle to turn our present arrangement of work and retirement inside out and literally reverse the order in which they come.

As it is now a guy works hard for years to lay aside enough to retire in comfort when he hits the Social Security plateau — at which time he's too pooped to enjoy the fruits of his labor.

Think what a Utopia it would be if we reversed that arrangement. I propose that a man start out by retiring at age 20 and that he pass the next 20 years puttering around the house, playing golf, fishing, and doing the other things Americans have come to regard as the good-life-in-retirement while he's young enough to enjoy them. Then after age 40, he'd spend the remainder of his alloted years and pay for his already-used retirement with a surtax based on income.

There would be a few details to be worked out, but I don't like to clutter up my mind with piddling particulars.

Once upon a time, in the long ago before we had Ann Landers and Dear Abby to help us with our self-improvement, New Year's Day was a time for the making of solemn, character-stabilizing resolutions. Since I'm so old-fashioned I think of Nehru as a statesman and not a designer of mod jackets, I still go the New Year's Day Resolution Route.

Honesty compels me to admit that I don't exactly have a perfect track record for keeping resolutions. Most have been broken outright, others badly sprained. A few, however, have been kept. It was on a New Year's Day, for instance, that I vowed never again to wrestle alligators and, from that day to this, I haven't. On another first of the year I resolved to give up spare-time testing of gasoline tanks by dropping lighted matches inside them. That took a lot of excitement out of my life, but man does not live by bangs alone.

At the present time I'm working on a resolution to be more tolerant, especially as it relates to those who may see fit to disagree with me. Although in the past I've been known to lapse into a combination temper tantrum and blue funk when a suggestion or idea I proposed was questioned, from now on I'm going to be one changed fellow. In fact, I'm going to be so tolerant of those who disagree with me that it will be sickening. After all, they do have a right to their ridiculous opinions.

I'm not out to knock miracles of these latter days — moon walkers, air-conditioning, never-fail-deodorants, etc. — but I wonder if children's literature doesn't prove we're actually newcomers when it comes to progressive accomplishments.

For instance, long before our astronauts had ever circled the moon, Mother Goose, that ancient and respected chronicler of childhood miracles, had recorded the feat of a talented cow that jumped all the way over the satellite.

We tend to think the war on poverty is new in our times, but actually it was started in the days of Mrs. Goose when the depleted cupboard of poor Old Mother Hubbard was restocked. A slum clearance and low-income housing program that far predated modern efforts dates back to that same time and was started to aid the Old Woman who lived in that shoe with all her children.

Mother Goose even wrote about a form of Medicare when she told of the valiant emergency attempt to put Humpty Dumpty back together again and to administer to the wounds suffered by Jack and Jill. She also traced the origin of the Animal Rescue League back to Little Tommy Stout, the kindly lad who pulled pussy cat out of the well.

The ancient rhymer also recorded other "firsts" some may think are of modern origin. Tom, the piper's son who stole a pig, the first juvenile delinquent; Little Tommy Tucker, who sang for his supper, the first child pro entertainer; Simple Simon, who, among a host of stupid

things, tried to carry water in a sieve, the first
kindergarten dropout.

In view of how our feats stack up against those
recorded by Mother Goose, it's enough to make a Little
Boy Blue.

This is an age of prepackaged, quick-draw conversation,
an era when all of us tend to resort at times to almost
patented words, phrases, and sentences in communicating
with each other in various situations.

The trouble is, often what we say is totally inane, and,
while perhaps relatively harmless, even *we* don't
necessarily believe a word of it.

Among others, here are a few samples of everyday
dialogue that should be taken with a king-sized grain
of salt:

"Gee, you're looking great!"

"Your sandwich will be ready in just a minute more."

"I haven't got a thing to wear."

"But the light was green when I started across, officer!"

"I used to walk five miles each way to school."

"If elected, I promise economy and efficiency in
government."

"When I was your age, I worked for every penny I had."

"I don't have a prejudiced bone in my body."

"But I couldn't have been going 85, officer!"

"Pay for it in 24, easy, low-interest installments."

"We didn't do things like that when I was a boy."

"You haven't changed a bit since I saw you last, 25
years ago!"

Conversation like that may fill a basic need to
communicate, but don't you believe it.

From the unbelievable number (and variety) of books
that spew off the presses, you'd have to conclude that
about all those who ever have said they have half a mind
to write a book really have done so, including me.

202

It likewise is unbelievable the number of books would-be authors have in mind that they're soliciting help in writing. In one month I was asked to contribute (for free) a chapter in books planned about odd place names, political humor, fishing and/or hunting incidents and, of all things, embarrassing moments. I've resisted the tempting offer to secure eternal fame via an agate credit line in the preface of those proposed books, but the one on embarrassing moments did recall a classic.

It concerns a lady who was on a strict diet and who went into a Louisville cafeteria, picked up the half grapefruit alloted her for lunch, and took a seat. Since the place was crowded, a man whose tray was loaded with soup, beef, potatoes, and three luscious blueberry muffins asked if he might share her table. It was all right.

As fate would have it, the lady had a passion for blueberry muffins and she drooled openly as the man wolfed down two of the three. After cleaning his dish, he left the table, leaving one muffin untouched. The lady stared at the muffin and the longer she stared the more irresistible it became until she no longer could resist the temptation. Impulsively she snatched up the muffin and took a big bite. No sooner was her mouth full of heavenly blueberry muffin than she looked up. There to her dismay stood the man, a pat of butter in his hand and a hopeless look on his face!

Every day when I get mired in the 5 p.m. bumper-to-bumper (and sometimes bumper-over-bumper) traffic, I wonder what comedian it was who dubbed that the "rush hour." For, what with everybody moving along like so many rheumatic snails, a rush hour it ain't.

However, that and similar traumatic peak traffic-load times makes it abundantly clear that talk of the two-car family no longer is idle conversation — it's a reality.

But that's just the beginning, folks. Since it has been stated that in the U.S. a baby is born every 12 seconds and a new car every five seconds, you can see that the machines rapidly are outnumbering the people. It won't be long before the manufacturers will have to start peddling the idea of two-car individuals instead of families.

This rapid breeding of automobiles points up the urgency of finding ways of disposing of them once they've outlived their life expectancy and have been stripped of all transplantable parts and the carcasses have been left to rust in peace. There are 20,000 junked cars abandoned on streets and in vacant lots in Louisville alone. That's a lot of junk and it will keep growing as production records for new models continue to be broken.

The point, if any, to this essay is that if you plan to cross the street, you'd better do it now.

To underscore our positive passion for littering, some learned person once observed that man is the only animal that will intentionally foul its own nest. We've done this for centuries to our own little planet, but now we've improved on that unenviable record by literally going out of this world to find new areas to litter.

Although we started visiting there a relatively short time ago, already we've turned the moon into a promising out-in-space junk yard. Left behind by our crops of explorers who have been there are remains of several TV cameras, bits and pieces of lunar modules, equipment that didn't function properly, and, most appropriately, two junked cars. I think it's only right that we left on the moon the lunar mobiles two teams of explorers used in getting around. For if one thing stands as absolute proof that Americans have been in any vicinity, it's junked cars. True enough, the moon cars might be overpriced models, but they had the same dented, flapping fenders and malfunctioning features as their counterparts which so colorfully decorate the countryside here on earth.

Thus, before we have any evidence of life on the moon, we've already littered up the place.

While the scientists seem convinced the moon can't sustain life, wouldn't it shake them if some future lunar explorer should stumble up on those two moon buggies and find they had been stripped of hub caps, tires, wheels, batteries, and other accessories just like cars back home?

Well, another April 15th passes and the trauma of income-tax settling up is over for another year.

All of which seems a good time for some pertinent, if perhaps ironic, comments concerning taxes in general in America, the land of opportunity where anybody can grow up to be a taxpayer.

It used to be said that only two things are certain — death and taxes. The way the Kentucky Legislature has been upping every levy known to man and beast in the past few years, there's one thing that can be said about death: it doesn't get worse every time the legislature meets.

As for the federal bite into income, it makes the etymology of the word "tax" easy to understand. It comes from the Latin "taxare," meaning "to touch sharply," and surely no one disputes that, a fact made more ironic when you recall that this country was founded partially to avoid taxes. If Patrick Henry nearly 200 years ago thought that taxation without representation was so terrible, I wonder what he'd think if he could see how it is today with representation.

But, after thinking it over and over, I can only conclude that the Internal Revenue Service, like God, must love poor people. After all, it makes so many of them every April 15th!

Perhaps the most meaningful thing I have ever done in all my life was to found a world-girdling society whose membership is restricted to only those of us whose first name is Joe and nothing more.

The society came about in this way:

Knowing, as I did in full measure, that for too long us Joes had been looked down upon and referred to as Josiah, Josephus, Joel, and especially Joseph because of a first name too simple to believe, I felt that it was time for the Joes of the world to unite.

Therefore, I announced formation of the most exclusive organization known to mortal man: Joes Only and Exclusively Society, or JOES.

The preamble which appears on JOES membership cards explains the purpose and exclusive nature of the society: "To all who shall come in envy to do honor, GREETINGS: Know ye that the bearer, having proved his full and sufficient first name to be JOE and nothing more, is entitled to the rights and privileges thereunto befitting one possessed of a name so simple and to be distinctive."

The society motto — "United we stand as Joes, divided we fall as Josephs" — is at one corner of the membership cards and my signature, as self-proclaimed king, is at the bottom.

Some may have wondered about my summarily taking over as JOES head. Although I did found the thing, it was not my intention to use that fact as a lever to seize power. I believe in democracy and at the outset I announced that members will have a chance to vote for another king if they wish. Just as soon as I can figure out a way to hold a South Vietnam-style election they can vote, that is.

Wallet-sized membership cards in JOES, printed on genuine paper, still are available, and all Joes who are not in the fold and who may wander this far into this book are invited to join. Just send me a self-addressed, stamped envelope and you'll get official proof that you belong to a society in which every Tom, Dick, and Harry really is named Joe.

Two or three times each month I take pen in hand and go through the agony of trying to make all the bills and the money in the bank come out even. Only on rare occasions do I succeed.

In view of the trauma involved in signing away one's treasure so often, I wish businesses would take into consideration the mental wear and tear on customers and make the statements they send out more humane. This being a credit card age, everything is tailored to be fed into a computer and there digested and balanced. That's the rub.

For instance, there are the statements that come in two halves which look identical except for a notation in the corner of one reading "Return this portion with check." Since this note obviously is written by the same man who engraves the Lord's Prayer on the head of pins, it takes one with eagle eyes — or a magnifying glass — to determine which half to return and which to keep.

Equally infuriating is trying to get along with the envelopes provided by some businesses that are too small to accommodate your check or the part of the bill you must send back without folding.

I've been known to fly into a nervous funk when confronted with return envelopes that demand name, address, and charge account number be recorded in the upper left corner. That charge number really bugs me because it's usually eight or ten digits that are impossible to sort from the mass of other numbers on the statement. I also detest return envelopes with a series of false flaps, bearing advertising, that must be torn away before getting down to the foul-tasting glue that seals the letter.

Most of all, however, there's the envelope that is blank on the front. It has a narrow slot into which the name and address of the firm on the return half of the statement must be carefully fitted. This fitting must be exact or nothing will show and the envelope may float around in postal limbo for days while service charges mount.

The alternative, I suppose, is cash, the poor man's credit card.

I long have been an open-mouthed admirer of Aesop, Ben Franklin, and others who invented all those proverbs, maxims, and good-old-horse-sense sayings folks are forever quoting to underscore assorted profound truths.

As a matter of fact, I was running around quoting "God helps those who help themselves," "Little strokes fell mighty oaks," and such from Franklin's *Poor Richard's Almanac* long before I learned to say my own name. And I wasn't a day over 14 at the time.

But much as I appreciate Franklin's sermonettes, I think they, as well as the sayings of the other great minds, should be modernized a bit for today's traffic, this being a different age indeed from times in which they wheeled and dealed.

For instance, I agree with the simple truth in old Ben's proverb "Remember that time is money," but to make it more relevant now perhaps this postscript should be added: "But try paying the milkman with a handful of minutes."

Other familiar old sayings that might be similarly updated include:

"There's no fool like an old fool; you just can't beat experience."

"Where there's a will there's a relative."

"If ignorance is bliss, why aren't there more happy people?"

"Money won't buy happiness; it won't buy poverty, either."

"A bird in the hand is worth two in the bush; a bird in the hand also is bad manners."

"People who get down to brass tacks rise rapidly."

"Early to bed, early to rise — until you get enough money to do otherwise."

"Oh, what is so rare as a day in May, except maybe an uncooked steak."

"Sticks and stones may break my bones, but words will never harm me; however, my defamation of character suit may."

"One swallow does not a summer make, but it sure ruins a New Year's resolution."

"No one is too old to learn, but some people keep putting it off."

"Birds of a feather flock together; how could they flock apart?"

"If thine enemy wrongs thee, buy his child a drum."

Fortunately, I'm not often given to making such changes in the accepted order of things, even sayings.

Among the most durable recollections of my boyhood in western Kentucky are the two or three Sundays each year we used to go to the farm of one of my mother's uncles for an old-fashioned family visit and country dinner. Counting all the uncles, aunts, children, in-laws, and stragglers I never could identify, these get-togethers would attract upwards of 50 people.

The serving of the dinner — and in that part of the country, dinner was the noon meal — was a ritualistic affair that started with someone offering a quick "Forwhatweareabouttoreceivemakeusthankful" blessing. Then the men would take a seat and be served by the women. They'd never heard of women's lib that far off the main road.

The children always had to eat at the second table. And you can imagine the choice morsels left after a swarm of robust men had had first crack at the vittles. It wasn't until I was old enough to graduate to the first table that I realized chickens in that part of Marshall County were constructed with anything but a neck, two wings, a scrawny back, and a gizzard.

But the thing I remember most from those dinners is watching my mother's uncles handle a knife and fork. To them, the fork was a secondary tool and the knife was the main implement. That is, they used the fork to sort of push food up on the blade of the knife and eat from it. There was poetry of motion and the balance of a tight rope walker or a juggler in the way they could eat something as elusive as green peas with a knife and not spill the food on their Sunday clothes.

I never mastered that art myself. But years later I heard a bit of doggerel verse that might explain the secret of their success:

> "I mix my peas with honey
> I've done it all my life
> It makes the peas taste funny
> But it keeps them on my knife."

There are certain inevitable "whens" that tell you the days are rolling by at a speed of 24 hours each and it's getting later than you think.

When everything appears to be farther away than it used to be.

When hills turn up in places you don't recall them being before and they seem twice as long going up as coming down.

When friends you knew from years ago have aged so much they don't recognize you.

When you marvel at how young college students are these days.

When you no longer can convince yourself that the strange gray cast your hair suddenly has taken is due entirely to the fact it bleaches easily in the sun.

When your idea of a good loser becomes a person who can diet successfully.

When all you want for your birthday is not to be reminded of it.

When the glass in the mirror you use for shaving begins to lie and the face staring back at you looks familiar but older than you remember.

When the circles under your eyes get so pronounced that associates can't tell whether you're wearing horn-rimmed glasses or not.

When friends refer to your western-style hair cut; that is, one with wide open spaces.

When the pretty girl who looks so familiar turns out to be her daughter.

These are a few of the "whens" that tell you that you are indeed getting older. Just you. I've already been through the "whens."

No two ways about it, this is a nation in which we, its citizens, are forever being surveyed about this, that, and the other thing: What TV show we're watching, what brand of toothpaste we prefer, what political candidates we favor, whether our deodorant has let us down lately, etc.

But I didn't realize how ridiculously low suveys had sunk until I read of a poll in California which revealed to a panting public that 31 percent of 1,552 housewives questioned said they "can almost always" count on the telephone ringing while they're in the bathtub.

Since I felt that, contrary to what met the untrained eye, there just had to be some significance, moral or otherwise, to the survey, I mulled it over for a couple of days. I read it backwards, turned the words inside out, even put them through my official Captain Midnight secret decoder ring.

Finally, I turned to that fount of all knowledge, the encyclopedia, hoping the answer might be buried somewhere in information regarding the bathtub and the telephone, respectively. And, sure enough, there I found a moral to the survey.

The bathtub, I discovered, was invented in 1850 and the telephone in 1875.

The moral? Well, if the housewives polled had been living in 1850 they could have soaked in their tubs for 25 years before the phone rang!

INTRODUCTION *It has been said that Kentucky represents America's last great repository of folklore, folkways and folk culture. Two reasons usually are cited to explain that reality: Kentucky's geographic location at more or less the nation's crossroads, and the steep, once-impenetrable mountains that cover the eastern quarter of the state.*

The latter reason is perhaps the most important. For it was in the mountains that the Scotch, Scotch-Irish, and English who appear more prominent on the Kentuckian's family tree settled because the land so reminded them of the Highland section of the British Isles where they or their ancestors had originated.

In the mountains, the settlers preserved the Old World superstitions, customs, stories, legends, myths, and way of life. And since the state was settled from east to west, in time those who located initially in the hills, or their children, moved into other sections and their background of folk culture was spread from the Big Sandy to the Mississippi.

Although Kentucky abounds in folk culture, it still would be difficult to define it in specific terms since it is nothing more, and nothing less, than the traditional knowledge and way of life Kentuckians have passed from one generation to the next.

Thus folk culture and folklore is the instinctive knowledge every little boy in Kentucky has that spitting on his bait before he drops it in the creek will attract fish; it is the home health practices seven generations have believed in; it is the good luck horseshoe that can be seen hanging over barns and sheds all across the state; it is the many Old World legends and fairy tales that have been given a local meaning.

Here, then, are random samples of Kentucky folk culture ranging from fairy tales to ghost stories and from superstitions to home health practices.

CHAPTER 11

THE WAYS OF FOLKWAYS

I have the strong feeling that if the American Medical Association ever held a full-scale investigation, upwards of half the people in Kentucky would be charged with practicing medicine without a license. For Kentuckians are great hands at do-it-yourself medicine and from one end of the state to the other great faith is put in home-style health practices that are deeply rooted in our folk culture.

I've heard it said in Leslie County that tea made by boiling a hornets' nest will cure asthma, while in Ballard County, 400 miles west, I've been told that the most severe nose bleed can be stopped by stepping backwards across a creek while you recite the first chapter of Ezekiel.

Some of the treatments — cornstarch for the heat, hot toddy for a cold — are reasonably logical, I suppose. But others — having a divorcée lay hands on an ailing person while she repeats her maiden name — are based on superstition only, it would seem.

But much of the strenth of home medicine is believing that it will work. For instance, an asafetida bag worn around the neck probably never kept disease from taking up residence within the body of the wearer. But who's to say the evil-smelling gum didn't keep germ carriers at a safe distance and thereby protected the practitioner?

And who's to doubt nine whiffs of a pair of dirty socks won't clear up a head cold as fast as the most powerful patented inhaler? Or that soup made from boiling an old pair of shoes won't make a sufferer forget lumbago?

Don't get me wrong. I'm not suggesting you tear up your doctor's telephone number and take something as folksy as a dose of elderberry leaves, cinnamon, and hog fat the next time you have a stomach ache. Still, if you feel a twinge of arthritis you might try carrying a buckeye seed. I do, and I'm not the least bit superstitious. I just don't like to take chances.

As mentioned, carrying a buckeye seed is one way, according to folk medicine, you can insulate yourself against arthritis. I heard another remedy for arthritis, or the "twinges," as it was described to me in the mountains many years ago, which I haven't yet tried.

The old man I was talking to said when he felt the twinges coming on, he would rush home and mix himself a tonic consisting of pokeberry juice laced with moonshine whisky. I told him that where I had come from I'd always been warned that pokeberries were deadly poisonous.

He thought on that one for a second or two, then laughed.

"Well, they might be, but not the way I take 'em," he said. "What I do is I mix the juice of one pokeberry in one gallon of moonshine!"

Although I'm not one to go strolling through graveyards at night, I've never put much stock in ghosts and witches and the like. Nevertheless, I must admit my incredulity is shaken somewhat when folks along the Kentucky-Tennessee line in Todd County tell convincing handed-down tales about their once-famous Bell Witch.

It's been more than 100 years since the witch last was heard from, but many still talk about her or it (or whatever personal pronoun fits a witch) with a present tense familiarity that comes from repeated retelling. Even Andrew Jackson enters into the story.

The witch story began after John Bell came from North Carolina and bought a large farm near Guthrie. The old woman from whom it was bought claimed he had cheated her, and on her death bed vowed to "hant John Bell and his kith and kin to their graves."

Sure enough, the Bells were tormented for years afterward by the malicious spirit of the old woman. No one ever saw the witch, but every visitor to the home claimed to have heard her as she threw dishes at the Bells, yanked their hair, poked needles into them, and cursed them in a high-pitched voice.

Eventually the fame of the witch spread to Nashville and Andrew Jackson, then just gaining political notoriety, determined, as he put it, "to face the terror and allay it once and for all." So he announced he would come to the Bell farm.

At the boundary of the farm, the horses pulling Jackson's carriage came to a sudden halt and no amount of urging would cause them to move. "Now, general," an eerie voice said from out of the darkness, "your horses can go on." And so they did.

All that night the witch kept the Bell house in an uproar. She sang, she swore, broke dishes, overturned furniture, and yanked the bed clothing from Jackson as he tried to sleep. The next morning a haggard and harried Andy beat a hasty retreat from the Bell farm.

"I would rather face the British again than have any more dealings with that torment," he supposedly said in departing the premises.

The witch vanished, never to be heard from again, the night John Bell died just before the Civil War.

Many Kentucky folklorists claim the severity and even pattern of an upcoming winter can be foretold by examining the color pattern on the coat of wooly worms in the early fall. The wider and more deeply colored the dark ends of the worm, the longer and more severe the winter will be.

Knowing that Omra Wesley of Casey County put great stock in this means of predicting the winter, some local joksters took a wooly worm, dipped both ends in black ink and narrowed the white stripe through the middle to a thin line. When the worm was dry, they took it to Wesley for his appraisal.

"Boys," he said after deep study, "either this is an awful sick worm or we're gonna have a helluva rough winter!"

It was in 1900 that John Luther "Casey" Jones died in the wreckage of the Illinois Central Railroad's "Cannonball Express" and in so doing took his place as an American legend alongside John Bunyan, Davey Crockett, Pecos Bill and others. His bravery in trying to stop the fast-mail train inspired "The Ballad of Casey Jones," one of the most familiar folk songs of all time.

How much a legend Casey has become is proven by the mass of stories about him one hears to this day in western Kentucky, Tennessee, and Mississippi, the areas where he operated. As befits a legend, his feats haven't suffered in the retelling, but grow as each teller tops the one before.

Casey grew up in, of all places, Cayce in Fulton County, and it was from there that he went on to fame. After he had taken over as an engineer, he fitted his engine with a six-tone calliope whistle that was loud enough to rouse the dead. It became his habit to open the whistle full throat to announce his arrival, early or late, at towns along the line as he sped by.

Finally the council of one town demanded that the railroad instruct Casey to stop blowing the whistle and roaring through at excessive speed in the wee hours. The next time Casey approached the town, he stopped the train. Then he hitched a mule he had arranged to have standing by to the front of the engine and, leading the way and ringing a hand bell, he slowly escorted his 100-car freight through town!

In less sophisticated times, in the weeks shortly before Halloween, ghost stories and tales of haunted houses would be in order in all parts of Kentucky.

For once upon a time, every town had at least one haunted house. These houses, located always at the end of a pine-bordered lane, were deserted except for assorted ghosts that came out after dark from wherever it is ghosts hole up during the day, to roam up and down cobweb-veined halls, moan, rattle chains and carry on in like manner. Many people, especially young boys, claimed to have seen these ghosts and any conversation from the middle of October to the last of the month would be spiced with sepulchral tales.

Two boys in eastern Kentucky were discussing their town ghost. Just the night before, one vowed, he was walking past the haunted house when the ghost, head conveniently tucked under arm, floated out a window toward him.

"What was that ol' ghost doin' the last time you saw him?" the other kid asked breathlessly.

"Son," came the logical answer, "he was fallin' behind, fallin' behind!"

They say that nowhere in the eastern United States do wild columbines grow in greater profusion than among the massive rocks and crevices along the Ohio River shore at Cave-in-Rock, Illinois. They also say that the columbines there are redder in color than elsewhere because the flowering plants probably came from seeds that were drenched in the blood of a Crittenden County, Kentucky, farmer.

The legend of the Cave-in-Rock columbines makes a fascinating story, one laced with enough truth to give it a ring of authenticity. It is fact that during pioneer days, from around 1790 to the early 1820's the deep, high-domed cave in the rocky bluff along the Illinois side of the river was the hangout for notorious river pirates who preyed on keelboats moving on the stream.

A succession of desperadoes, including Sam Mason, the Harpe brothers, Jim Wilson, and Jim Ford, led the pirates, who would swoop down on the boats, rob and sometimes murder the crews and then scurry to safety in the fort-like cave.

The episodes involving the columbines began about 1820 when James Love, a Crittenden County farmer, set out to deliver a load of potatoes to New Orleans. Before leaving, he asked his wife and two daughters what he might bring them from the big city. One daughter wanted a new blue silk dress, the other a doll, while his wife wanted only a few seeds of the columbine, a beautiful plant that had been brought to this country from France only a few years before.

Weeks passed. Then late one afternoon, a Love slave came running to the house with tragic news. Love had been found near the river, strangled to death. He had been robbed and everything — his wallet, the presents for his children, even the columbine seeds — had been taken from his body.

It was never known who murdered Love. The Cave-in-Rock pirates were prime suspects, perhaps with reason.

Shortly wild, blood-red columbines, which hadn't been there before, began to bloom in great abundance around the cavern hangout of the pirates.

The pioneers who settled Kentucky brought with them many tales that originated in the Old Country and had come to the New World with their Anglo-Saxon ancestors. Here they were kept alive by word-of-mouth retelling, and they still are repeated to this day in some parts of the state.

Such a tale is the mountain version of Pluto's kidnapping of Persephone, a classic of mythology that the ancient Greeks used in explaining why there is a summer and a winter. In being retold from generation to generation in the hills, however, the myth was changed somewhat, and was given a local setting and a modern cast of characters.

According to the original Greek tale, Persephone, the daughter of Demeter, the goddess of vegatation, was kidnapped by Pluto, the ruler of Hades, and taken to the land of the dead. Demeter searched for her daughter, and during the time she searched no vegetation grew on earth. Finally she found Persephone in Hades, and the gods ruled that if she had eaten nothing she might return to earth. She had eaten just one pomegranate seed, so it was decreed that she could spend half of every year on earth with her mother, but that she must spend the remainder of the time in Hades. Thus, the myth concluded, while Persephone was on earth vegetation bloomed and it was summer; while she was in Hades and her goddess mother grieved, nothing bloomed and it was winter.

The mountain version goes this way:

"Onct they was this widder woman who had a mighty purty girl child. The widder was a great hand at helpin' her neighbors with their crops and when she done that they turned out uncommon good. When she went away in the mornin' to help, the widder always told her girl not to wander off.

"But one day she did wander off and an old man who lived in a big house on the underneath side of the mountain grabbed her up and runned off with her. The widder was heartsore and looked high and low for her girl. When she found her in this big old house underneath the mountain, it was said that if she hadn't et nothin' since bein' there she could go home. All she had et was two little old plum granny seeds — not much, but enough to argue on.

"Finally they said that she could live part time with her maw, but that she'd have to live part time with that old man. The time she was with her maw was the time it was warm and things growed. But when she had to go back underneath the mountain, that was the time when the cold winds blowed and nothing' growed."

In the early spring, it is said, the restless spirit of a long-dead Indian princess can be heard — even seen, some say — roaming the inky-darkness of the corridors of Saltpetre, one of the four caves within the boundary of Carter Caves State Park near Grayson.

The restless spirit belongs to Manuita, a Cherokee princess who died and was buried inside the cave more than 200 years ago. Legend holds that Manuita died of a broken heart when the brave she loved was lost in battle.

Grief-stricken, she went into Saltpetre Cave to mourn alone, died, and was buried there by her people.

Still to be seen on the tourist route through the cave is the grave from which her body supposedly was taken when the tribe moved westward. But you'll hear it said by old timers in the region that the princess never really left — that she still roams the darkness of the corridors of the cavern in endless search for her lost lover.

A prank played by nature more than 180 years ago was responsible for part of Lawrence County, more than half of Pike County, and all of Martin County winding up in Kentucky when by all rights they were supposed to belong to Virginia.

When Kentucky was preparing to separate from Virginia and become the 15th state in 1792, surveyors were sent to determine the boundary. Their instructions, according to legend, were to start at present-day Catlettsburg and plot the line along the Big Sandy River to the village of Levisa, now called Louisa.

At Levisa, where the Tug and Levisa Forks join to form the Big Sandy, they were told to lay the boundary along the larger of the two tributaries of the main stream. Normally the Levisa, the westernmost of the two forks, is much the larger. But shortly before the surveyors arrived at the junction, heavy rain fell in the mountains spreading out from the Tug and it was in violent flood, while the Levisa Fork was normal.

So, presuming the Tug was the larger fork, the surveyors obediently drew the boundary along its course.

And that's how, by legend or otherwise, nearly 1,000 square miles of territory was added to Kentucky, thanks to a freak of nature.

From time to time, various western Senators exert pressure on the Treasury Department to give a boost to one of their basic natural resources by adding more real silver to minted coins. In view of this, the "crusade" a Kentuckian of another era made on exactly the same basis marks him as a man ahead of his times.

There was one slight flaw in the use-more-silver plan of this Kentuckian: He made his own coins, a short cut viewed with considerable suspicion then as now.

The man was Josiah Sprinkle, and his homemade coins began circulating in the early 1800's when he appeared in Mason County and started passing out silver dollars he admitted weren't government-made. The coins, slightly larger than normal and with an owl stamped on one side and a star on the other, were perfectly all right, Sprinkle hastened to assure one and all, and they were accepted.

In time, news of the competition he was giving the U. S. Mint reached Washington and he was arrested, charged with counterfeiting and brought to court. During the trial which followed, Sprinkle claimed to have found a secret silver lode from which he mined the metal to make his coins. Assayers examined the dollars and, when it was discovered that they contained more than a dollar's worth of pure silver, he was acquitted. Sprinkle continued making the coins until his death in the early 1830's. The "Sprinkle Dollars," as they became known in northern Kentucky, marked perhaps the first time in American history counterfeiting was condoned.

Let me tell you a ghost story that is not original with me. Where it came from I'm not sure, but one shouldn't be picky about ghost tales.

It was a foggy October night some years ago and a misty rain was falling when two young men set out to drive from Winchester to Lexington to attend a dance. About midway to Lexington, they were startled to see a pretty girl in a pale-blue evening dress, but without a wrap, standing beside the road in a lonely spot. The boys stopped and asked if they might give her a lift. She accepted and, as fate would have it, she was going to the same dance. Her name, she told them, was Eleanor and, although her escort had failed to show up at the appointed time, she was determined to go to the dance anyway.

They delivered Eleanor to the dance and later both saw her several times. In fact, one of the boys asked her for a dance. He found, significantly, that she danced light as a spirit, but that her skin seemed cold to his touch. The boys lost her in the crowd before the dance ended, but then on the way home they once again were startled to see her standing beside the road on the edge of town. They stopped and asked if they might drive her home. Again she accepted and, since the early-morning air was cold, one of the boys offered her his tweed overcoat, which she slipped over her shoulders and pulled close about her.

Near the Clark County line, the girl directed the driver to turn down a side road to her home. The house was dark and Eleanor thanked them profusely before disappearing silently inside the house. It wasn't until they had reached Winchester that the owner of the overcoat realized she had gone into the house still wearing his wrap.

"Never mind," he said, "that will give me an excuse to come back."

Next day he did return. He found the house, rang the bell, and a woman appeared at the door.

"I drove your daughter Eleanor home from the dance last night," he said. "She was wearing my overcoat but forgot to return it to me when we got here. I've come to get the coat and say hello to Eleanor."

The woman began to sob softly.

"You're mistaken," she replied. "I did have a daughter named Eleanor but she died exactly five years ago last night in an accident on her way to a dance in Lexington."

"But my coat," the young man objected. "I know I saw a girl in a pale blue evening dress walk into your home with it over her shoulders."

"I see you don't believe me," the woman said sadly. "Eleanor is buried in the family cemetery behind the house. You'll find her grave there if you care to see for yourself."

The young man followed directions and had no trouble finding the cemetery. Nor did he have any trouble finding Eleanor's grave.

For draped over the tombstone bearing her name was his tweed overcoat!

One of Kentucky's most legendary figures was Mike Fink, the self-styled "king of the keelboaters" on the Ohio River in the pioneer period. While there was really a man named Mike Fink, his exploits have been wrapped up in such a cocoon of folklore that it's difficult to tell where fact leaves off and fiction begins.

Two things certain about Fink is that he was a notable rifle shooter and he loved a good fight with no holds barred. His ability with a long rifle was such that posters up and down the river announcing shooting matches always carried a postscript: "Matches open to all but Mike Fink." Needless to say, countless tales concerning him have been perpetuated. One of the best took place in Louisville and it concerns the only time in his wild career he ever was arrested.

Seems Mike and crew were poling down the Ohio and, having tired of the menu of sowbelly and roasted potatoes, he longed for fresh leg of lamb. Somewhere below Louisville the keelboat passed a riverside farm where young lambs were cavorting about. Fink, a tin of snuff in his pocket, swam ashore and powdered the faces of several lambs with snuff. Then he found the owner and called his attention to the lambs as they coughed and leaped wildly into the air. They were, Fink confided, afflicted with deadly black Murrain and would pollute the entire flock unless eliminated. The distraut owner begged Mike to weed out his flock, and for several days the keelboaters enjoyed fresh lamb.

When the crew eventually returned to Louisville, a warrant for Mike's arrest had been issued. Fink agreed to go to court without a fight on one condition — that he go in his keelboat. The relieved sheriff complied and the flat-bottomed keelboat was mounted on wooden wheels and hitched to a team of oxen. All boatmen stood in place on deck as the oxen pulled them through the streets to court.

Once the trial started inside, it was apparent that things weren't going well for Mike.

"To your places, boys," he shouted suddenly, leaping to his feet.

With that, the boatmen jumped out the window and pushed their boat — wheels, oxen and all — to the river. Before the startled judge could issue an order to bring them back, they were poling rapidly back down the river to safety.

The king of the keelboaters had done it again.

I wish I had a nickel for every time a TV or nightclub comedian has done a variation of the aged routine in which a patient goes to the doctor to be treated for a cold.

"About the only thing I can suggest you do is let this cold develop into pneumonia," the doctor in the skit always will say. "I can't do anything for a cold, but I can cure pneumonia almost every time."

C. K. Reid, Madisonville, offers a variation of that variation in a crossroads story concerning a self-taught veterinarian named "Uncle Wash" whom he knew in western Kentucky. One time, Reid says, he went with the "doctor" to make a stable call on a sick mule.

The mule did indeed seem rather peaked, and offered little objection when Uncle Wash started his examination. He carefully looked at each hoof of the beast, uttering almost inaudible and knowledgeable-sounding "ummmms" at what he detected. He thumped on the mule's stomach and clucked loudly at the ripe watermelon-sound he heard. He looked at the eyes, teeth, and ears and what he finally diagnosed caused him to shake his head with apprehension.

"You got a mighty sick mule here," he announced to the farmer, "and I'm kinda uncertain about what he's got.

"But I tell you what," he continued, reaching into the black satchel he always carried and extracting a bottle of something. "You start dosin' him with this stuff. It'll give him the bots, and I can cure the bots nine times out of ten!"

Another example of an Old World fairy tale that was brought to Kentucky by the Anglo-Saxon people who settled so much of the state and which has been kept alive in the oral tradition is the regionalized version of "Snow White and the Seven Dwarfs." I heard the story first in the late 1940's in Knott County, but later I heard the story, told in almost identical style, 250 miles due west in the Mammoth Cave region. Bearing in mind that this is another story that never was written down, merely passed through seven generations by word of mouth, you can appreciate the changes that have been made over the years in the story line, cast of characters, and even in its length. As preserved in Kentucky, the story, in its oral version, goes this way:

"Onct upon a time, away back in the ancient years, they was this man and this woman, not nobody you likely ever heard tell of since you ain't from around here. Anyways, they had an onliest child, a little girl who was smart as could be and purty, too, from all folks has told. They named her Snowwhite on account of her skin was as white as any snow you ever seed drifted on the barn roof.

"When Snowwhite was a baby her maw died and left the old man to do the best he could fer his little youngun'. After a while he hired hisself a nurse maid to come in and do the needful things fer little Snowwhite. Now this nurse maid she acted real nice to Snowwhite at first and finally the old man ast her to marry up with him and she done it. Now that was about the worst thing the old man ever done 'cause soon as she got him married up she showed her bad side and become poison mean to little Snowwhite.

"Now this stepmaw she was a vain woman, too, and she hanged a magic lookin' glass on the wall and she used to spent hours a-starin' at herself in that lookin' glass and askin' it who around the place was the purtiest. Some has

said the lookin' glass sassed her and told her Snowwhite
was a heap the purtiest, but I don't never tell the tale that
way 'cause I can't put no faith in lookin' glasses that
sasses people.

"Well, finally the stepmaw got all she could hold of that
lookin' glass sassin' her and tellin' her Snowwhite was the
purtiest. So she hired herself a mean hunter to grab up
Snowwhite and take her on the fur side of the mountain
and leave her there in the wilds, hopin' she would die and
then she would be the purtiest one around the place and
the lookin' glass would hush mean-mouthin' her.

"But when the hunter left Snowwhite there in the wilds,
his best hound dog, that had took up with her, stayed
behind and as night was comin' on he led her to a little
cabin set way up a deep holler that had seven little beds
and seven little chairs in hit.

"Now Snowwhite she was plum tuckered out from the
long tramp she had took in the wilds so she plopped down
in one of them little beds and taken herself a nap. Later
that day the seven little men who lived there comed in
from workin' in the woods and they found her. They was
purty much surprised and didn't much like her bein' there
until Snowwhite cooked up a big supper to show them she
was more than just purty. They liked her supper so good
they said she could stay on and board with 'em as long as
she done the washin' and cooked all the meals. They even
let the old hound dog stay, too.

"Years later the evil-hearted stepmaw, who still was
gettin' sassed by the lookin' glass, learnt where Snowwhite
was livin' and she fixed up a big poke full of pizen apples
and pears and stuff and sent this spiled fruit to her, hopin'
she'd eat it and die and then she would be the purtiest one
and that would hush up the lookin' glass.

"But when this spiled fruit comed, the old hound dog,
that still was livin', barked so loud when Snowwhite
started to bite into a pizen pear that she didn't have no
appetite for it no more.

"Right after that the stepmaw got her self kilt and that
way she finally got rid of her meanness. I don't rightly
know how she got herself kilt. Some says she felled in the
creek and drowned while she was fishin' and some says
she got kicked in the head while she was milkin' the cow.
But it don't make no difference to me, I'll tell you that.

226

"Right after the stepmaw got herself kilt, a big man named Prince, who was a drummer for a bolt goods store over at the county seat, come ridin' by the house of the seven little men on a big white mule. The minute Prince cast his eyes on Snowwhite he fell in love of her. Prince got off his mule, runned up to her and asked her to marry up with him and go live with him in a big white house he owned in town opposite the courthouse.

"So, the mean-hearted stepmaw got herself kilt in the end. And that hunter, you know he had a mighty troubled life, too. He had his bad doin's on his mind all of them years, and on top of that he lost his best hound dog!"

Perhaps the best known of all Kentucky folk medicines is the sipping of tea made from the aromatic root of the sassafras tree as a means of chasing that tired-blood, rundown, no-energy feeling that comes in the late innings of winter.

I practically grew up with the aroma of sassafras tea in my nostrils. From the time the first migrant robin appeared in her backyard in the early spring, my Grandmother Cross, who was wiser than a roomful of Philadelphia lawyers in such matters, would have me gulping down large quantities of this home-brewed tea that for ages has been a seasonal must in rural regions of Kentucky. And out in the plowed ground you'll still find thousands who swear by sassafras tea as a system-toning tonic that thins the blood and renews energy.

I guess I've drunk enough of the stuff to float a medium-sized canoe. Not that I ever really liked it, mind you, but my grandmother was a first-rate psychologist and so convinced me that the tea was exactly what the doctor would have ordered. Strangely, as soon as the sweet-sick taste of the tea cleared my taste buds, I could imagine that wondrous things were taking place deep within my depleted carcass and soon I was surging with renewed vim and vigor.

Maybe the sassafras tea worked. I don't know. But, then, I've always been a sucker for the power of positive thinking.

In Crittenden County, it is said that nowhere in the world do mockingbirds sing sweeter than in the cottonwood and locust thickets along the river near the now-extinct village of Ford's Ferry. Why that is true is explained in a fascinating legend that is pure Kentucky, but which isn't too well-known.

Early in the last century, Ford's Ferry was the stronghold of a notorious band of river pirates headed by Jim Ford. While he was a brigand and cutthroat, buried deep inside Ford was something of the poet and he liked nothing more than to sit in the late afternoon and listen to the mockingbirds sing in the trees along the river.

One afternoon, the legend goes, he was listening to the birds when John James Audubon, then a penniless mill operator upstream at Henderson, but eventually to become world-famed as a bird artist, pulled his canoe into the landing and was invited to spend the night.

"Audubon," Ford said later as they sat and listened to the mockingbirds, "did you ever hear music to beat that?"

"Only one place," Audubon supposedly replied, "and that's a little valley near the Bay of Biscay in western France."

"When you go back to France," Ford pressed, "promise to bring me six of those birds. I want to turn them loose here and let them mate with our Kentucky mockingbirds so that in my old age I can listen to music a man could hear only in his dreams."

It isn't known whether or not Audubon kept his promise. As for Ford, he was killed by one of his own men a year or two later.

Nevertheless, the story concludes in fitting legend fashion, only in the cottonwoods and locusts in the vicinity of Ford's Ferry do the mockingbirds today really make the kind of music a man hears in his dreams.

Unlike any other day, there is an eerie air of supersition surrounding a Friday that has the misfortune to fall on the 13th day of a month. Because of that, draw near and hear about a Kentucky club that refused to be intimidated by Friday the 13th and even begged to be cursed by the evil spirits that supposedly stir uneasily on that day.

The club was founded in 1899 at Covington on a Friday that was the 13th. Everything about the club pertained to the numeral 13 — it had 13 members, each with 13 letters in his name; they met only when a Friday the 13th appeared on the calendar; the meeting place was a building on Madison Street, which contains 13 letters.

To show their disdain for jinxes, the name members chose was "A Black Cat Club," which, needless to say, has 13 letters. On top of that their slogan was "We Defy The Jinx," which has you-know-how-many letters. On meeting days members walked under a ladder with 13 rungs in it in reporting for a dinner that always included a menu of 13 dishes. Once convened, members thumbed their noses at two other ancient curses by opening an umbrella indoors and then smashing a mirror.

The club continued for six years, during which time Friday the 13th showed up 13 times. On the Friday the 13th it met for the last time, each member invited a guest whose named contained 13 letters. The souvenir program for the disbanding contained 13 pages and the story of the club's origin was told in 169 words, which is 13 times 13. The dinner was served by 13 waiters and the room was illuminated by 13 lights. At exactly 12:01 a.m., the president rapped his gavel 13 times, the 13 lights were turned out and 13 black cats were loosed in the room. The club then was declared officially disbanded.

The members had defied the Friday the 13th jinx. Or had they?

It may have been pure coincidence, but the first of the 13 charter members to pass on died 13 months later on, of all days, a Friday the 13th!

More than to any state except Missouri, the legendary Jesse James was drawn to Kentucky. Not only were both his parents and his brother Frank born in Kentucky, his wife also was from this state as were many members of his band of desperadoes who terrorized the middle border from after the Civil War until his death in 1882.

At least four robberies were pulled off in Kentucky by Jesse James and various members of his band before he was gunned down by Bob Ford in St. Joseph, Missouri. In one of the Kentucky jobs, the robbery of the Bank of Columbia in 1882, the cashier was slain as the bandits escaped.

During the late 1920's and 1930's, various Jesse James pretenders showed up in Kentucky, usually as an after-feature at tent shows. For a price, these pretenders would tell that he was the real Jesse, and that he had entered into an elaborate plot with Ford to have him shoot a total stranger wearing James' clothing, thus enabling him (the real Jesse) to escape the sheriffs, marshals, and detectives hounding his trail.

Shortly before World War II, a forgetful James pretender appeared with a traveling show at Columbia. As soon as the man entered town, U.S. Marshal Evan Akin met him.

"Are you Jesse James?" Akin asked point blank.

When the man admitted he was the one and only, the marshal pulled a yellowed piece of paper from his pocket.

"In that case," he said, "I have here a warrant for your arrest, charging you with the robbery of the Bank of Columbia and the murder of the cashier."

The stranger turned pale.

"However," the marshal continued, "on the off chance that you just may not be Jesse James, I'm giving you ten minutes to get out of town."

"Marshal," the man shouted, taking off to the south, "I can beat that time with five minutes to spare!"

Because of the ever-present threat of the mine roof collapsing, a pocket of gas exploding, or some other mishap occuring, men who go far underground to mine

230

coal have developed certain superstitions and legends that are all their own.

The most common legend is that of "Old Joe," a short-tempered giant who sometimes walks the mountain ridges and makes the earth shudder under his weight. When he stomps his foot in anger, the top of the mine may give away and cause a cave-in, an eventuality that causes many underground miners in time to develop a totally fatalistic philosophy.

The legend of Old Joe found its way to Kentucky in the early part of the twentieth century when Welshmen, among other European groups, were imported to work in the mines of eastern Kentucky. In Wales, Old Joe supposedly was a real miner, fired without good cause. Angered at the injustice, he vowed to knock down the supporting pillars and cause the roof of the mine to collapse. A short time later, when an earthquake occurred and the roof did indeed fall in, the miners credited the feat to Old Joe and the legend was born.

I came into contact with the legend of Old Joe indirectly the first time I went into a coal mine. When the men on the shift took time off for the noon meal, they unpacked their lunch pails and proceeded to eat their desserts first. When I asked why, the answer was one I've never forgotten.

"Because," the oldest man in the lot replied tersely, "the roof might fall."

INTRODUCTION   *No examination, however cursory, of what Ken-*
tucky is all about would be worthy of the effort without devoting some
space to such odds and ends as short outbursts of crossroads philos-
ophy, signs, classified ads, and the priceless communiques provided
weekly newspapers by their country correspondents.

Although the beautiful scenery of Kentucky is justly famous, I've
also been fascinated by the wonderful signery of the state — advertising
come-ons displayed by stores, mini-sermons on bulletin boards out-
side churches, and the like. As the series of crudely-lettered signs about
10 feet apart along the boundary of a farm near Owensboro that read,
in order: "No Hunting . . . No Fishing . . . No Swimming . . . No Tres-
passing . . . No Asking."

Some of the great humorous writing of our times is buried in the
classified ad section of newspapers, large and small. Because those
placing the ads are trying to conserve words, the result, as these sam-
ples show, often is downright hilarious, if unintentionally so:

FOR SALE — apples, come pick your own; remember the early bird
gets the worm.

NOTICE — to whoever stole my step ladder. It is old, rotten, and
unstable and I will not be responsible if you fall off and break your
#*!#* neck.

As for philosophy, after he retired and settled in Louisville following
40 years of teaching in Illinois and Ohio, Fred J. Tuttle started mem-
orizing the Bible. To those who asked why, he had a standard school-
teacher answer ready: "I'm cramming for the finals!"

More bits and pieces of wit and wisdom follow.

CHAPTER 12

WIT, WISDOM AND OTHERWISE

Speaking of crossroads philosophers, of which
Kentucky abounds, the best bit of self-analysis I've ever
heard was offered by an old gent outside the Perry
County Courthouse at Hazard years ago.

"I've really got just two bad faults," he admitted. "I
chew tobacco and cuss when necessary!"

When it was suggested that each taxpayer set aside $1 of
the amount he coughs up in federal income tax to finance
the campaigns of candidates for president, Morehead
publisher W. E. Crutcher was all in favor of the idea.

"In no other way," he figured, "could a person receive
so much entertainment for $1."

The perfect lament to winter was underlined succinctly
in a one-line editorial offered by Richard G. Potter of
Louisville after we'd undergone a particularly severe
season. "Wouldn't it be terrible," he said, "to survive a
winter like this and die on the first day of spring?"

Charles Aaron, the sage of Russell Springs and the Lake Cumberland country, was talking about a friend. "Put us together," he concluded, "and I guess we're the two smartest men in the United States. Take us apart and we don't know anything!"

There are many ways to get across the idea that one never should be too critical of things that are gotten for nothing, the eternal "Never look a gift horse in the mouth" maxim being one. Ray McDonald, Owensboro, expressed that idea a bit differently.

"Don't ever," he advised, "thump a free watermelon."

Mrs. E. P. McMinn of Louisville went to a district church meeting that was poorly attended. In leaving, she overheard a somewhat portly lady talking to a friend.

"If I had known the crowd would be this small," she sighed, "I sure wouldn't have worn my tight girdle!"

The price of eating out being what it is these inflated days, at last I've come to realize why the waiter always presents the check to you face down.

It just never pays to underestimate people regardless of their circumstances, as a man who should know once told me.

Seems he was teaching in a Kentucky school system where an important bond issue for schools was to be voted on. The principal asked him to visit an impoverished

234

area in the district where the educational level wasn't very high and try to sell the people on the need to upgrade the schools.

In order not to talk over the heads of the voters, the teacher spiced his conversation with a few ain'ts, deliberately mispronounced words, and mangled the mother tongue in general.

The bond issue was defeated badly in the district.

"That man who come down here to talk to us talked so bad and seemed so stupid," one parent explained later, "that we figured if he was educated, we didn't want our kids to have none of it!"

Fred J. Kissinger of Lexington went to be measured for a new suit and the experience left him somewhat shaken.

"It was only when the tailor told me what my waist measured," he said, "that I realized a Douglas fir with that much girth would be 90 feet tall!"

The Kentucky Farm Bureau convention in Louisville one year was a series of late-to-bed, early-to-rise meetings, all of which led R. O. Wilson, a director from Livingston County, to make this yawning appraisal:

"It sure doesn't take long to spend the night in Louisville."

A somewhat aged observer of the marital scene heard of a young couple's plans for marriage, reports Elizabeth Spalding of Bardstown.

"More's marryin' now," the old man mused, "than's doin' well."

Louisville businessman Thomas A. Ballantine ran into a
hotel waiter in Philadelphia who, judging from the way
he could apply clear, cold logic to his actions, should
have been from Kentucky.

Ballantine had gone to the dining room and was
undecided what he would order. The breast of capon
sounded good and so did the veal cordon bleu. Finally he
chose the latter and gave the order to his waiter. In due
time the entrée arrived, but it turned out to be the breast
of capon. Thinking that because of his initial indecision
he might have given the waiter that choice, he didn't ask
to return it for the veal. However, when the bill was
delivered he noticed "cordon bleu" entered on the check.

"Why," he asked the waiter out of curiosity, "when I
ordered the veal did you bring me the breast of capon?"

"Well," the waiter answered, resorting to a classic bit of
Kentucky-style inverse logic, "they are both the same
price!"

The prayer of an old mountain man as told to me by
Norman Allen, the Prestonsburg editor, is worth repeating:

"Lord, I don't ask for a faith that would move yonder
mountain. I can take enough dynamite and move it if it
needs movin'. What I pray for, Lord, is enough faith to
move me."

An elderly woman came into Johnson's Department Store
in Hazard and told Mrs. J. O. Harper, who waited on her,
she wanted to buy a dress. After trying on several and
looking at herself critically in the mirror, the customer
sighed and delivered this dissertation on the fashions of
the day:

"They used to make dresses long enough to cover a
body's instep. Now they make 'em so they just barely
cover the step-ins!"

Two old-timers were talking in the shade outside the
Taylor County Courthouse at Campbellsville when one
unloaded a conversational gem.

"The old woman ain't talkin' to me," one of the men
said, "and I ain't in no mood to interrupt her!"

I can barely remember my Great Grandmother Dotson,
a peppery little woman who remained extremely
outspoken to the day she died at the age of 101.
However, I didn't appreciate how outspoken she really
was until my uncle, E. T. Cross of Gilbertsville, recalled
her comments about a preacher she didn't care for.

"But, after all," someone argued with her, "he was
called by the Lord."

"That preacher," she snapped back, "was called by a
jackass!"

As I was saying, you always should read the classified ads
in your newspaper for at least two reasons: You not only
come across some real bargains, you also are exposed
at time to flashes of rare, if unintentional, humor. For
instance, these culled from Kentucky papers:

FOR SALE — wedding dress and veil; also bassinet.

LOST — stainless steel lady's watch.

FOUND — tan ladies billfold.

FOR SALE — blue bridesmaid dress.

WILL TRADE — once-used skis for adult-size crutch.

WANTED — summer cottage for small family with
good drainage.

FOR SALE — boys' pants — 1/3 off.

LOST — upper plate of false teeth; badly needed.

FOR SALE — used electric typewriter by secretary
with wide carriage.

Those who say the day of personal journalism is no more just don't read reports sent to weekly papers by correspondents who live in various crossroads communities in the counties they serve. For these local reporters see and tell all.

For instance, this item from one paper in central Kentucky:

"Mrs. ------ went to town to see the doctor. She has been having mouth trouble for years."

The evolution of a relapse was perhaps inadvertently, but clearly, explained in this item which appeared in one of the community columns written for a western Kentucky paper:

"Mrs. ------ has returned home from the hospital, but is feeling worse at this writing. All her children visited her over the weekend. Also lots of neighbors."

No doubt there was some hurried apologizing around the office of a Bluegrass-area paper when a picture showing the mayor and the eight new town councilmen bore a cutline with one embarrassingly garbled word:

"The mayor of ------ was sworn in and with him tight councilmen . . ."

This social note was lifted from a Purchase-section weekly paper:

"Mr. and Mrs. William ------ have returned from St. Louis. While there they attended a family reunion at the Forest Park Zoo."

A rousing big time by all hands was pointed up in this
item from a Green River country paper:
   "Mr. and Mrs. ------ drove around a while Sunday."

Even though one letter was misplaced in one word of a
sign outside a Louisville parochial school, it still made
pretty good sense since it read:
   "PTA BROAD MEETING TONIGHT."

This ad, complete with implied warning perhaps, appeared
in a weekly newspaper in west central Kentucky:
   "PUBLIC AUCTION — Located 12 miles west of town
on Indian Creek Road. Watch for the arrows."

In these times, it's pretty easy to get all tensed up —
grammatically as well as otherwise — as two signs seen in
eastern Kentucky prove. One outside a rural church in
Bell County read: "All Is Welcome," while the other in a
roadside grocery went: "Cigarettes Is Cash."

A neighborhood tavern in the western section of
Louisville displays this cordial notice: "We have an
agreement with the banks — they serve no beer, we cash
no checks."

All the eventualities were nailed down in this sign that appeared on the door of a drive-in restaurant in Lexington: "WE OPEN PROMPTLY EVERY DAY AT 6, USUALLY."

Some years back a roadside café near Renfro Valley in Rockcastle County was named "Belly Acres Café." Nearby was a combination café-filling station that sported this double-feature sign: "GOOD FOOD AND HIGH GRADE GAS."

It always seemed to me somewhat ironic that the Jefferson County Jail in Louisville should be located on Liberty Street. And appropriate that the old County Workhouse, now razed, should have been on Payne Street.

New Year's Day traditionally is a time for making resolutions. Fred Homra, Fulton, knew a man in his town whose resolution one year was: "I will drink no more this year — nor any less."

Being a psychiatrist, Dr. William Keller of Louisville naturally believes in one and all blurting out the truth rather than keeping it caged inside. Like in a conversation he had with a waitress in a café at Elizabethtown.

"I ought to pay you double for this," he told her after she had served him an especially good meal.

"Well," she replied honestly, "you are!"

240

"When I started in my job years ago, I was told that I'd have to work for peanuts until I proved my salt," Warren Everett, Lexington, reported, "Now I'm working for salted peanuts."

Landon Wills, a former Calhoun editor, told about a merchant in his town who was about ready to resort to desperation measures in an effort to get some action from a customer who was especially slow in paying his bills.

The last resort did get some action when the dun included this PS: "If you don't pay your bill, I'll tell your other creditors you did."

I thought I'd really stumbled on something big when Edwin Portwood of Louisville insisted he had a cat that could say its own name. It really could. Its name was "Meow."

Ever since she saw the play "Arsenic and Old Lace," Walter G. Duncan, Louisville, said his wife had been acting like Teddy Roosevelt in the play.

"Every time she goes into a store," he moaned, "she yells, 'Charge.'"

Usually the loss of a letter produces a grotesque word that is easily recognized as being garbled. On occasion, however, dropping a letter still leaves a complete word that makes sense. Consequently there may have been something prophetic in a jewelry store ad in a central Kentucky paper which I assumed contained a misspelled word.

"1½ carat diamond for $305. You'll be thrilled at owing so much for so little."

The sign outside a Louisville tavern read: "Dancing
Every Night — Music Fri. & Sat."

In Grayson County they tell about a man who fell off the
wagon with a thud and went off on a protracted drunk.
After several days, he dragged home, deathly sick,
and asked his wife to offer up a short prayer on his behalf.

"Oh, Lord," she began, "my husband's been on a big
drunk and now he's bad sick . . ."

"Hold on," the man interrupted, "Don't tell Him I've
been drunk; just say I'm terrible sick."

The Glenmore Distillery plant at Owensboro offered $25
cash to employees whose suggestions would save the
company money. One of the most original suggestions was
from a guy who proposed lowering the award to $10.

In Russellville they tell about a woman who went into the
post office and asked for 50-cents worth of stamps.

"What denomination?" a clerk asked.

"I sure never thought religion would go this far," she
answered, "but if you must know, I'm Baptist."

A Covington tailor shop displayed this window sign:
"Pants pressed in the rear while you wait." Just the place
for the man who wants to look well-groomed going
but baggy coming.

Louisvillian Ralph Day reported seeing a woman who drove a car painted green on one side and blue on the other. And she had a reasonably logical explanation for the two-tone job.

"I'm rather accident prone," she understated, "and you should hear the witnesses contradict each other!"

A Louisville wholesale jewelry dealer sends items to be repaired to an expert who obviously likes to work alone since on the wall of his shop this breakdown of charges is posted:

"Repair work — $8 an hour.
"If you watch — $10 an hour.
"If you help — $12 an hour."

A sign erected on US 421 north of the point the road enters Jackson County once offered this warning: "Proceed with caution. The next 29 miles of US 421 are extremely dangerous. Jackson County has one doctor, no hospital. We do have good wrecker service and a good funeral home."

Sherman Hinkebein, a former Louisvillian living in Evansville, Indiana, has the perfect yardstick for measuring the various levels of the national economy. "It's a recession," he figures, "when your neighbor loses his job, a depression when you lose your job, and a panic when your wife loses her job."

When one of the secretaries at a large Louisville
wholesale firm arrived late for work one morning,
she offered the perfect alibi: She had taken her coffee
break before coming in.

I've always thought that Smith Broadbent, Jr. owns a
mailing address that couldn't be improved upon.
Broadbent, who started one of the nation's largest
hybrid seed-corn operations, lives at Cobb.

A sense of humor is a wonderful thing. To underscore
that, the residents of Dosker Manor, a splendid housing
project for senior citizens in Louisville, have their own
private name for the place: "God's Waiting Room."

Bill Mayer of Buechel saw this sign in the office of the
Pulaski County tax commissioner: "I know that you
believe what you think I said, but I am not sure you
realize that what you heard is not what I meant."

The idea that if you aren't part of the solution you're part
of the pollution is expressed in a slightly different way
by a sign, done jingle style, that stands in the parking lot
at Jefferson County's Chenoweth Park:
        "Let no one say
           And feel to your shame
           That all was beauty here
              Until you came."

Central City's tell-it-all Larry Stone reported that the cops there arrested a drunken citizen who demanded his right to make one telephone call. The call was to his bootlegger.

Aside from the fact they keep a lot of people inside, out of the cold, the outburst of football games — pro playoffs, bowls, all-star clashes — on TV during the holiday season is beneficial for still another reason, according to Roy McDonald of Owensboro. "I saw the start of so many games and heard the National Anthem so many times one holiday," he says, "that I almost learned all the words."

It's amazing how much better your old automobile looks after you price new ones.

A sign outside a Louisville go-go joint provided a pretty good idea of the cultural level of the place since it read: "No shorts or T-Shirts — We Don't Want No Competition For Our Dancers."

This line from the "Personals" column in a western Kentucky weekly paper: "Miss ------ has come home from the U. of Kentucky where she is taking home economics and some education."

Sometimes I think horsepower may have been better when it was concealed under old Dobbin's hide and not the hood of an automobile. Anyway, after I had taken my car in for a simple tune-up and the bill was tallied, this thought flitted through my mind: When people in the old days took a horse to the blacksmith to be shod, did he find a couple of dozen other things that ought to be done to the nag?

A new way of shaming customers into paying their delinquent bills was tried by the operator of a Russellville service station who posted this sign: "Please pay your bill — my wife is PREGNANT."

Classified classic from an eastern Kentucky weekly paper:
    FOR RENT — house with bath opposite courthouse.

Jess Anderson, long-time Mayfield newspaperman, recalled how in 1923 when his town celebrated its centennial the Mayfield Cemetery Association set up a food stand on the courthouse lawn to serve the large crowds that gathered. A canvas sign stretched over the stand had an almost prophetic ring to it since it read: "Eat Here and Help the Cemetery."

Perhaps more than most, I know how typograhpical errors can creep into printed matter and change things more than just somewhat. As in this line from a rural correspondent's report in a Bluegrass weekly:
    "------ Church was host to a singing last Sunday night. A large crowd was on hand and everyone enjoyed the wonderful sining."

Gordon Finley, a Louisville attorney, told about an old man in eastern Kentucky who was advised by his doctor to go to Arizona for health reasons. But after being there less than two weeks, he died and the body was brought home for burial. Two long-time friends were the first to visit the funeral home.

"My, don't he look nice," one friend mused.

"Sure does," the other agreed. "Arizona sure done him good!"

A three-hole golf course was laid out inside the fences at the Kentucky State Reformatory at LaGrange. The inmates immediately gave it an appropriate name: "The Links of Steel."

"We laid down the law and we don't have coffee breaks at our place," claimed the office manager of a large Louisville firm. "Instead, we have an occasional work break."

The conversation was about birthdays and Ray Wimberg, Louisville's number one booster, admitted he feels a bit nervous every time his personal anniversary rolls around.

"We sit there at the breakfast table," he said, "and the first thing Mamma does is look at me closely and ask, 'How much Social Security did you say I will get?'"

Paul Camplin of Frankfort and Greenville knew a fellow who visited in Arizona and returned with a batch of cactus which he started raising as a hobby. At first the pastime caused him trouble because he never knew when the plants should be watered.

However, ingenuity won out in the end and he hit on the solution by subscribing to a Phoenix newspaper. When the paper reported it had rained in Arizona, he watered his cactus!

Sometimes a place was destined to have a particular address. As in the case of Christ the King Church in Lexington. It's located on Providence Road.

Ralph Day, Louisville, told about a man who was discussing the greatest disappointment of his life. "It was the time," he confessed, "I slipped under the tent to see the circus and found I was in a revival meeting."

This from the classified section of a Frankfort paper:
LOST — brown and white cocker spaniel; either return pup or adopt our children.

Why is it we seem to feel obvious things need to be emphasized? Thus eggs always are proclaimed to be "extra fresh eggs;" an announcement always is a "special announcement;" an order blank is a "handy order blank;" and keep-out signs read "Positively No Admittance."

This persuasive reason for not leaving, decorated the wall of a Louisville Preston Street oasis:

"Your wife can only get so mad, so why not stay for one more?"

The adding or dropping of one letter in a key word in a news story often produces a word that still is complete but which gives the item an entirely different meaning. A good example is this line from a society page story in a western Kentucky weekly:

"Mrs. ------ was high player at duplicate bridge with 23 pints."

A friend was considering early retirement until an acquaintance advised him to stay home a week before taking the step and watch the daytime TV programs. If that wouldn't keep a man on the job, he was told, nothing would!

A small store on Preston Street in Louisville opened one week and closed the very next week. Thus a sign on the door was entirely fitting: "Opened By Mistake."

It seems this man was in jail for having broken into a smokehouse near Pleasureville and taken several sides of bacon. His wife went to the county judge and pleaded for him to be released.

"He ain't no account in that jail and he ain't no account out," she admitted.

"If that's true," the judge reasoned, "why do you want him out?"

"Well," the wife said honestly, "we're about out of meat again!"

Strange things happen to people when they're in their cups, as proven in an incident related by Woodrow Burchett, a Prestonsburg attorney.

"I was driving home last night," he quotes this fellow, heavy with hangover, as having said, "when the car began going thump, thump, thump."

"Sounds like you had a flat tire," his listener cut in.

"Right," he who had tied one on last night replied. "I got out and changed the tire, but when I started up again there was that same thump, thump, thump."

"Don't tell me you had another flat tire," said his listener.

"Nope," he sighed, "I'd fixed the wrong tire!"

Peter Turner of Louisville figures that hot — really hot — weather helps him cut down on his golf score. He doesn't play any better, just fewer holes.

It was in Salyersville that Bob Prater told me about the man, protesting his absolute innocence in a loud voice, who was brought before the judge on a charge of stealing a big batch of lumber.

"This is your third offense," the judge ruled, "so I'm going to ask you to make a retribution."

"I don't rightly know what a retribution is, Judge," the accused said, "but if you've got the blueprint, I've got the lumber."

I'm glad I have forgotten who it was that laid this one on me: If all the cars in the United States were painted white, what would we have? Why, a white carnation, of course.

Some years back a young fellow was charged in
Muhlenberg County with having killed a man by striking
him with a rock. When the case was tried, the prosecutor
started by calling on several witnesses to establish the
size of the death weapon.

"Was the rock as big as my fist?" he asked one witness.

"No, it was bigger."

"Well, was it as big as my head?" the prosecutor pressed.

"I guess it was about as big around," the witness
replied after some thought, "but not nearly as thick!"

N. L. Rost, Louisville, tells about a friend who was taken
in by one of those fly-by-night firms whose "your money
refunded if not satisfied" ad appeared in a cheap
magazine. When the item he bought didn't pan out,
he wrote to the company, calling attention to the wording
of its guarantee. In due time he received a reasonable
answer:

"Your money was entirely satisfactory so no refund can
be made."

This bit of philosophy liberally laced with an appropriate
moral was displayed on the bulletin board outside a
Louisville church: "Few people are led into temptation —
most of us are able to find our own way."

The women's golf group at a country club in a
southwestern Kentucky town held a pantry and
bake sale that no doubt drew a near-record turnout
of male golfers that day since the event was headlined
in the local newspaper thusly: "PANTY AND BAKE
SALE TODAY."

Not particularly apropos of anything, but did you hear about the aged millionaire who was constantly changing his will? He was a fresh heir fiend.

Years ago, according to Perry Cross, of Albany, a Clinton County farmer was all but peeling the paint from nearby houses with the outburst of salty remarks he was directing at a team of balky mules.

"Don't talk like that to those poor, dumb animals," a passer-by reprimanded him, "they can't understand what you're saying."

"If they don't understand what I'm sayin'," the man spat, "then how in the world did Noah get these #'+*!* things on the ark!"

Only when he watched a solitary golfer putting out on the final hole one afternoon did it dawn on Frederick M. Nichols, Madisonville, why so few par chasers play alone. Just imagine the mental anguish that would arise if a player made a hole-in-one with no one watching!

The matter of an ace in golf reminds me of the old story about the player who always wore two pairs of pants just in case he got a hole in one.

Since the sky is full of the things now, it may be difficult for some to realize it wasn't too many years ago that airplanes were a positive novelty. Moreover, on the belief that if God had intended for man to fly He would have given him wings, many in those days regarded going up in a plane as roughly the equivalent of suicide.

Slim Pickins, the resident newspaper gossip of Greensburg, tells about a plane landing in his town in those bygone days. A large and curious crowd immediately gathered to stare at the flying machine. Before he took off, the pilot asked an old man in the throng if he'd like to go up.

"I don't know," the old party mused, "How much do you pay?"

According to Mrs. Emily Vaught, Louisville, you know you're getting too stout when you're the last person on the bus other passengers choose to sit beside.

When Mrs. Edith W. Annunziata of Pleasure Ridge Park reached her 100th birthday, she expressed herself in a most profound way: "Every birthday is the best one of all."

For some uncomfortable reason, I feel Ed Mardis, Louisville, had me in mind when he passed on this thought: "Maybe what you don't know won't hurt you, but it may make you look pretty stupid."

Ed Stagner of Louisville figures he's just naturally snake bit, and he can cite bad luck to prove his claim. In a fit of affluence, he bought himself one of those expensive, shockproof, waterproof, unbreakable, anti-magnetic, self-winding calendar watches guaranteed to last a lifetime — at least.

The next day he lost it!

Index

Aaron, Charles, 46, 140, 181, 234
Abbott, H. P. Almon, 139
Adams, Ed, 139
Alice Lloyd College, 153
Allen, Mrs. James, 91
Allen, James Lane, 15
Allen, Norman, 111, 236
Allen, Sonny, 137
Allison, Young E., 31
Anderson, Jess, 246
Annunziata, Mrs. Edith W., 253
Armstrong, George, 111
Arnett, "Goosebite", 110
Arnett, Oakley, 109
Arnold, Barney, 126
Audubon, John James, 228

Bacon, Barry, 97
Bailey, Clay Wade, 52, 69
Ballantine, Thomas A., 236
Baptising, 15
Barkley, Alben W., 47, 169
Barnstable, Dale, 122
Barry, Mike, 130
Barry, Paul, 13
Beam, Mrs. T. Jeremiah, 30
Bell, J. Earle, 130
Bell, John, 214
Bell Witch, 214
Benjamin, Sister Joseph, 92
Benton, 40, 165
Betting Systems, 125
Bimble, 149
Boeck, Peggy, 80
Bogard, Quentin, 153
Boles, S. A., 127
Booe, Charley, 91
Boone, Daniel, 12, 157
Bootlegger, 68, 73
Bourbon, 17, 64, 134, 155
Bradley, E. R., 174
Bradshaw, Charley, 136
Bratcher, John, 179
Bray, Mary Helen, 95
Breathitt, Edward, 62
Breckinridge, Mrs. Mary, 175
Broadbent, Robert, 79
Broadbent, Sarah, 79
Broadbent, Smith, Jr., 244
Broadbent, Smith, III, 79
Broida, Mrs. H. B., 13
Brown, George, 103, 185
Brown, John, 164
Brown, John Young, Sr., 58
Bryant, Paul, 133
Buchanan, Bill, 139, 178
Burchett, Woodrow, 250
Burke, Frank W., 46
Burkhard, Fred, 21, 28
Burlew, Mrs. Daniel M. III, 101
Butler, Wendell, 33

Campbell, John, 12
Campbell, R. B., 72
Campbell, William C., 56

Camplin, Paul, 181, 247
Carpenter, James, 109
Carr, Paul E., 125
Carroll, Julian, 73
Carter Caves State Park, 219
Carter, Dr. Tim Lee, 44
Cary, Arthur, 185
Catlettsburg, 148, 171
Cave-in-Rock pirates, 217, 218
Centre College, 134, 142
Chandler, A. B. "Happy", 54
Chandler, Arthur, 21
Cheek, Waynetta, 79
Chinn, George, 134
Churchill Downs, 124
Civil War, 156, 161, 173
Clark, Diane, 81
Clark, Dr. Thomas D., 169
Clay, Henry, 162
Coal Mine Superstitions, 230, 231
Cobb, Irvin S., 66, 134
Cochran, A. M. J., 69, 177
Coleman, Robert M., 135
Combs, Bert, 53, 61
Combs, "Preacher" Sam, 108
Commonwealth, 177
Congleton, Dr. Ralph, 15
Cook, Alice, 96
Coon hunting, 178, 181, 183, 188
Cooper, John Sherman, 49, 58, 59, 169
Corns, Arthur, 126
Craig, Elijah, 64
Creason, Bill, 84
Creason, Joe Cross, Sr., 197
Creason, Peggy, 114
Cross, E. T., 237
Cross, Perry, 113, 252
Crutcher, Catherine, 84
Crutcher, W. E., 233
Curran, Mary Ann, 100

Davis, Elmer, 66
Davis, Jefferson, 168
Dawkins, Truthful, 179, 191
Dedman, T. C., 29
DuPont, T. Coleman, 172
Day, Ralph, 182, 243, 248
DeBoe, Bob, 127
Deters, Ward, 101
Diddle, Ed, 129, 130, 141
Doll, Angie, 97
Dougherty, Jack, 16
Dudley, Mrs. Ambrose, 155
Duncan, Walter G., 241
Durrett, Reuben T., 163

Eades, Tommy, 128
Easterley, Ed, 149
Eighty Eight (88), 152
Elizabethtown, 27
Eslinger, Dr. Troy, 22

Fern Grove, 163
Fields, Margie, 81
Filson Club, 40

Filson, John, 12, 157
Fink, Mike, 120, 223
Finley, Gordon, 247
Fish bait, 127, 139, 140
Fisher, Jack E., 36
Flag, 60
Flint, Mrs. Nina, 95
Foley, Dr. Ernest, 114
Fontaine Ferry Park, 88
Ford, Jim, 228
Ford, Judge H. Church, 67
Foster, Bobby, 123
Fourth of July, 60
Fox hunting, 125, 135, 138, 185
Fox, John, Jr., 169
Friday the 13th, 229
Frizzell, Roger, 87
Frontier Nursing Service, 175

Gentry, Dorothy, 83
Ghent, 86
Ghosts, 217, 219, 221
Gibson, Jeanne, 158
Gibson, Mallie, 158
Glen Dean, 148
God, 87, 89
Golden Pond, 69
Goodman, C. A., Sr., 34
Goodman, Izzy, 38
Goodman, Julian, 34
Grafton, Arthur W., 46
Grand Hotel, 14
Greensburg Art Club, 23
Grimes Mill, 139
Gullion, Carroll, 86

Hargan, John L., 100
Harmon, Henry, 21
Harper, Mrs. J. O., 236
Harrelson, John, 184
Hasenour, Ed, 21
Heer, John E., Jr., 93
Hell-for-Certain, 116, 145
Helm, Mrs. Ben Hardin, 173
Helm, Elodie, 173
Henderson, W. B. "Big Six", 66, 68, 70, 74
Henson, "Uncle" George, 108
Hickman, Peck, 131
Hinkebein, Sherman, 243
Hodapp, Mary Ellen, 82
Hollis, Dr. Ben, 36
Holmes, Mark, 66
Homra, Fred, 240
Horne, Edwin W., 106
Hoop Snake, 180
Horse Cave, 148
Hughes, Mrs. Nancy, 96
Hust, Ed, 81
Huter, David, 89

Imorde, George, Sr., 31
Iroquios Hunt Club, 139

Jackson, Andrew, 164, 215
Jackson, Ed. P., 35
Jackson, Dr. V. A., 88
James, Frank, 230

James, Jesse, 170, 229
Jarboe, Joe C., 42

JOE'S, 206
Johnson, Cal, 57
Johnson, Joe R., 110
Johnson, Mrs. Keen, 49
Jones, "Casey," 216
Joseph, Brother John, 34

Karnes, G. H., 149
Keller, Dr. William, 240
Kelly, Dr. B. W., 185
Kelly, John Sims, 126
Kellytown, 147
Kentucky Derby, 124, 133, 174
Kentucky, name, 157
Kentucky, University of, 122, 126, 136, 150
Kinnaird, William H., 68
Kirke, Jay, 136
Knott, J. Proctor, 171

Laughlin, Bob, 129
Latham Hotel, 176
Lawrence, Dr. David, 143
Ledbetter, Mrs. Joe, 154
Lees Junior College, 22
Lepping, Buddy, 130
Lewis, Bill, 27
Lincoln, Abraham, 168
Lincoln, Mrs. Abraham, 173
Logan, M. M., 57
Logsdon, David, 85
Long, Bob T., 93
Love, James, 218
Lunker Fish, 138, 184, 191

Mammoth Cave, 170
Man o' War, 121, 130
Masters, Cindy, 85
Mayer, Bill, 244
Mayo, John C. C., 170
McAfee, J. R., 24
McBride, Beth Ann, 92
McCarthy, Joe, 137
McConnell, J. Ed, 179, 191
McCreary, James B., 54
McDonald, Mrs. Emma, 95
McDonald, Erwin, 83
McDonald, Ray, 234, 245
McDonough, Thomas J., 26
McFarland, Mrs. Raymond, 96
McKay, William, 13
McKinney, Garland, 39
McLane, Hardin, 27
Mead, Larry, 150
Merrick, David, 158
Mint Julep, 133
Mobley, Tom, 52
Moneyham, Daniel, 161
Monkey's Eyebrow, 151
Monroe, James, 164
Moody, Thomas J., 183
Moonshine recipe, 72
Moran, Charley, 134, 142
Morehead State University, 129
Morris, Dick, 115
Morrisey, Jim, 30

255

Morrow, Edwin P., 51
Moss, John McKenize, 48
Mountain Farming, 109
Mountain men, 110, 112
Mudd, "Guinea", 37
Murphy, Sister Bona Vita, 19
Musselman, Johnson, 14

Nazareth, College, 19
Nichols, Frederick M., 252
Norton, Letcher, 126
Nunn, Fred, 135, 183, 184
Nunn, Louis B., 52, 60, 62

Old Christmas, 156, 166

Paint Lick, 148
Paradise, 153
Parkinson, Jack, 122
Parsons, Mrs. Lloyd, 93
Pearl, Quinn, 65, 66
Phillips, Mrs. Russell, 23
Phobias, 195
Pickins, Slim, 253
Pippa Passes, 153
Pogue, Kevin, 91
Pollution, 93, 154
Potter, Richard C., 233
Prater, Bob, 250
Purdy, T. C., 117
Purvis, Mrs. Kate, 20

Quinn, Tom, 70

Rains, Lowry, 120
Ramsey, Frank, 122
Read, Joe, 88
Read, Lee S., 89
Read, Mary Louis, 82, 99
Reid, C. K., 165, 224
Rheumatism, 111
Riddle, Samuel D., 121
Roberts, Harry, 124
Roberts, Red, 134
Rogers, Will, 63
Roosevelt, Franklin D., 194
Rose Island, 163
Rost, N. L., 251
Rothert, Otto, 40
Rountree, R. H., 170
Rupp, Adolph, 122, 123, 136
Russell, John, 161

Sandlin, John, 187
Salt River, 161
Sermonettes, 208
Shakespeare, William, 102
Shane, Mrs. Robert V., Jr., 94
Shelbourne, Judge Roy M., 46, 72
Shelbyville, 33
Shely, Wyatt, 112
Shepherdsville, 147
Short, William, 73
Signs, 239, 240, 242, 243, 245, 246, 249
Silliman, George, 62
Sisk, Mack, 60
Smith, Daniel Boone, 55
Smith, J. M., 183, 184
Smock, Coleman E., 37, 186

Snake handlers, 159
"Snowwhite," Kentucky version, 225
Southworth, Billy, 132
Spalding, Elizabeth, 32, 80, 235
Sparks, Dr. Paul, 87, 190
Speech glossary, 119
Sprinkle "Dollars", 221
Stanley, A. O., 51
Stengel, Casey, 131
Stone, Larry, 18, 26, 123, 245
Strip mining, 76
Stuart, Jesse, 167, 168, 169
Summers, Charles, 65, 66

Tartar, Roscoe, 48
Tater Day, 165
Taylor, Zachary, 164
Terrell, Clara, 89
Thanksgiving, 100, 145
Thomas, W. W., 22
Thompson, Brent, 82
Thompson, Dr. Kelly, 141
Thompson, Wallace, 187
Timmons, W. B., 26
Tobacco, 199
Tolu, 150
Towles, Harry, 139
Townsend, William H., 169, 173
Travis, Joe, 52
Trotter, George, 16, 112
Trout, Allan M., 54
Tully, John, 109

Uno, 145, 148

Van Winkle, Julian, 25
Vaught, Emily, 253

Waller, Thomas S., 36
Ward, Henry, 61
Warren, Clay, 89
Watkins, Sam Houston, 39
Welshmen, 156, 162
Western Kentucky University, 129, 141
Whistling, 193
Whitehead, Don, 109
Whittle, Charles E., Sr., 19, 56, 57, 183, 188
Wildcat, 108
Wilgus, Dr. D. K., 189
Wilhite, O. G., 107
Williams, Mrs. Marge, 86
Wills, Landon, 241
Wilson, Mrs. George W., III, 31
Wilson, Phil, 112
Wilson, R. O., 235
Wimberg, Ray, 22, 247
Wolfe, Carl, 183
Wombwell, Andy, 101
Woods, G. G., 18
Woodson, William T., 133, 143
Women's Lib, 81
Wooton, George, 116
Wooton, John, 114
Wright, "Devil" John, 170
Wyatt, George Homer, 41
Wyatt, Wilson, 61

Yancey, Mrs. L. J., 98
Yeager, C. Robert, 41